Spiders & Stardust
a tribute to david bowie

Welcome to SPIDERS & STARDUST!

This is a passion project from a collection of comic book writers and artists, paying tribute to the work of the late David Bowie. For this project, we wanted to create a collection of comic book stories inspired by David Bowie and honoring the creativity of his music. I wanted as many fans of both comics and Bowie as possible to be able to enjoy the stories we've created, inspired by the power of Bowie's music. We hope we did his spirit justice and made a comic with stories as diverse as his life and career.

Thanks for supporting us. Now on to the stories!

-Kurt Belcher, Editor

FIRELIGHT COMICS

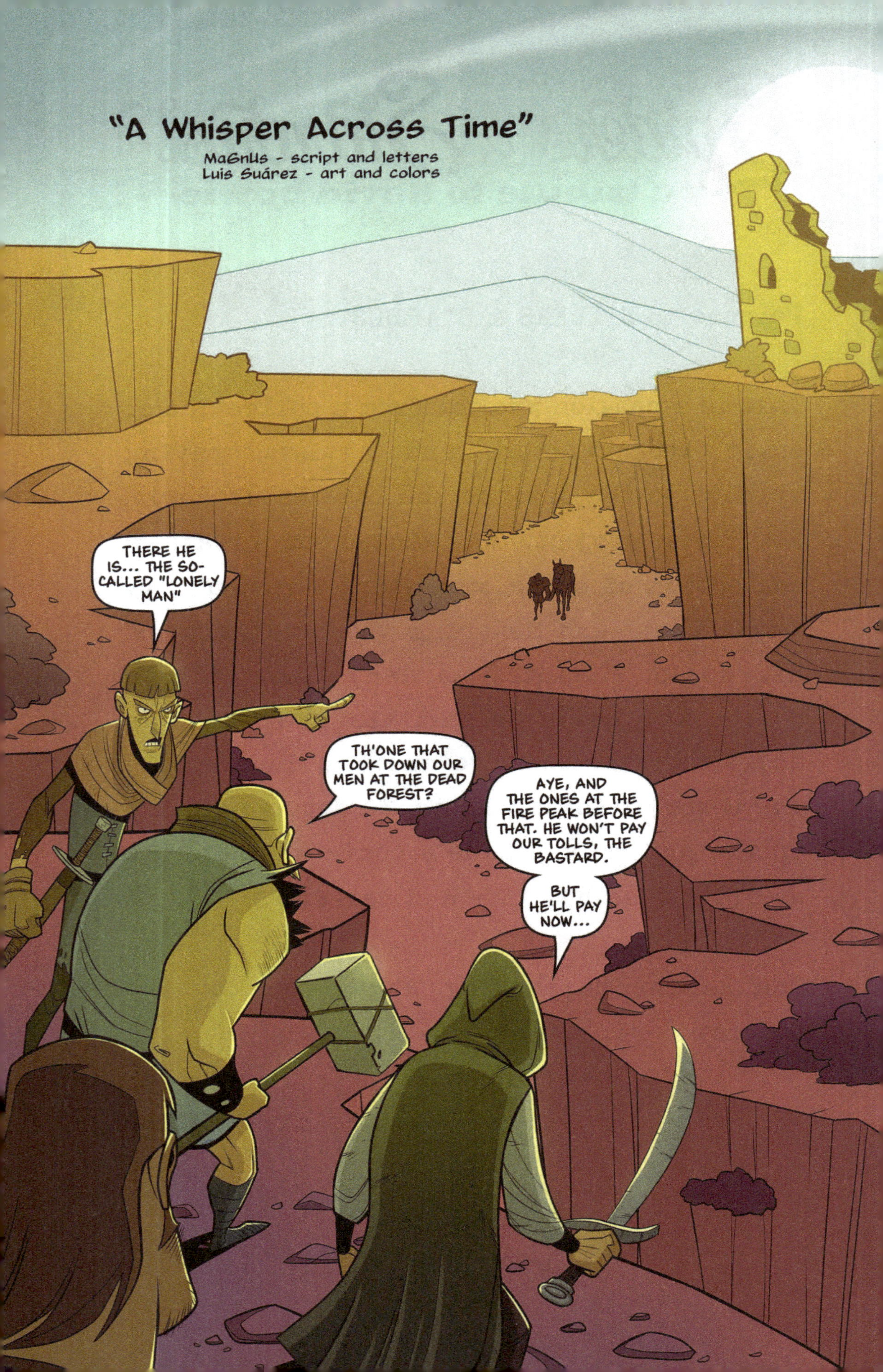
"A Whisper Across Time"
MaGnUs - script and letters
Luis Suárez - art and colors
THERE HE IS... THE SO-CALLED "LONELY MAN"
TH'ONE THAT TOOK DOWN OUR MEN AT THE DEAD FOREST?
AYE, AND THE ONES AT THE FIRE PEAK BEFORE THAT. HE WON'T PAY OUR TOLLS, THE BASTARD.
BUT HE'LL PAY NOW...

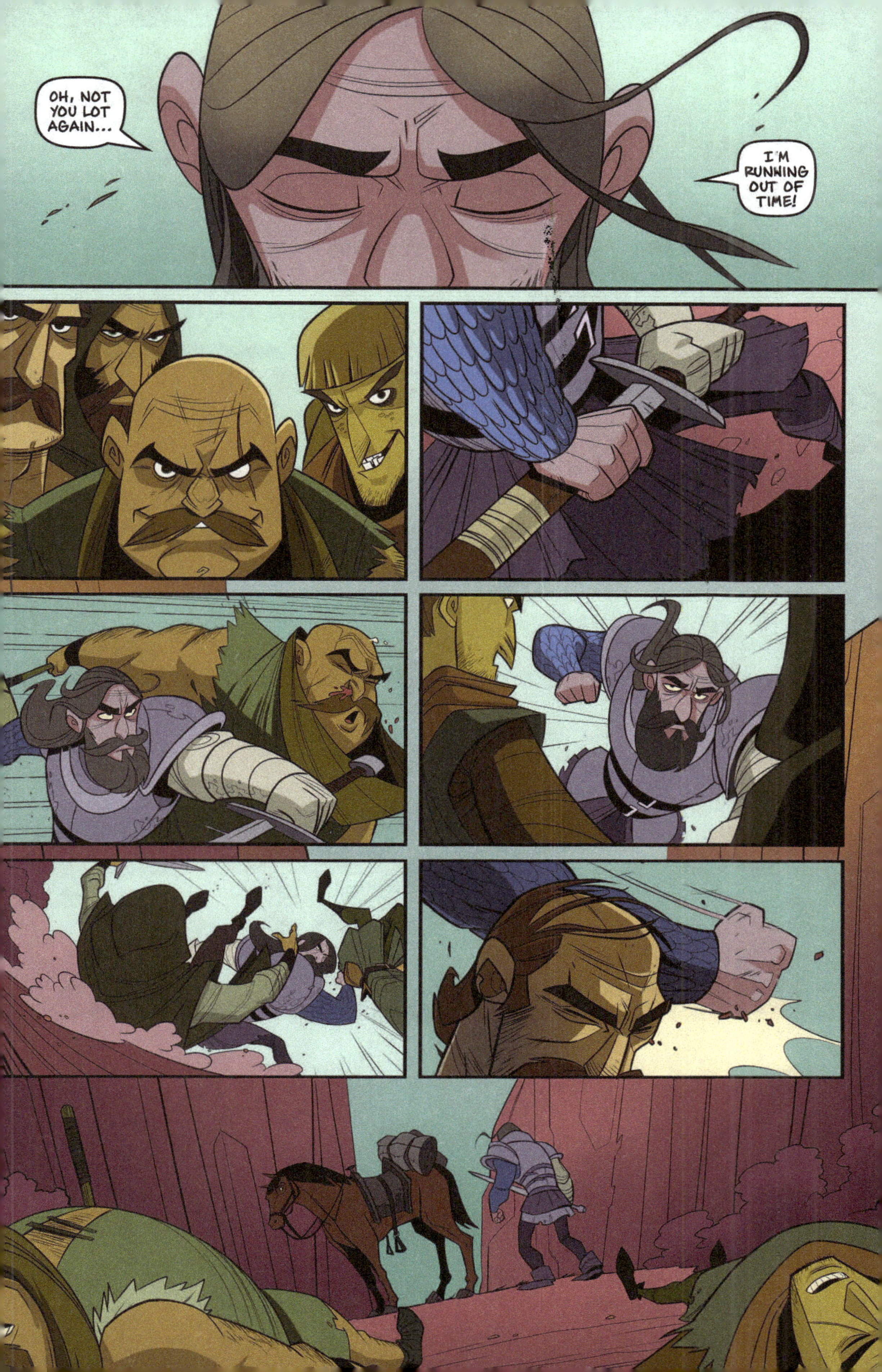
OH, NOT YOU LOT AGAIN...
I'M RUNNING OUT OF TIME!

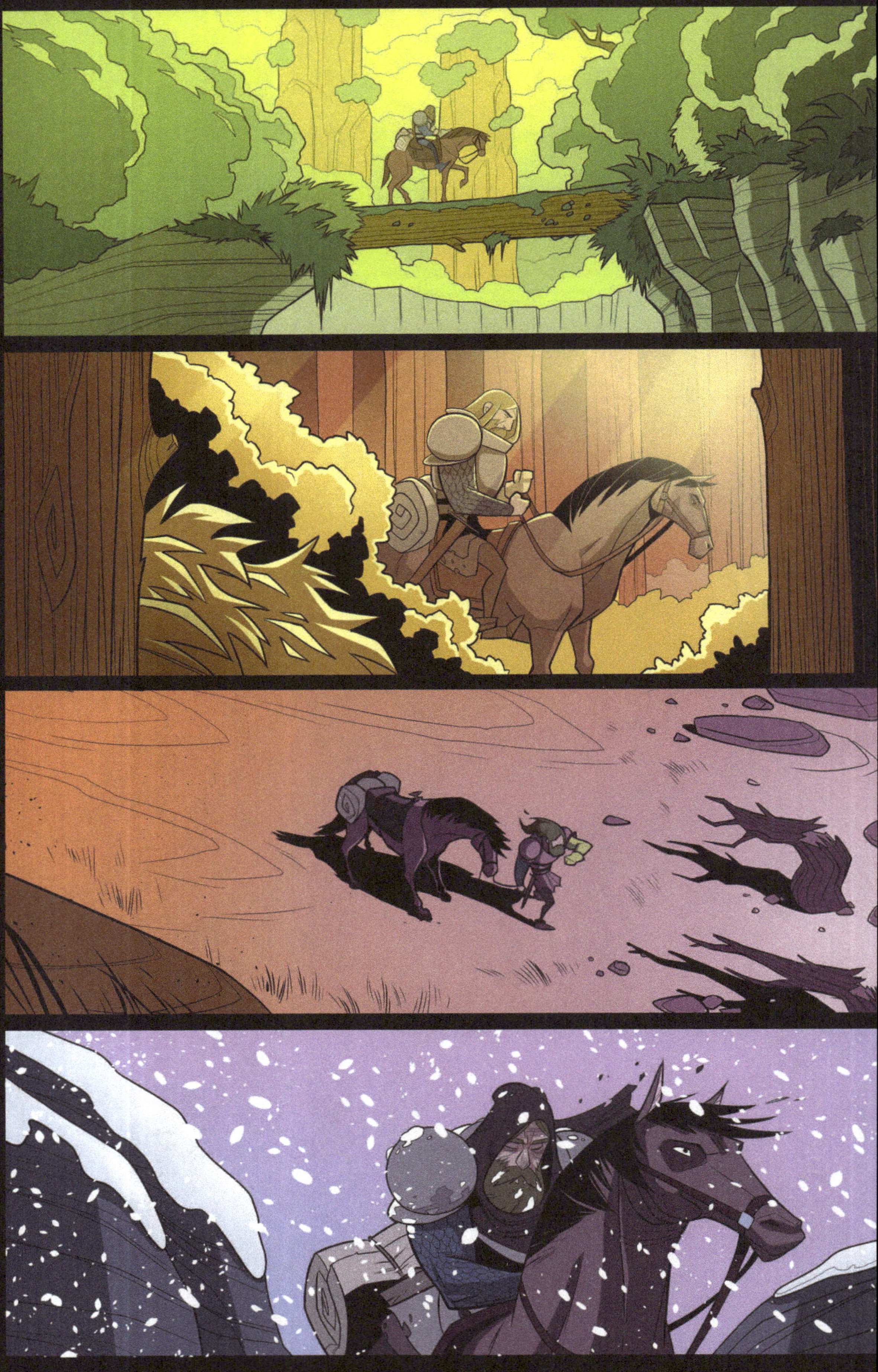

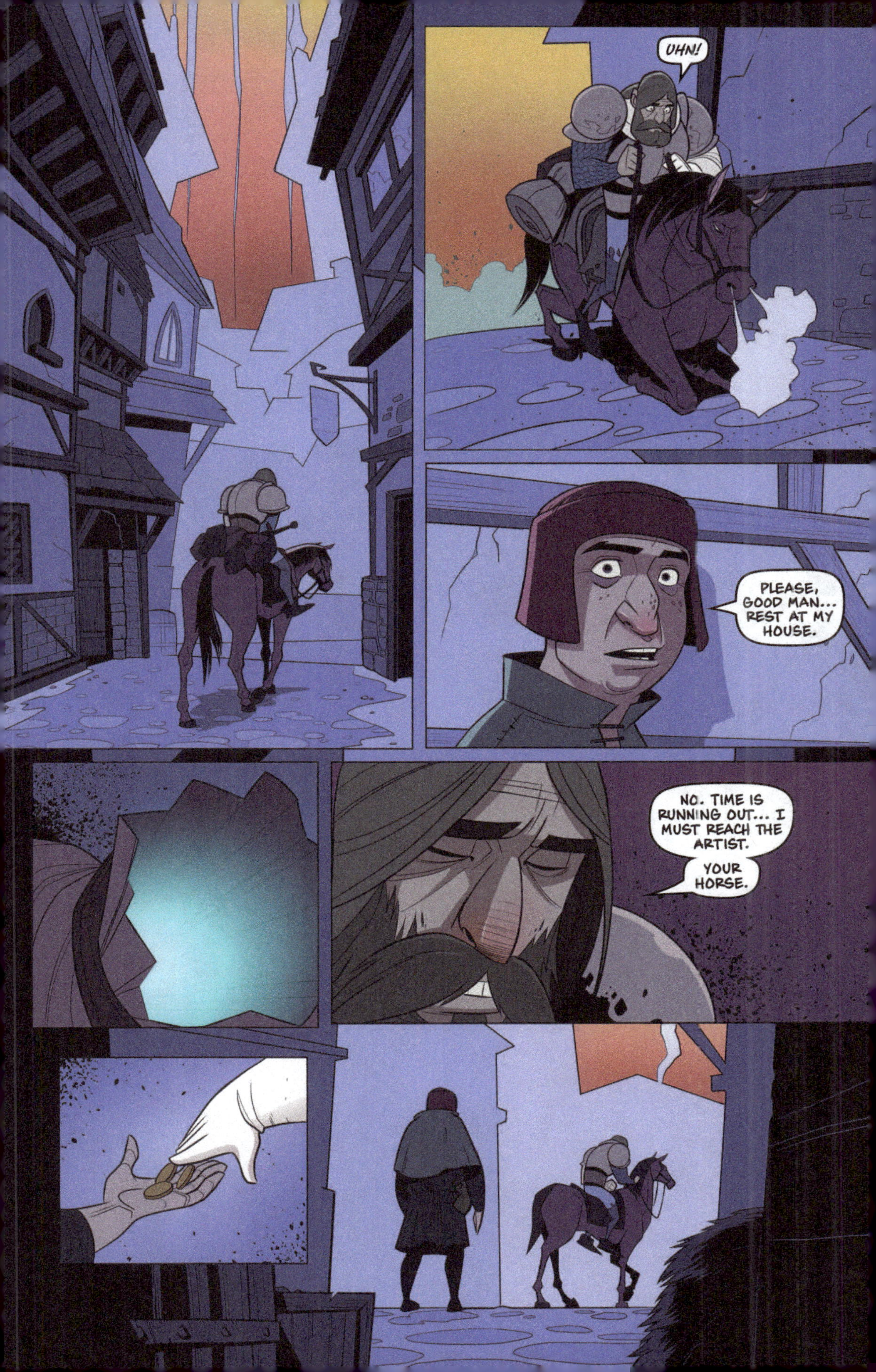
UHN!
PLEASE, GOOD MAN... REST AT MY HOUSE.
NO. TIME IS RUNNING OUT... I MUST REACH THE ARTIST.
YOUR HORSE.

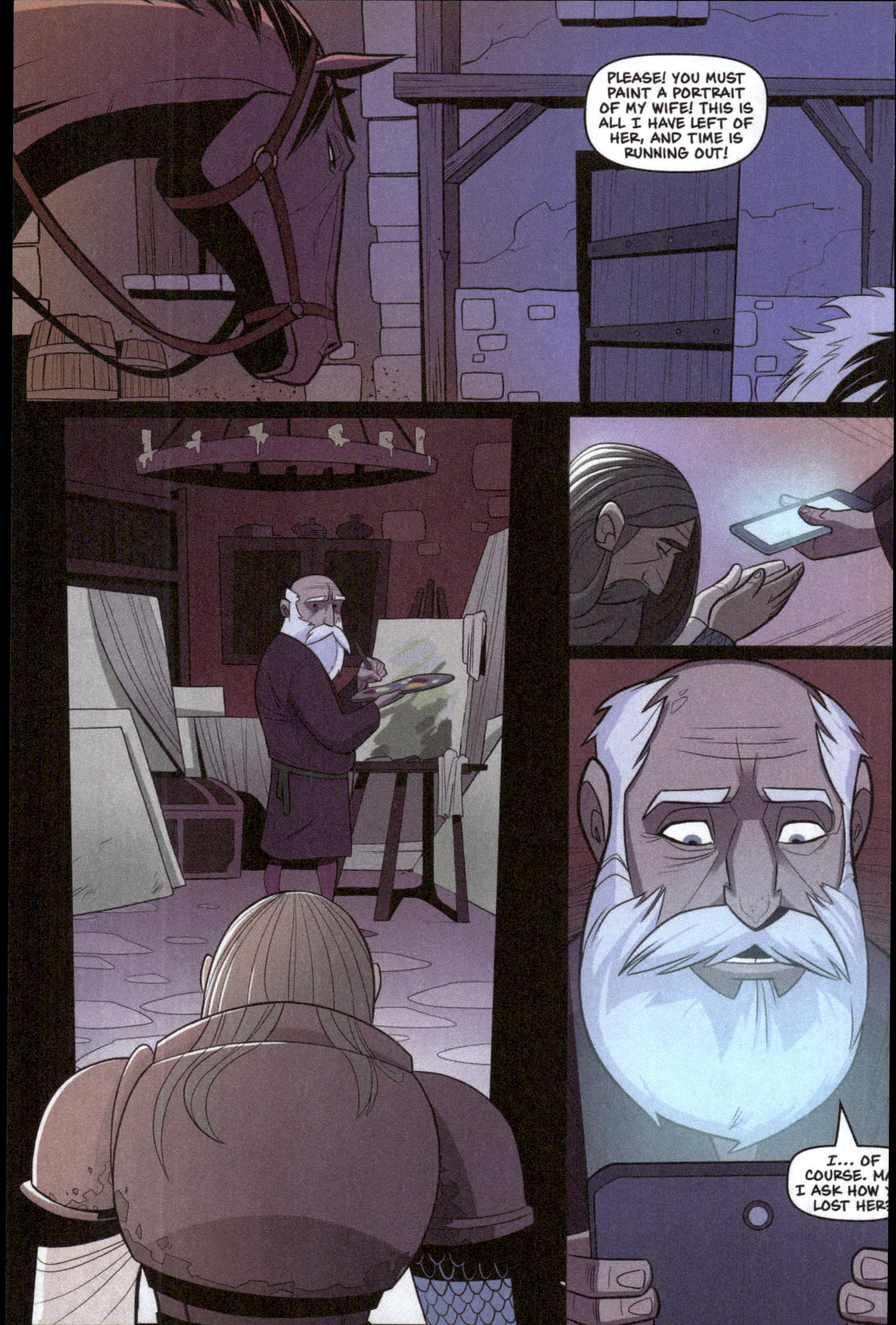
PLEASE! YOU MUST PAINT A PORTRAIT OF MY WIFE! THIS IS ALL I HAVE LEFT OF HER, AND TIME IS RUNNING OUT!
I... OF COURSE. MA I ASK HOW Y LOST HER?

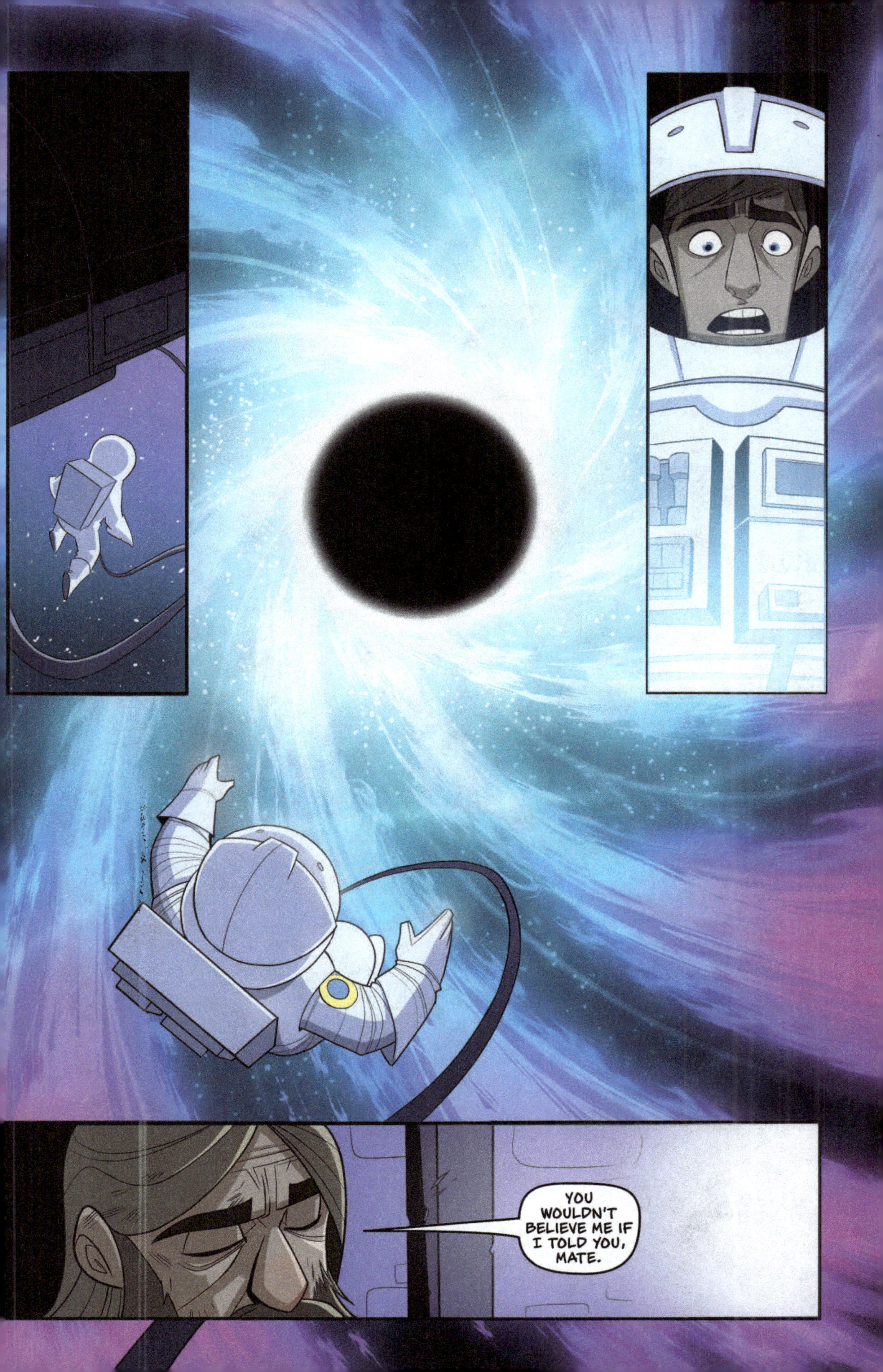
YOU WOULDN'T BELIEVE ME IF I TOLD YOU, MATE.

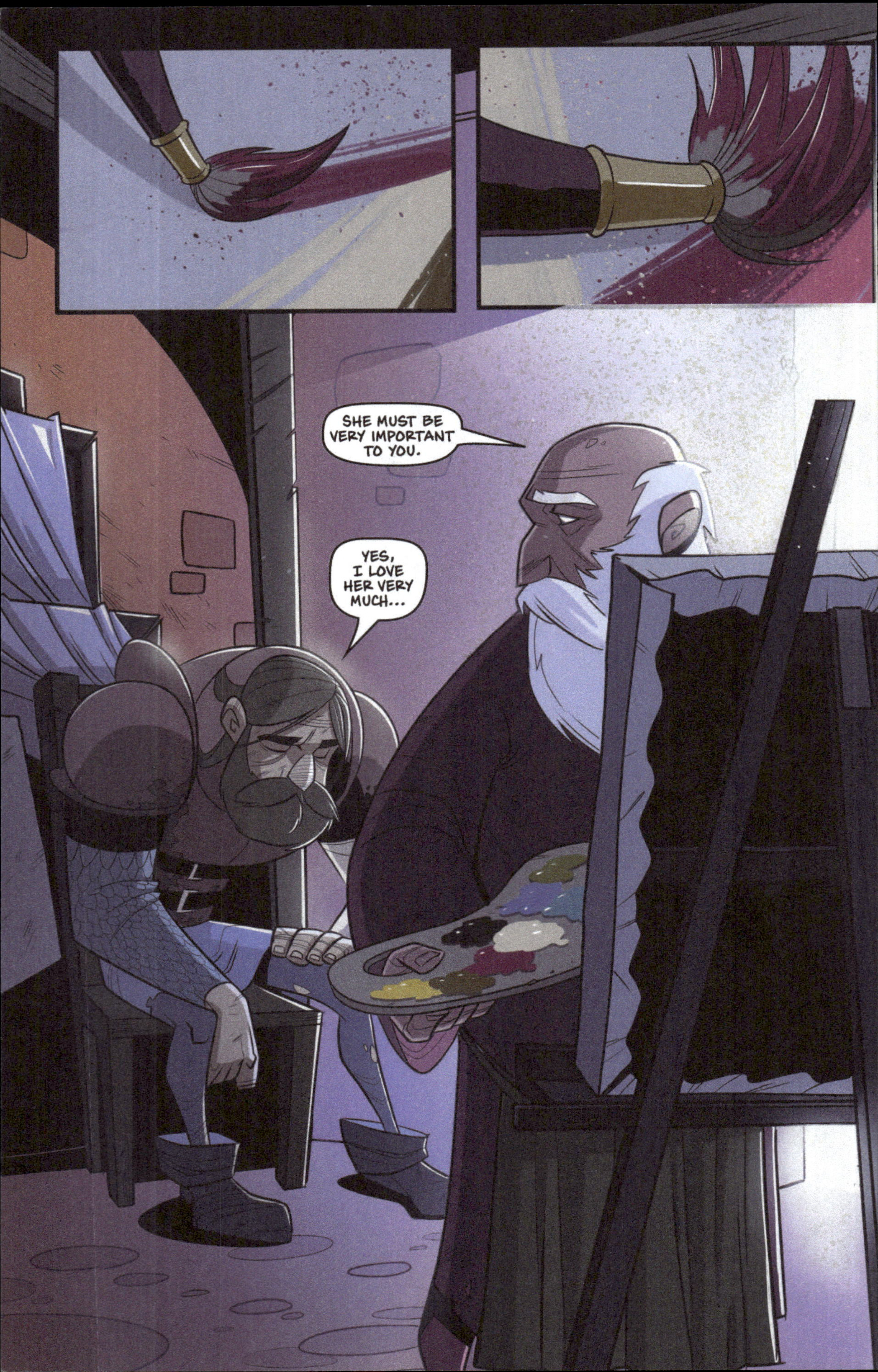
SHE MUST BE VERY IMPORTANT TO YOU.
YES, I LOVE HER VERY MUCH...

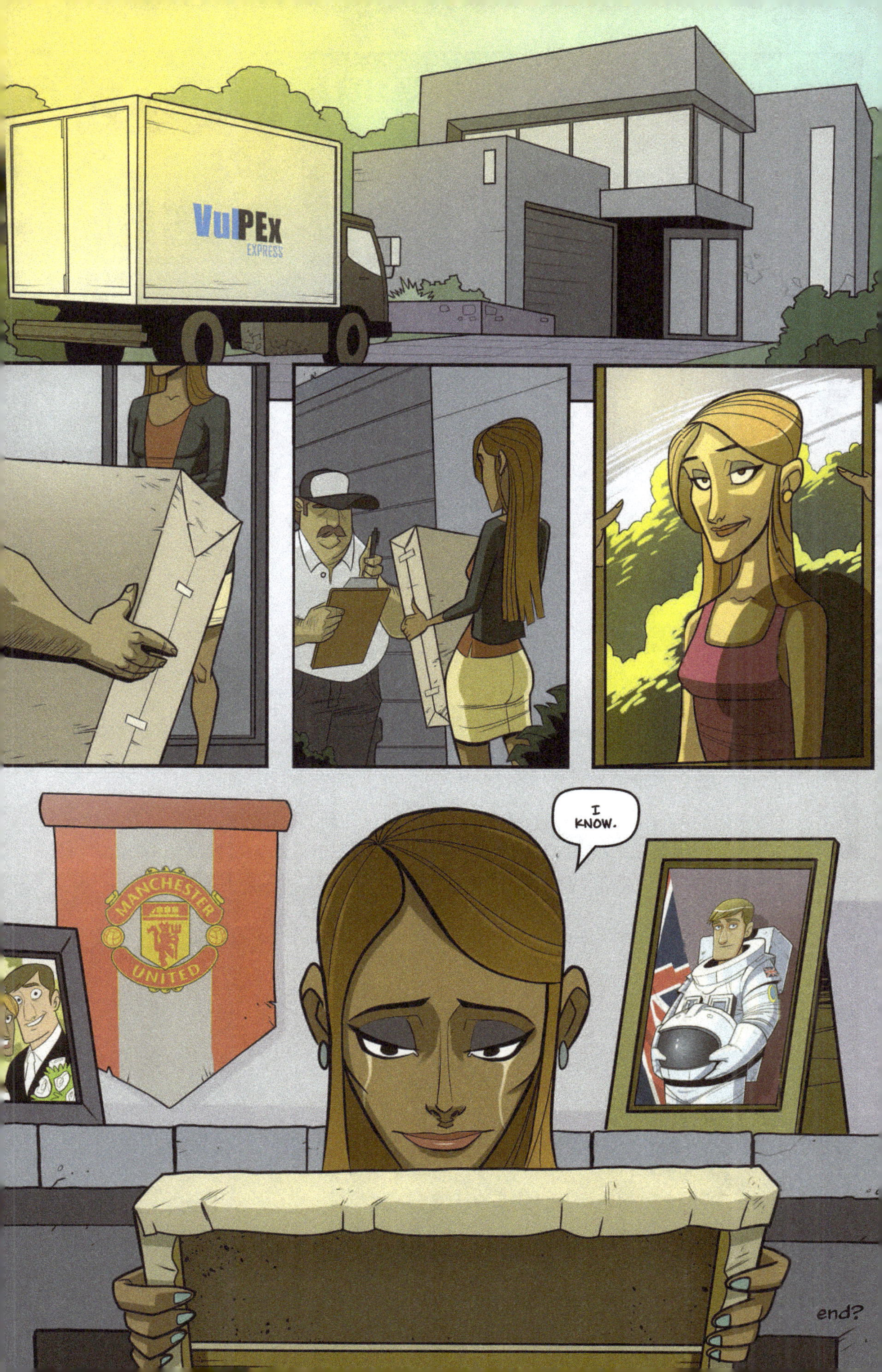
VuPEx
EXPRESS
I KNOW.
MANCHESTER
UNITED
end?

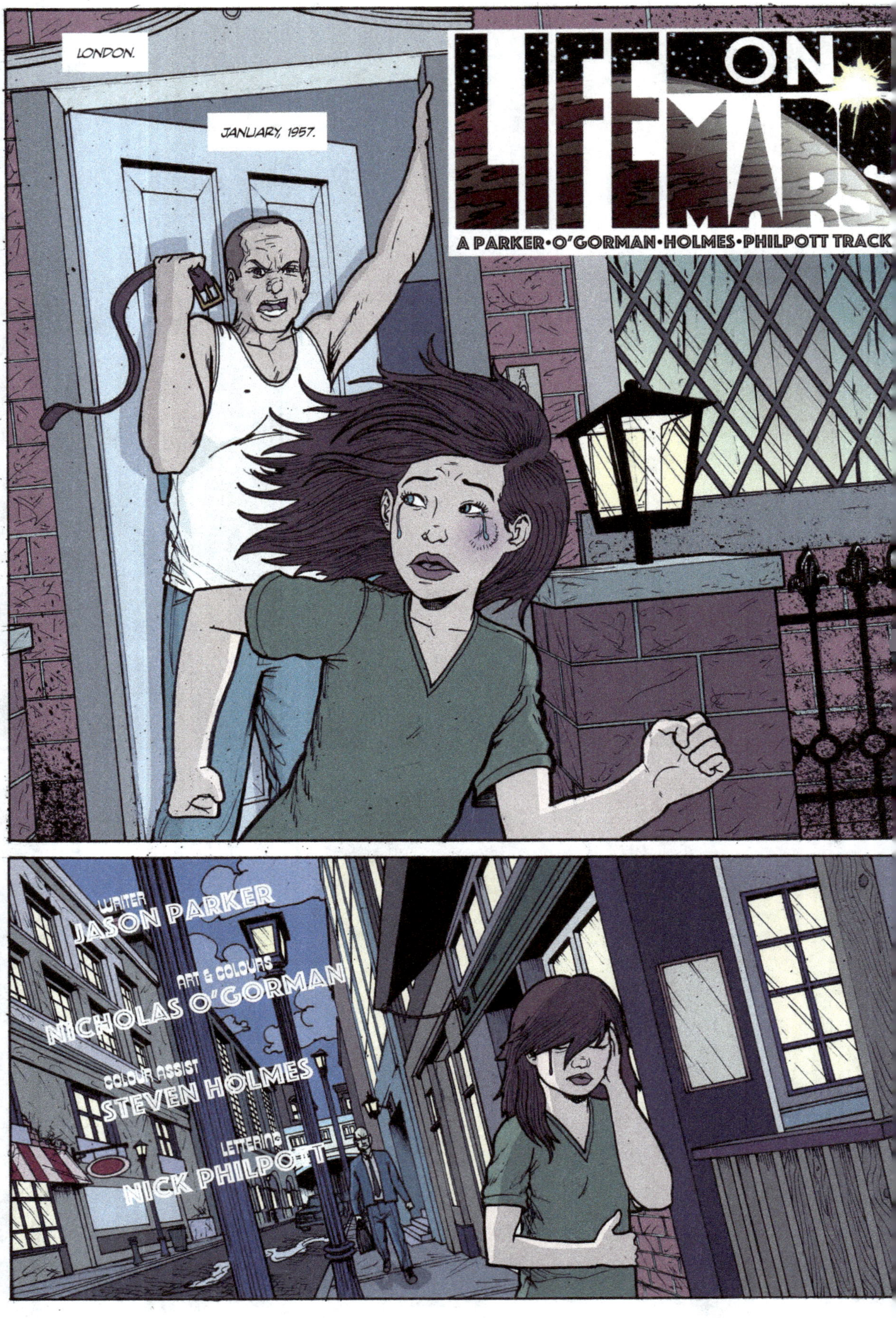
LONDON.
JANUARY, 1957.
LIFE ON MARS
A PARKER·O'GORMAN·HOLMES·PHILPOTT TRACK
WRITER
JASON PARKER
ART & COLOURS
NICHOLAS O'GORMAN
COLOUR ASSIST
STEVEN HOLMES
LETTERING
NICK PHILPOTT

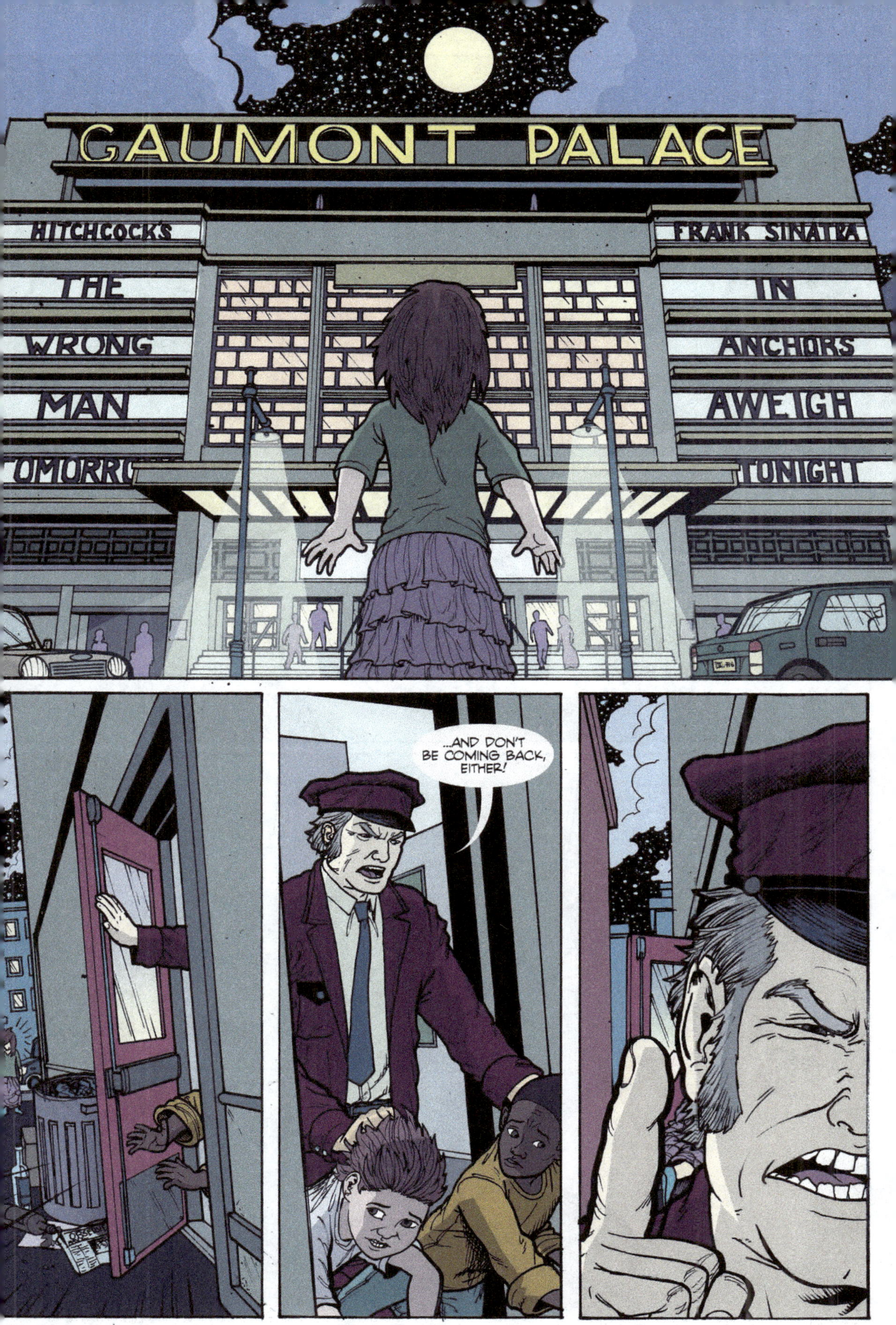
GAUMONT PALACE
HITCHCOCKS THE WRONG MAN
FRANK SINATRA IN ANCHORS AWEIGH TONIGHT
...AND DON'T BE COMING BACK, EITHER!

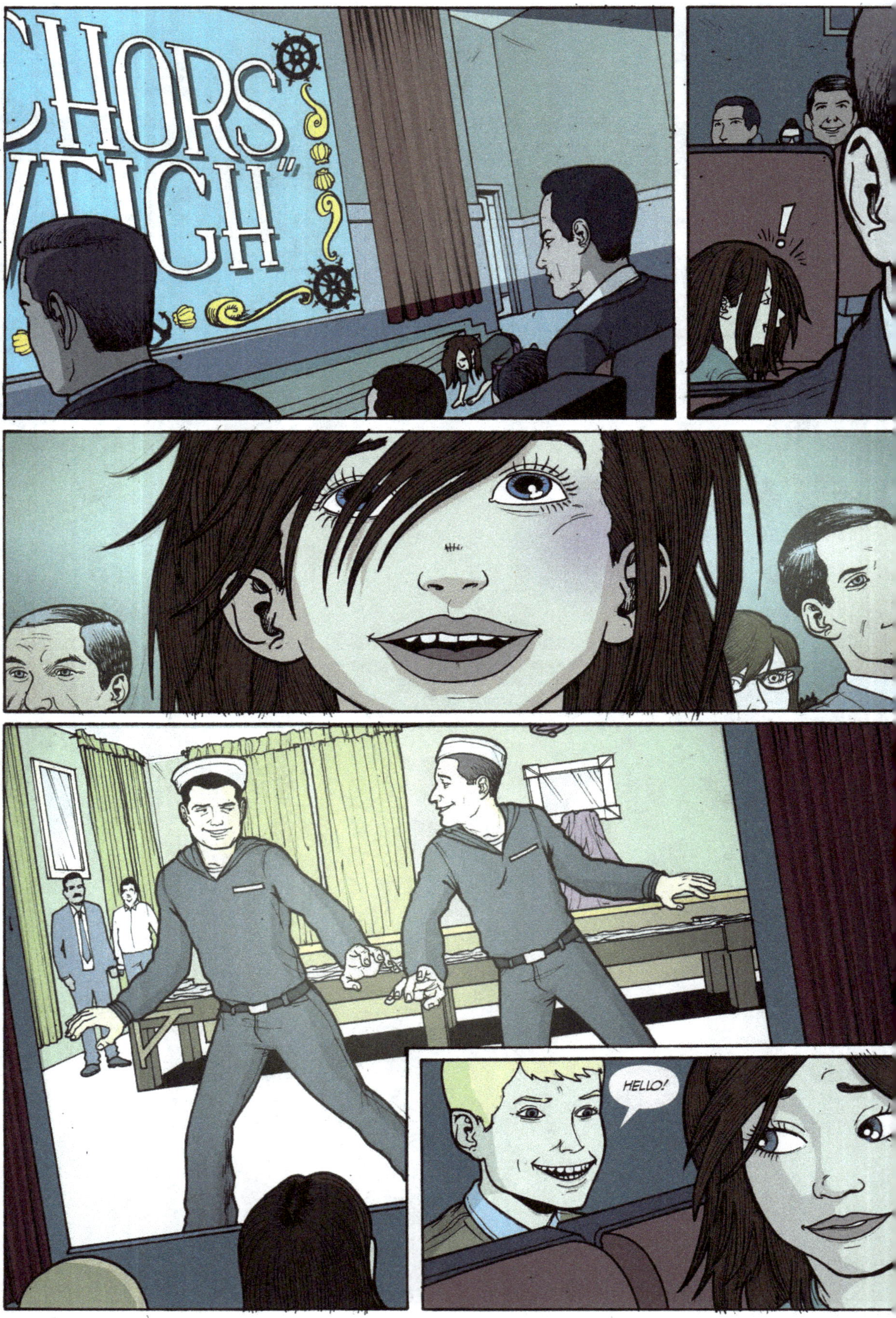
CHORS
VEIGH"
!
HELLO!

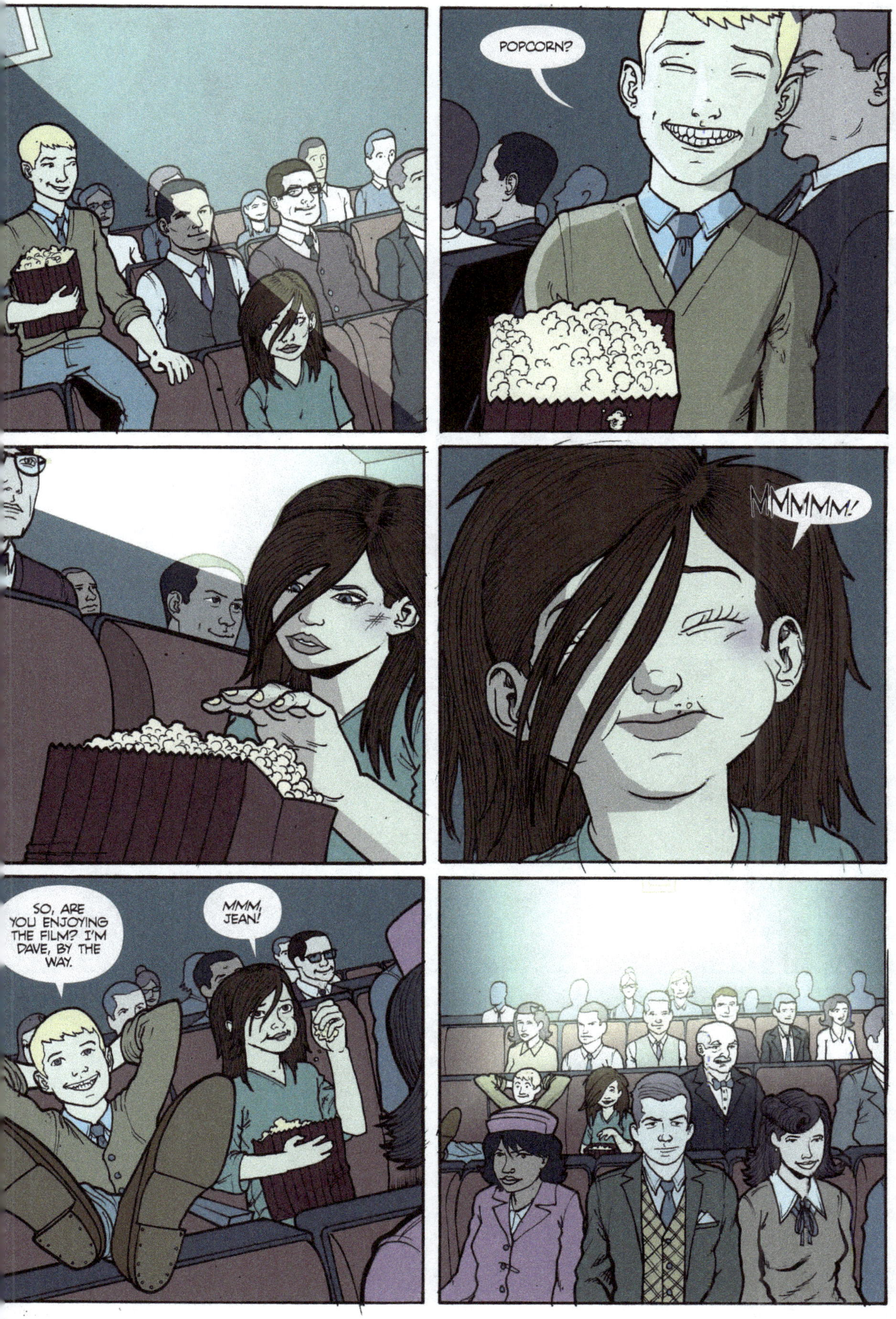
POPCORN?
MMMMM!
SO, ARE YOU ENJOYING THE FILM? I'M DAVE, BY THE WAY.
MMM, JEAN!

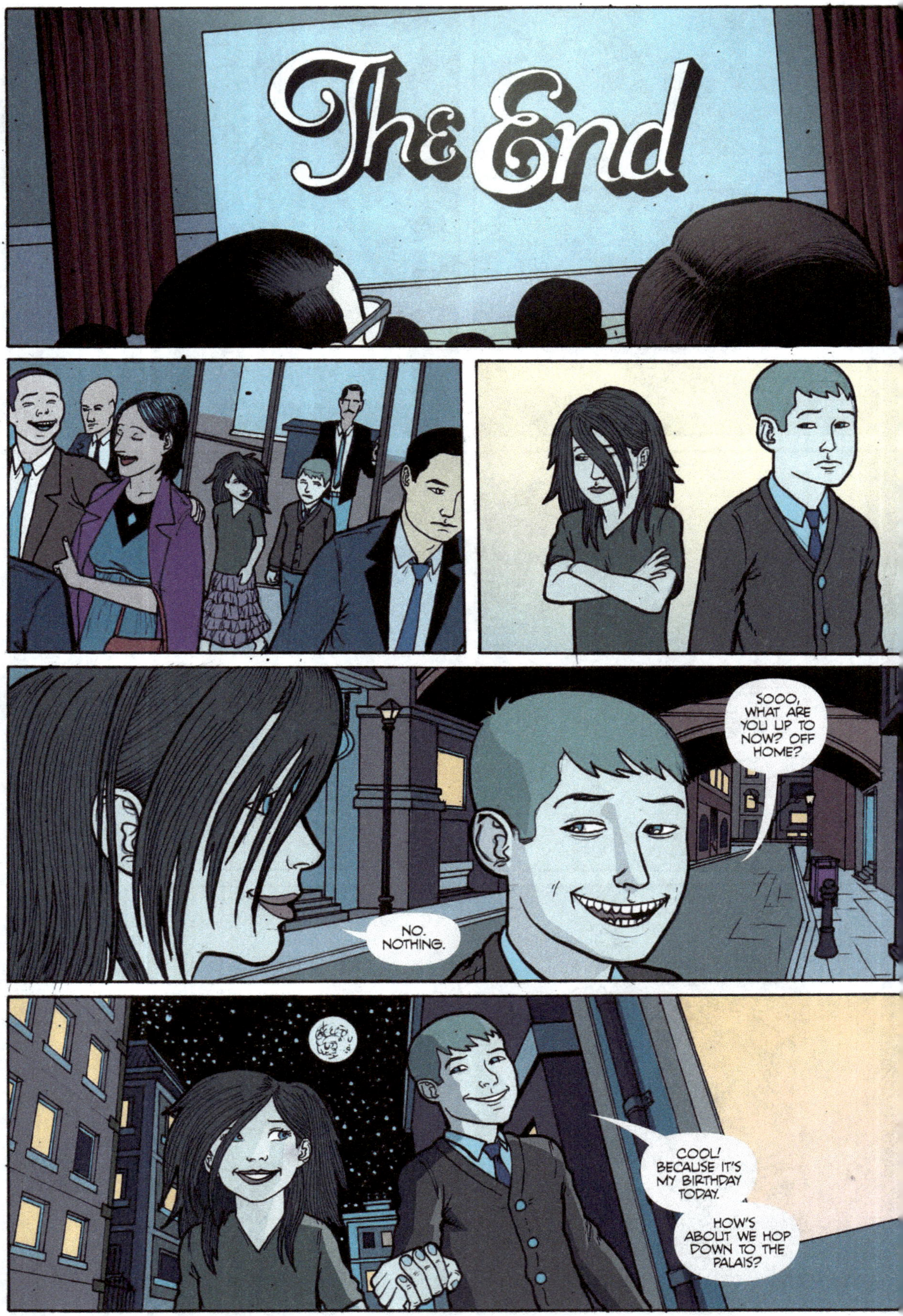
The End
SOOO, WHAT ARE YOU UP TO NOW? OFF HOME?
NO. NOTHING.
COOL! BECAUSE IT'S MY BIRTHDAY TODAY.
HOW'S ABOUT WE HOP DOWN TO THE PALAIS?

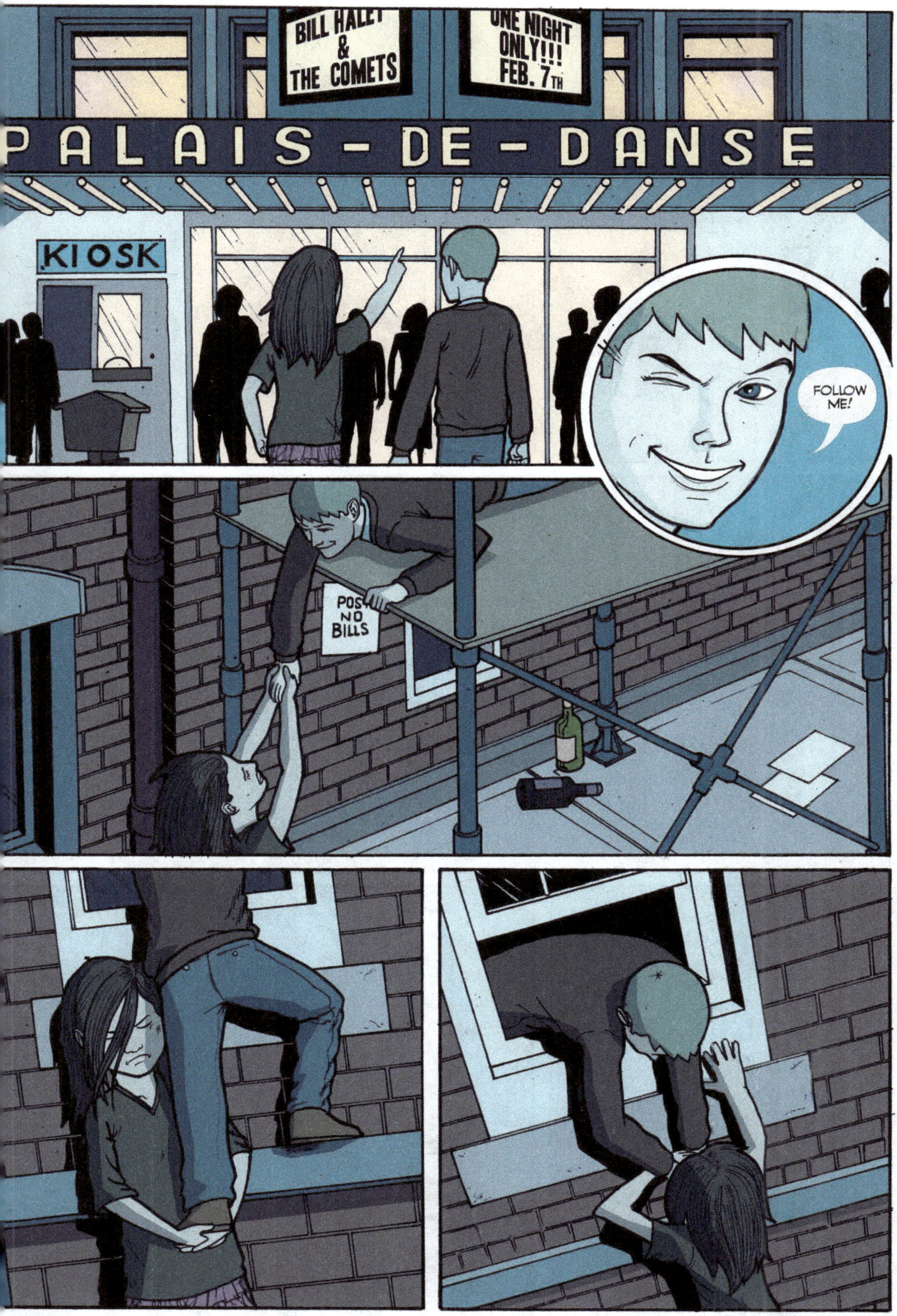
BILL HALEY & THE COMETS
ONE NIGHT ONLY!!! FEB. 7TH
PALAIS-DE-DANSE
KIOSK
FOLLOW ME!
POST NO BILLS

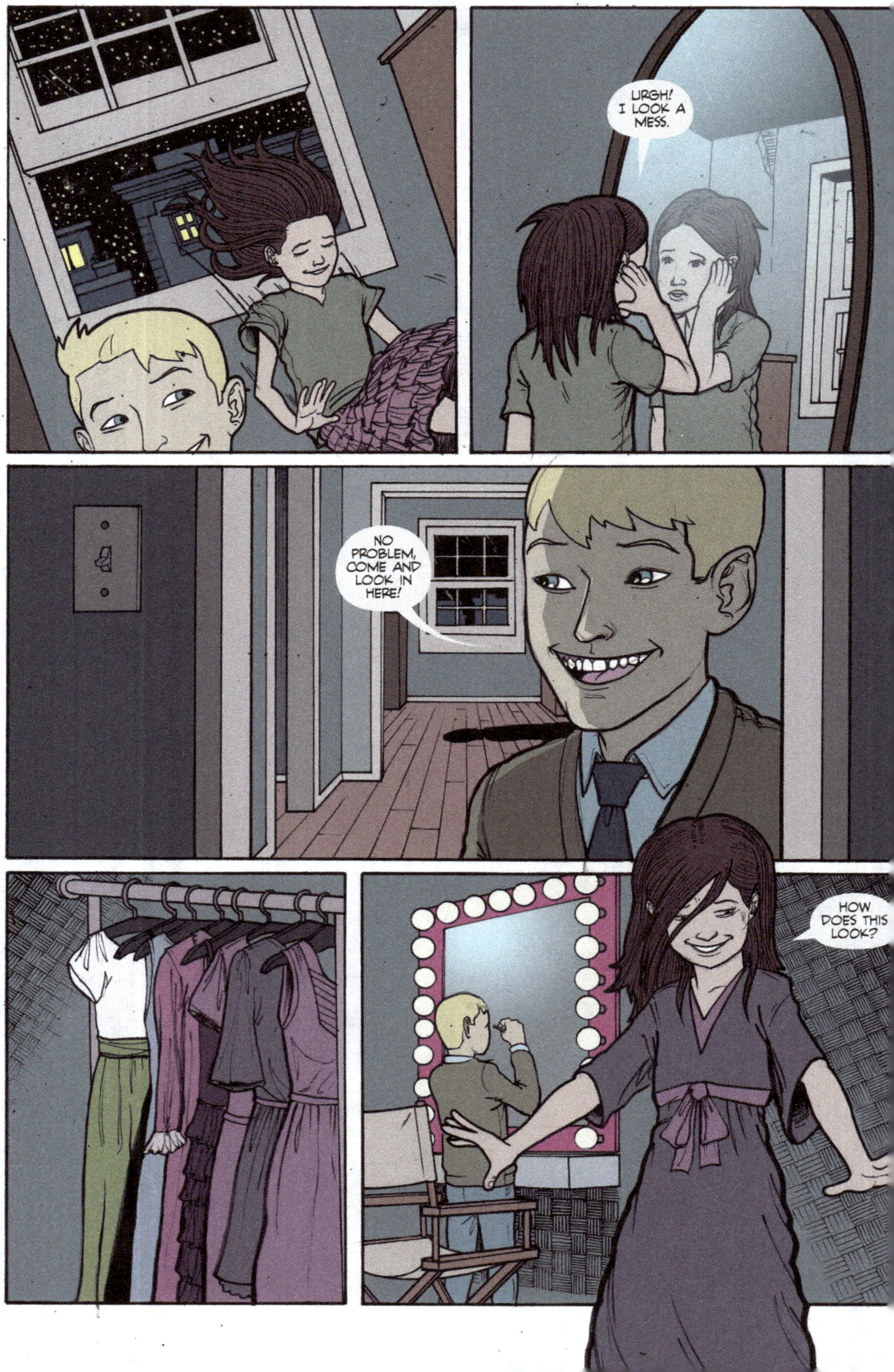
URGH! I LOOK A MESS.
NO PROBLEM, COME AND LOOK IN HERE!
HOW DOES THIS LOOK?

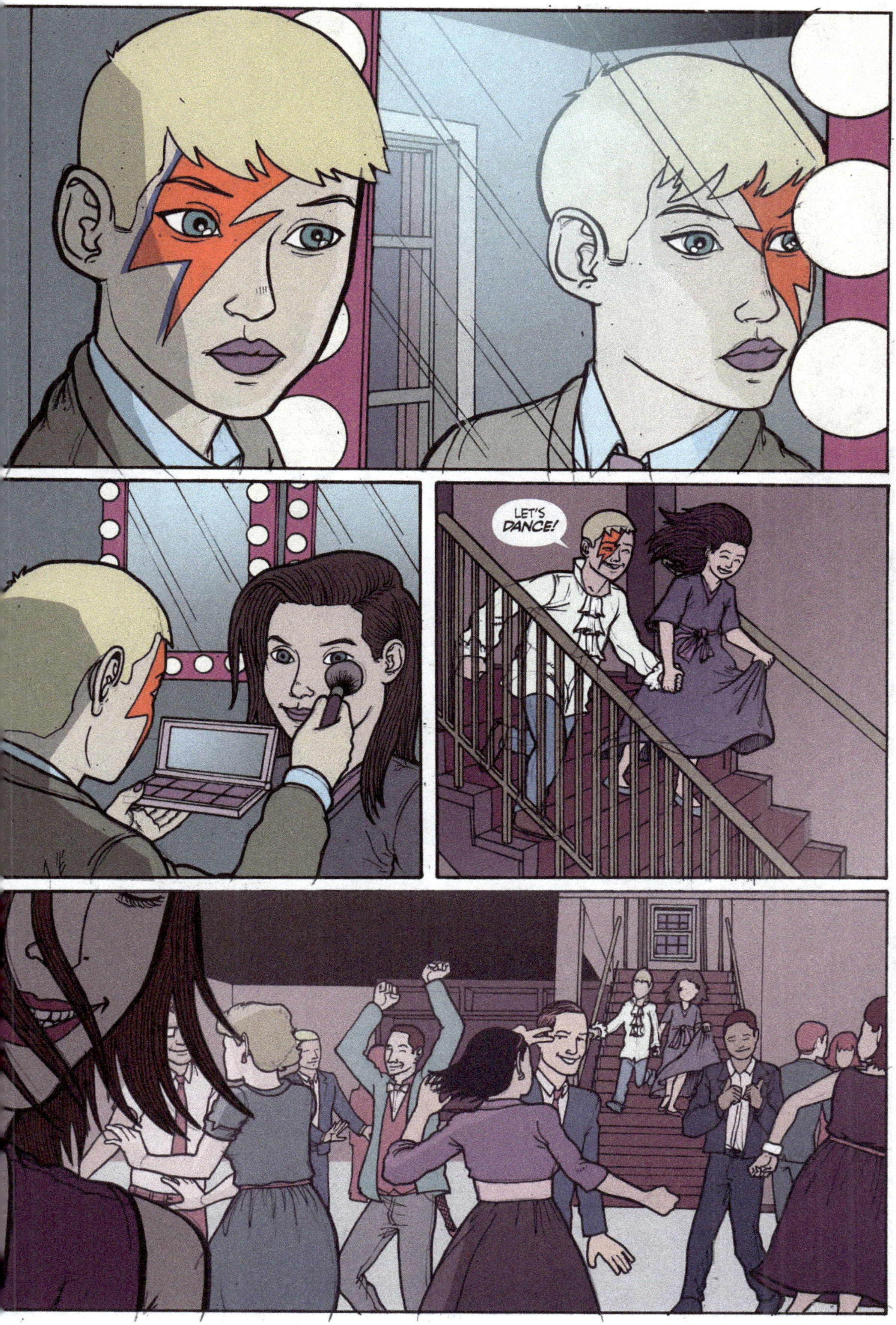
LET'S DANCE!

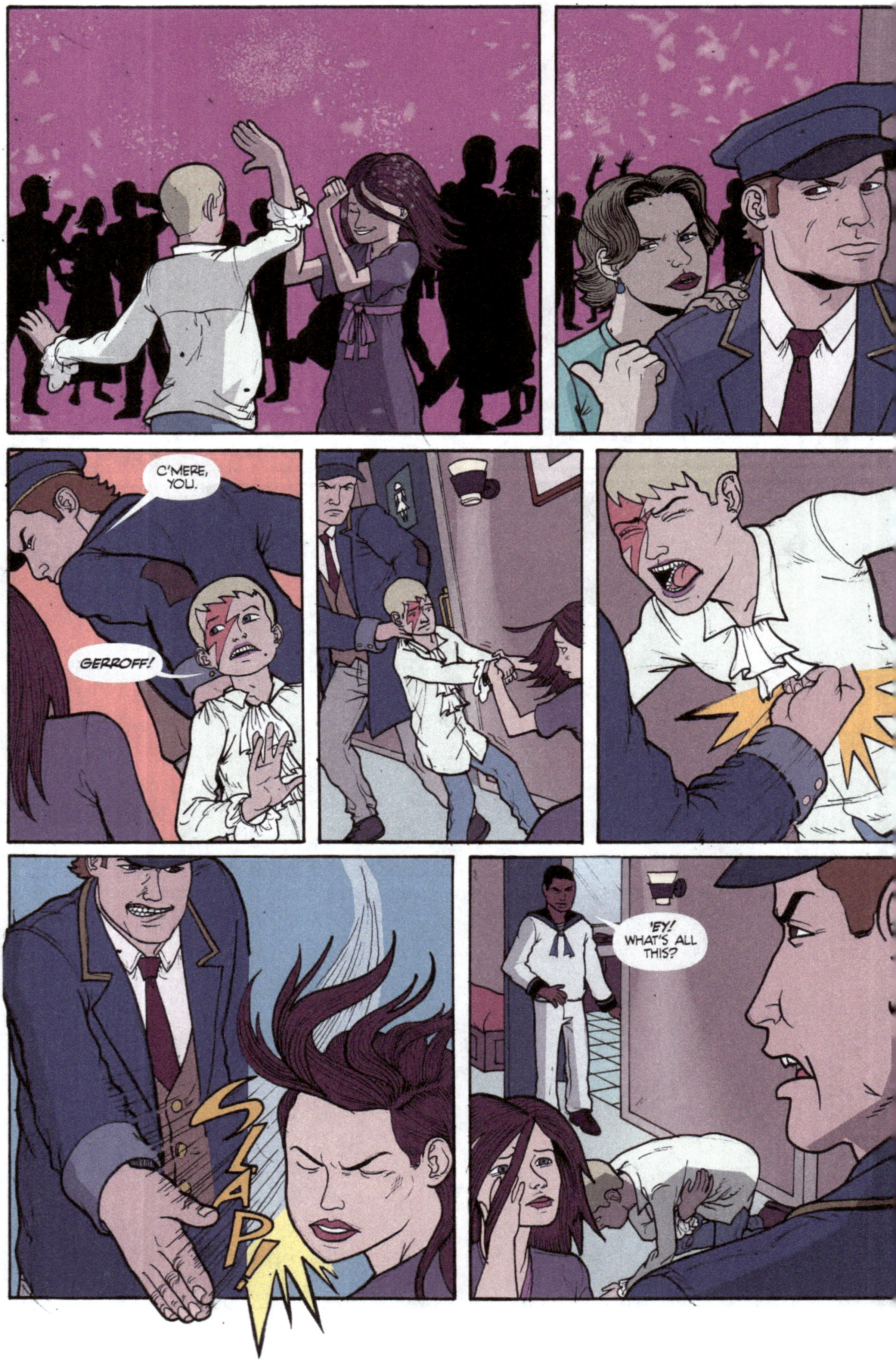
C'MERE, YOU.
GERROFF!
SLAP!
'EY! WHAT'S ALL THIS?

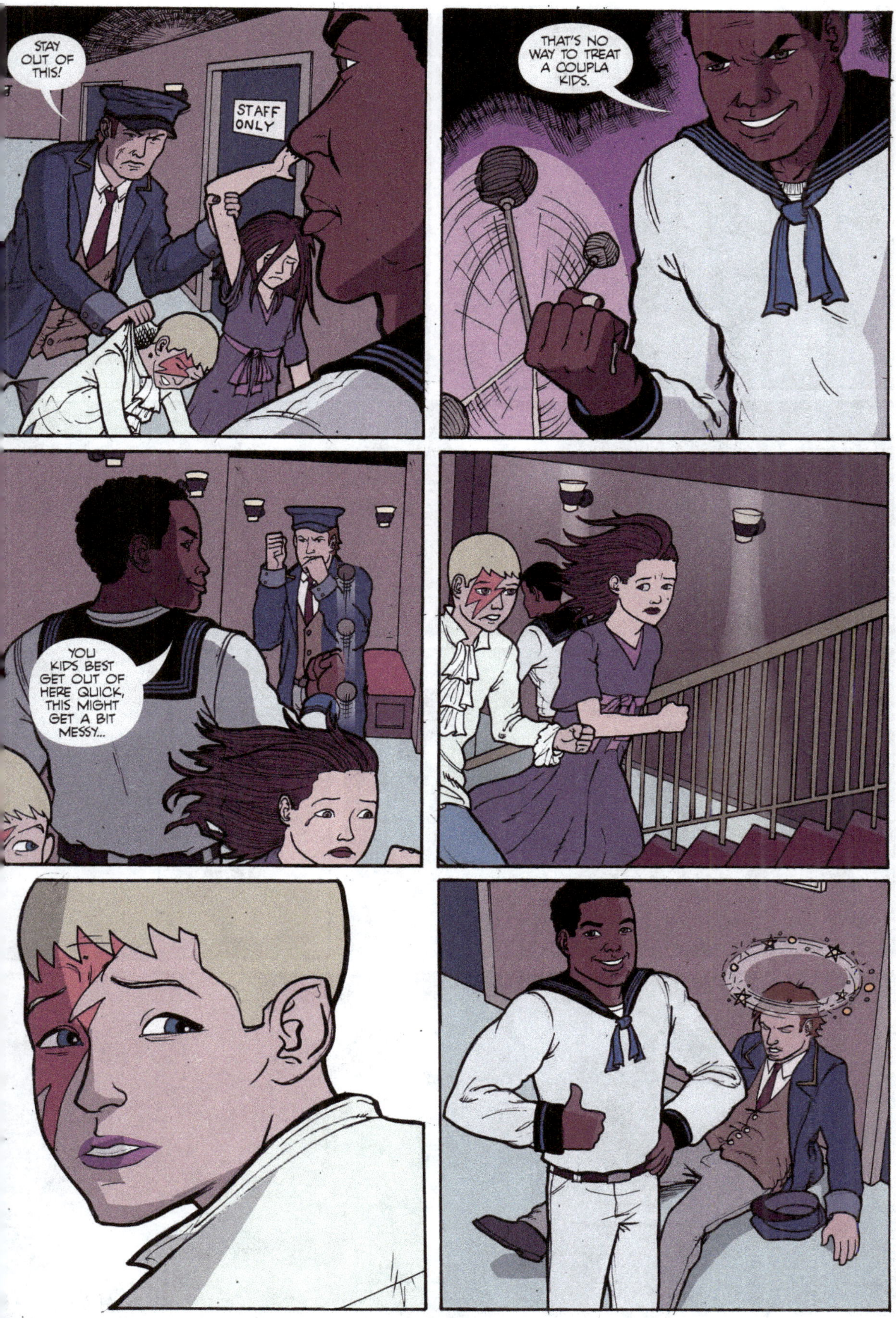
STAY OUT OF THIS!
STAFF ONLY
THAT'S NO WAY TO TREAT A COUPLA KIDS.
YOU KIDS BEST GET OUT OF HERE QUICK, THIS MIGHT GET A BIT MESSY...

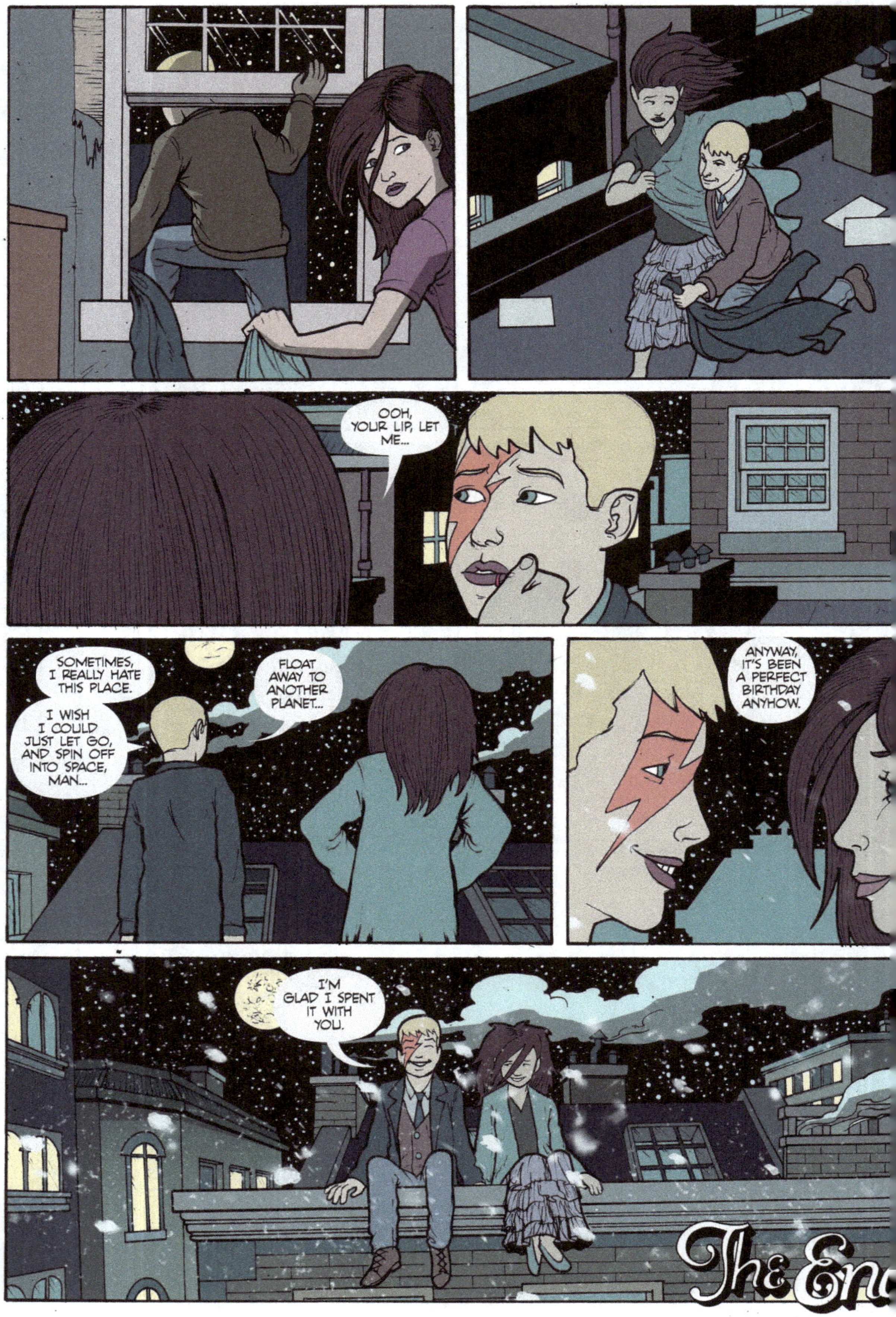
OOH, YOUR LIP, LET ME...
SOMETIMES, I REALLY HATE THIS PLACE.
I WISH I COULD JUST LET GO, AND SPIN OFF INTO SPACE, MAN...
FLOAT AWAY TO ANOTHER PLANET...
ANYWAY, IT'S BEEN A PERFECT BIRTHDAY ANYHOW.
I'M GLAD I SPENT IT WITH YOU.
The En

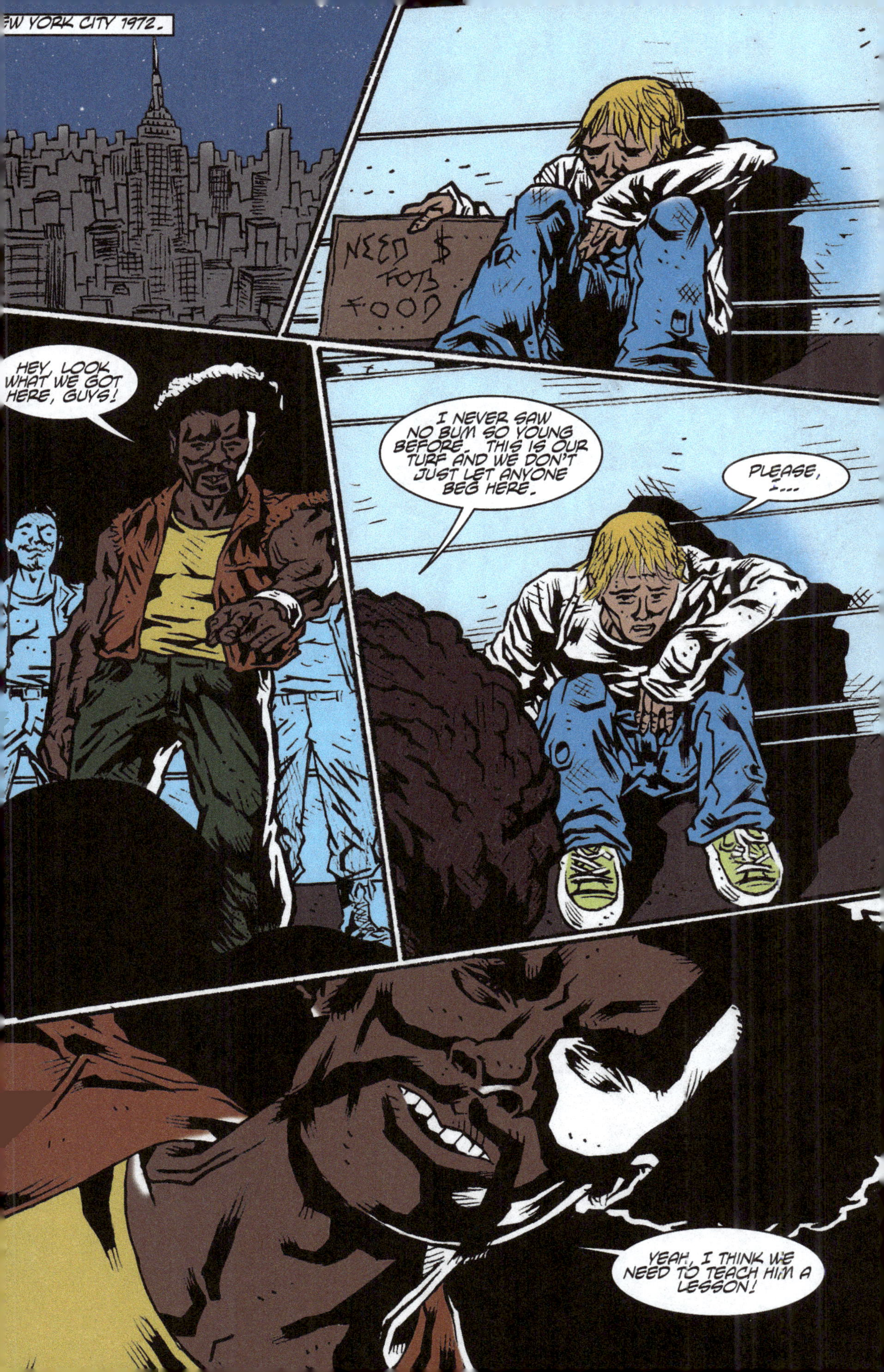

EW YORK CITY 1972.
NEED $ FOR FOOD
HEY, LOOK WHAT WE GOT HERE, GUYS!
I NEVER SAW NO BUM SO YOUNG BEFORE. THIS IS OUR TURF AND WE DON'T JUST LET ANYONE BEG HERE.
PLEASE, I...
YEAH, I THINK WE NEED TO TEACH HIM A LESSON!

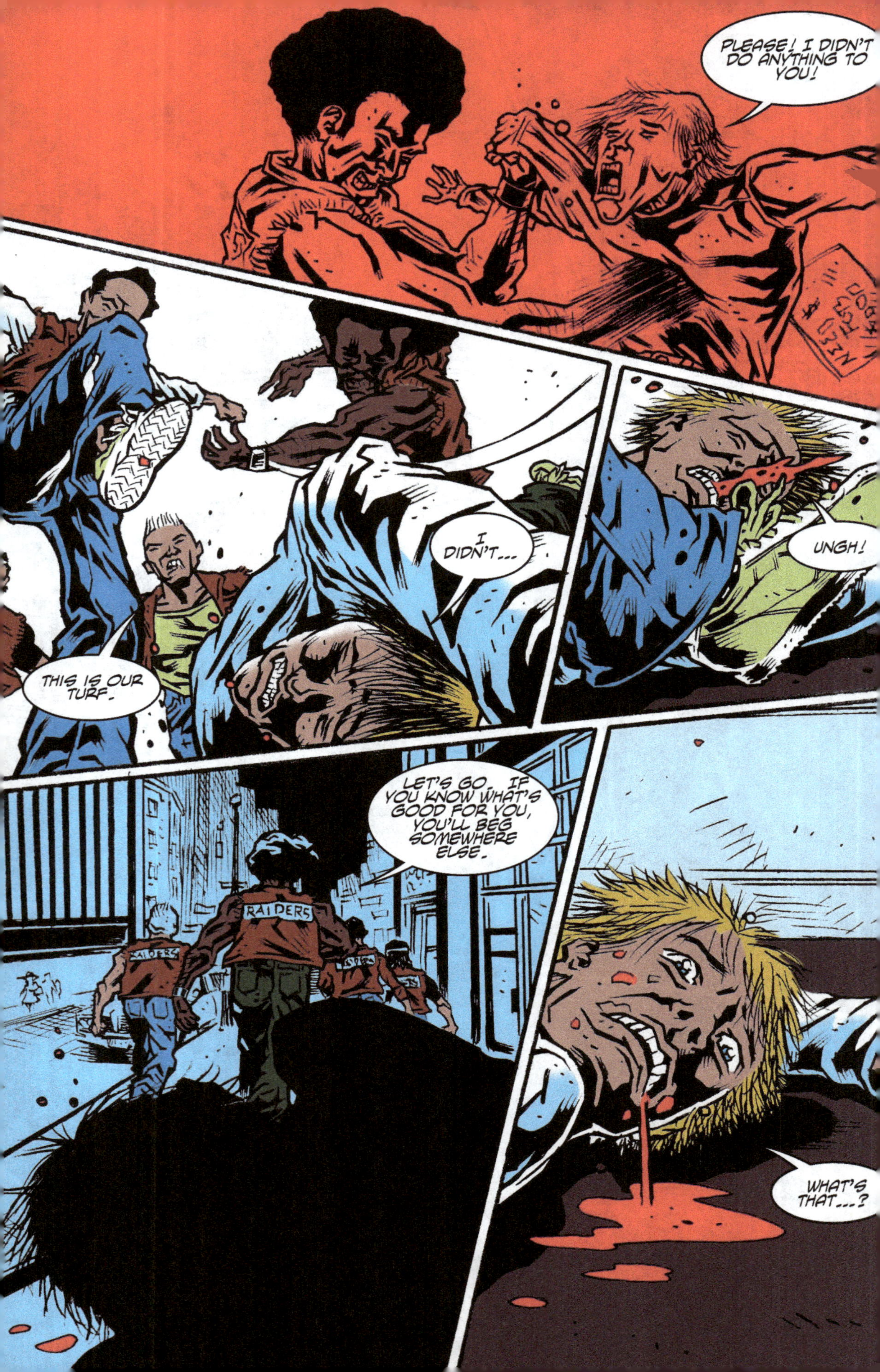
PLEASE! I DIDN'T DO ANYTHING TO YOU!
I DIDN'T...
THIS IS OUR TURF.
UNGH!
LET'S GO. IF YOU KNOW WHAT'S GOOD FOR YOU, YOU'LL BEG SOMEWHERE ELSE.
RAIDERS
RAIDERS
WHAT'S THAT...?

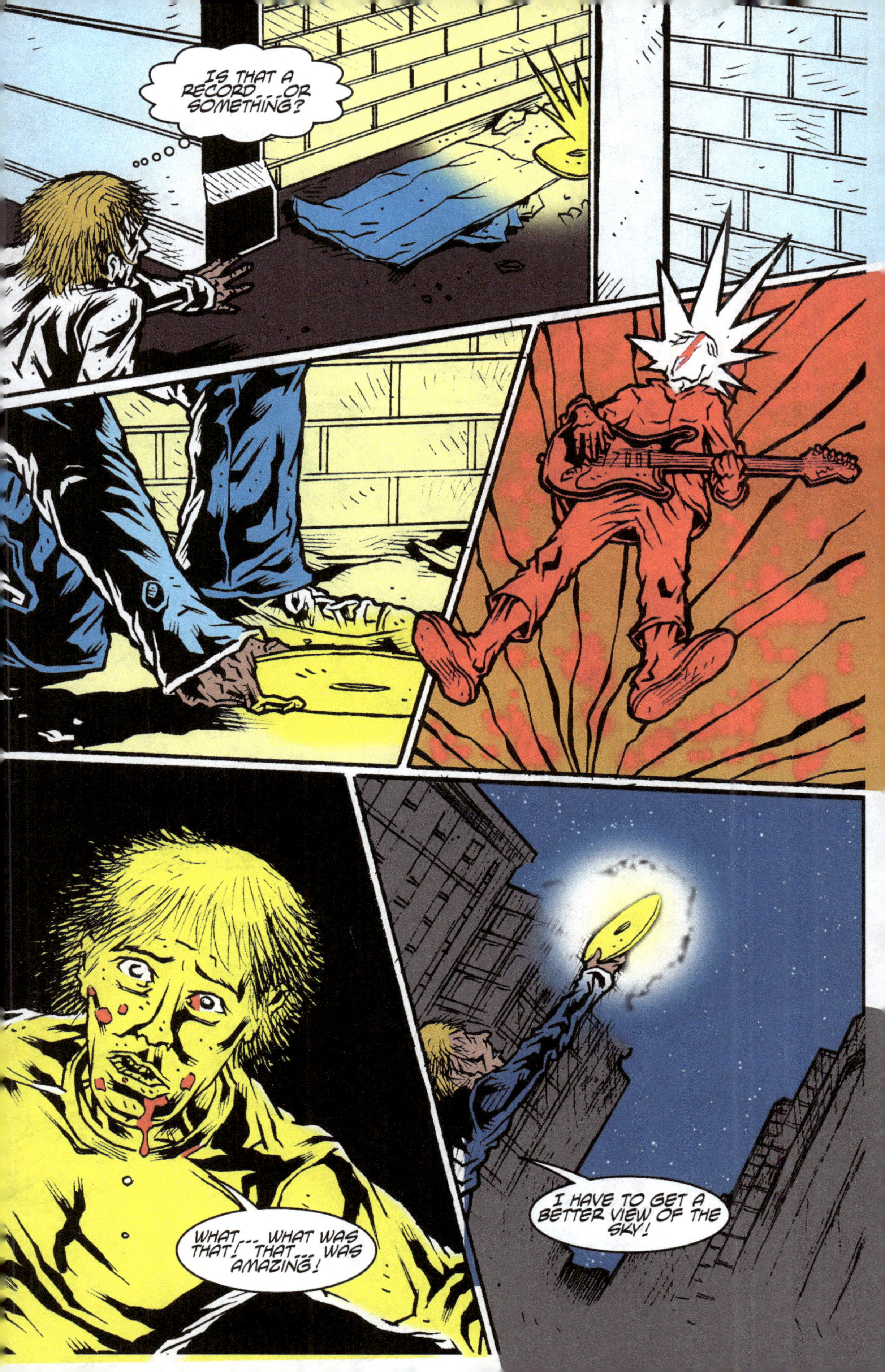
IS THAT A RECORD . . . OR SOMETHING?
WHAT--- WHAT WAS THAT! THAT... WAS AMAZING!
I HAVE TO GET A BETTER VIEW OF THE SKY!

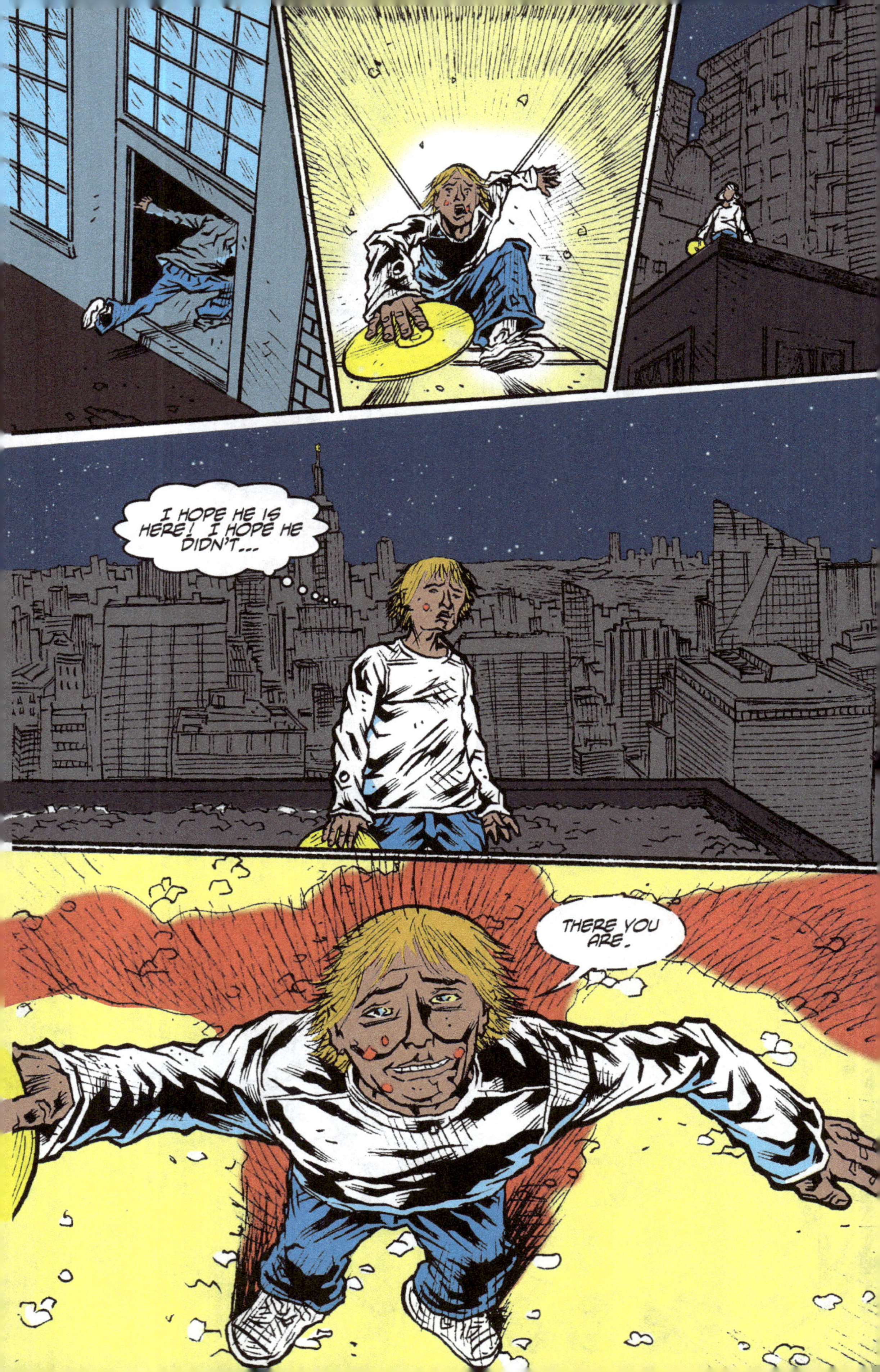
I HOPE HE IS HERE! I HOPE HE DIDN'T...
THERE YOU ARE.

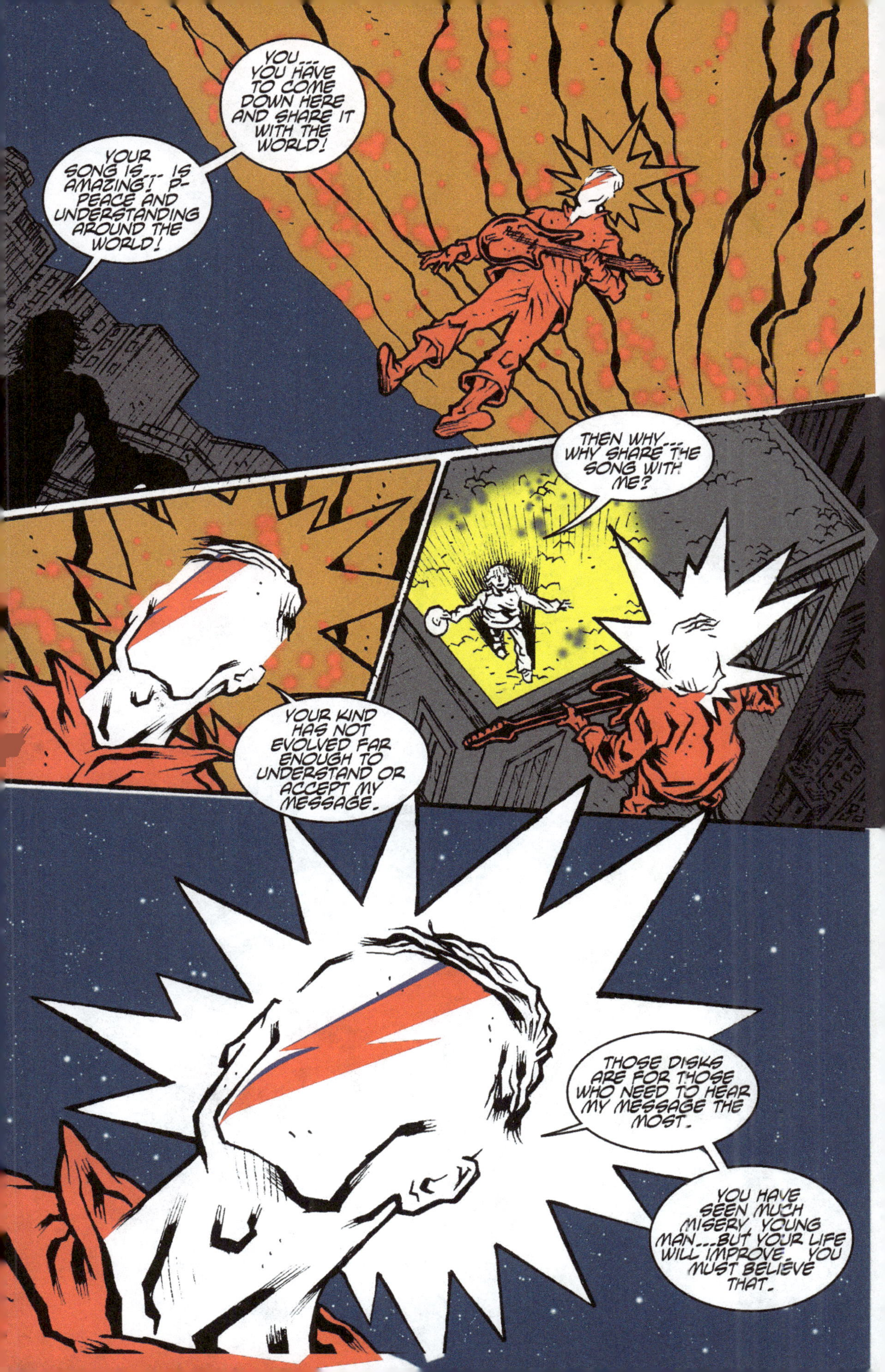
YOU... YOU HAVE TO COME DOWN HERE AND SHARE IT WITH THE WORLD!
YOUR SONG IS... IS AMAZING! P-PEACE AND UNDERSTANDING AROUND THE WORLD!
YOUR KIND HAS NOT EVOLVED FAR ENOUGH TO UNDERSTAND OR ACCEPT MY MESSAGE.
THEN WHY... WHY SHARE THE SONG WITH ME?
THOSE DISKS ARE FOR THOSE WHO NEED TO HEAR MY MESSAGE THE MOST.
YOU HAVE SEEN MUCH MISERY, YOUNG MAN...BUT YOUR LIFE WILL IMPROVE. YOU MUST BELIEVE THAT.

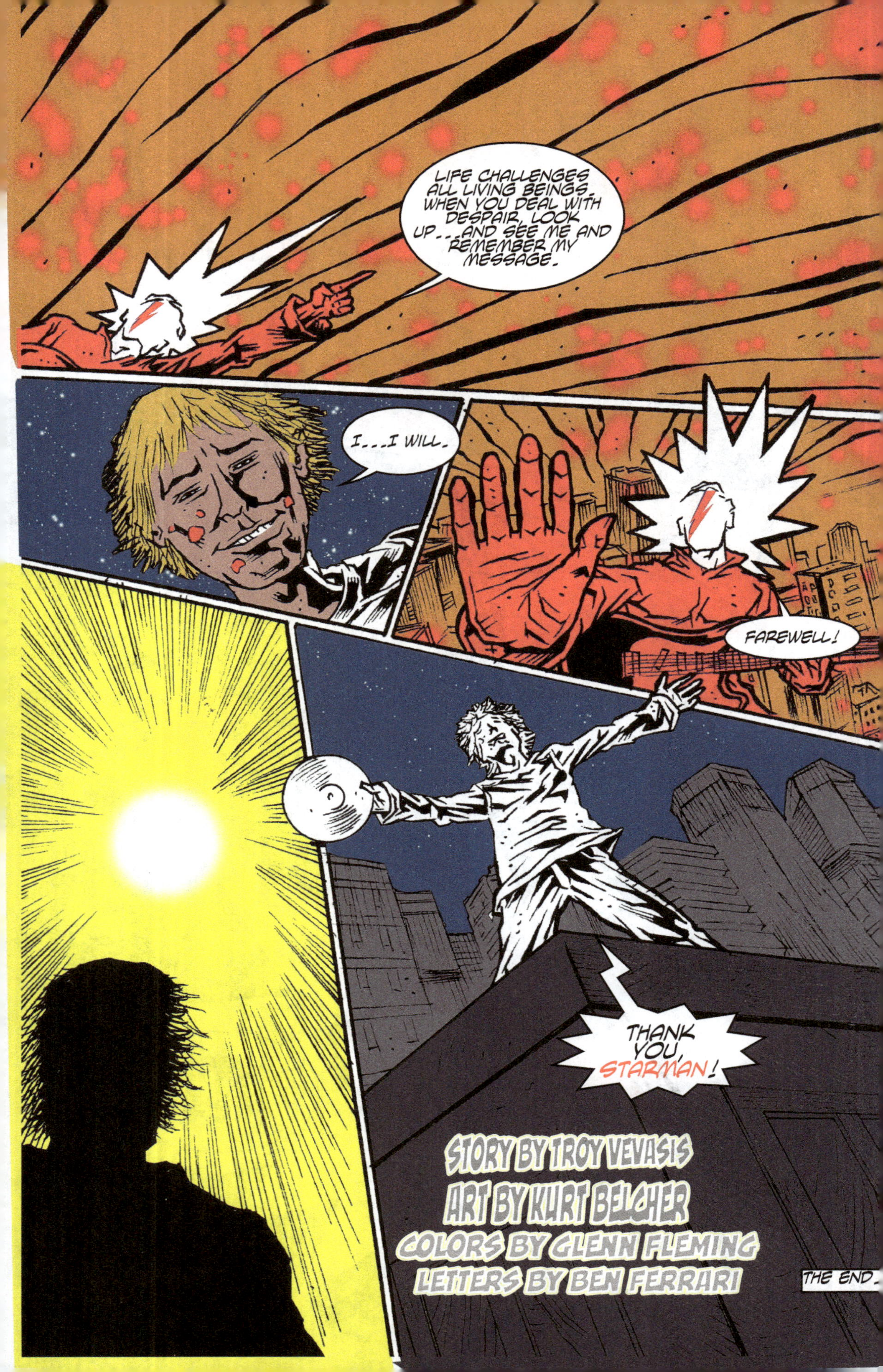
LIFE CHALLENGES ALL LIVING BEINGS. WHEN YOU DEAL WITH DESPAIR, LOOK UP...AND SEE ME AND REMEMBER MY MESSAGE.
I...I WILL.
FAREWELL!
THANK YOU, STARMAN!
STORY BY TROY VEVASIS
ART BY KURT BELCHER
COLORS BY GLENN FLEMING
LETTERS BY BEN FERRARI
THE END.

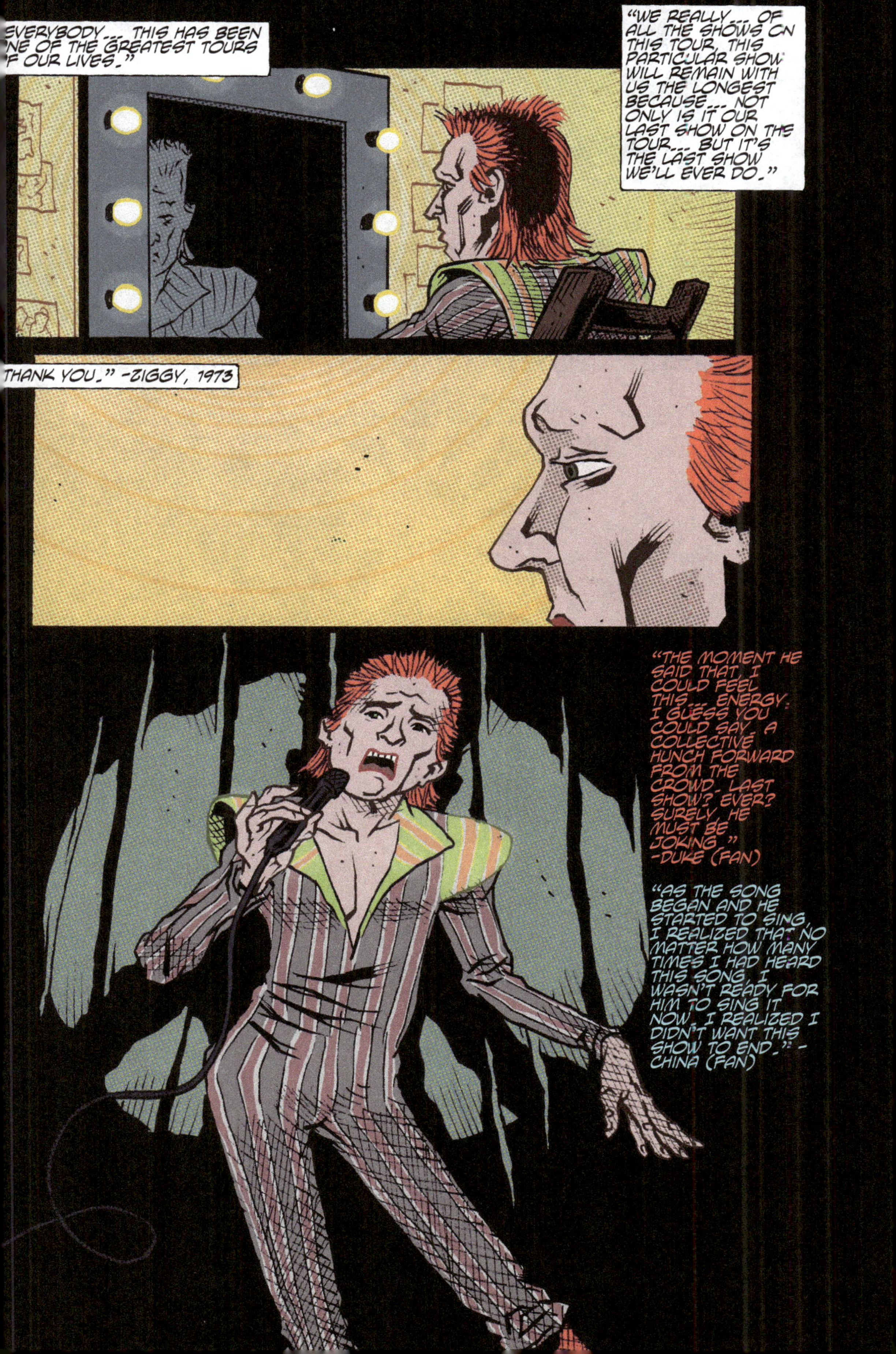
EVERYBODY... THIS HAS BEEN
NE OF THE GREATEST TOURS
F OUR LIVES."
"WE REALLY... OF ALL THE SHOWS ON THIS TOUR, THIS PARTICULAR SHOW WILL REMAIN WITH US THE LONGEST BECAUSE... NOT ONLY IS IT OUR LAST SHOW ON THE TOUR... BUT IT'S THE LAST SHOW WE'LL EVER DO."
THANK YOU." -ZIGGY, 1973
"THE MOMENT HE SAID THAT, I COULD FEEL THIS... ENERGY. I GUESS YOU COULD SAY, A COLLECTIVE HUNCH FORWARD FROM THE CROWD. LAST SHOW? EVER? SURELY, HE MUST BE JOKING." -DUKE (FAN)
"AS THE SONG BEGAN AND HE STARTED TO SING, I REALIZED THAT NO MATTER HOW MANY TIMES I HAD HEARD THIS SONG, I WASN'T READY FOR HIM TO SING IT NOW. I REALIZED I DIDN'T WANT THIS SHOW TO END." -CHINA (FAN)

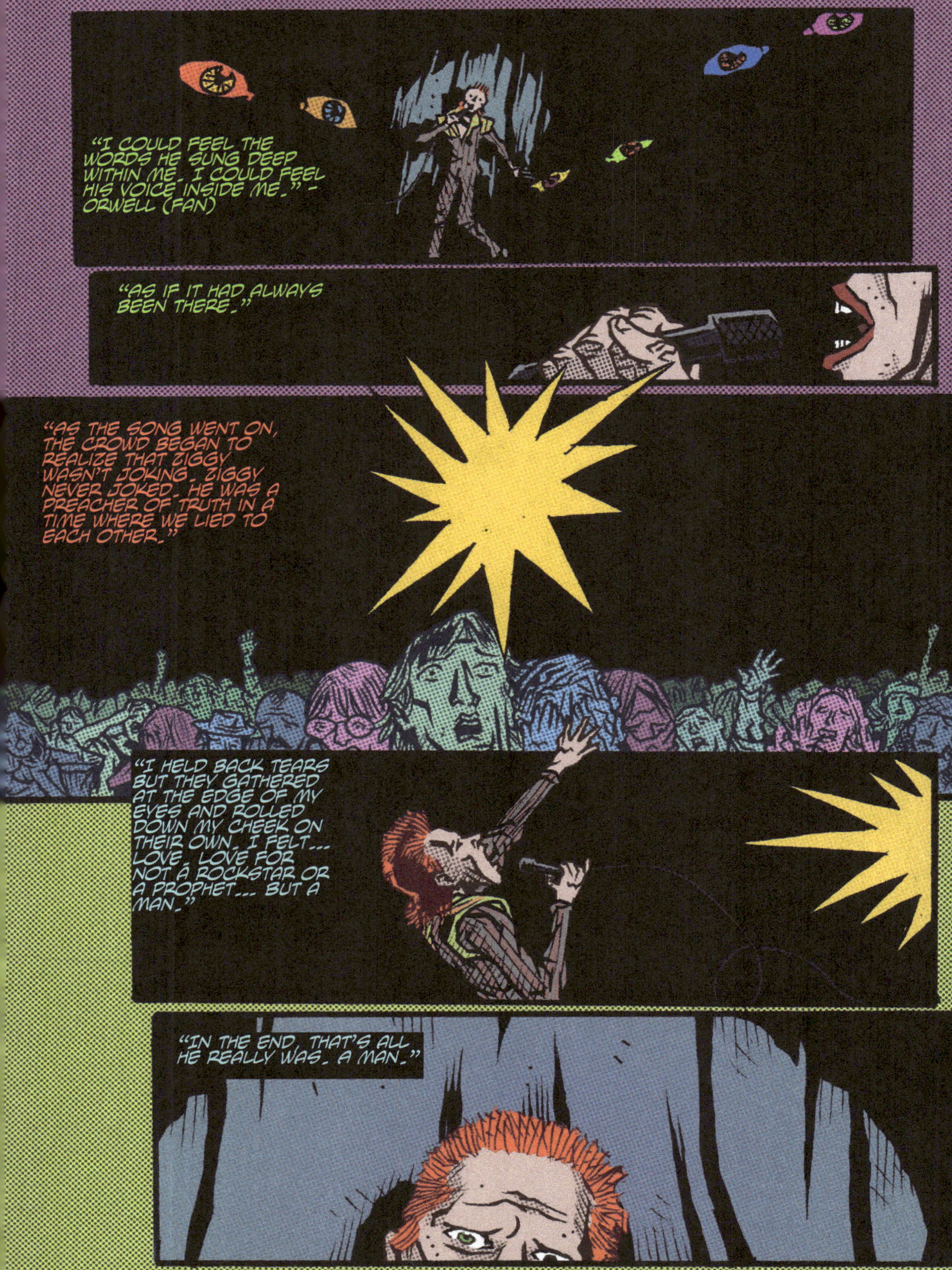
"I COULD FEEL THE WORDS HE SUNG DEEP WITHIN ME. I COULD FEEL HIS VOICE INSIDE ME." - ORWELL (FAN)
"AS IF IT HAD ALWAYS BEEN THERE."
"AS THE SONG WENT ON, THE CROWD BEGAN TO REALIZE THAT ZIGGY WASN'T JOKING. ZIGGY NEVER JOKED. HE WAS A PREACHER OF TRUTH IN A TIME WHERE WE LIED TO EACH OTHER."
"I HELD BACK TEARS BUT THEY GATHERED AT THE EDGE OF MY EYES AND ROLLED DOWN MY CHEEK ON THEIR OWN. I FELT... LOVE. LOVE FOR NOT A ROCKSTAR OR A PROPHET... BUT A MAN."
"IN THE END, THAT'S ALL HE REALLY WAS. A MAN."

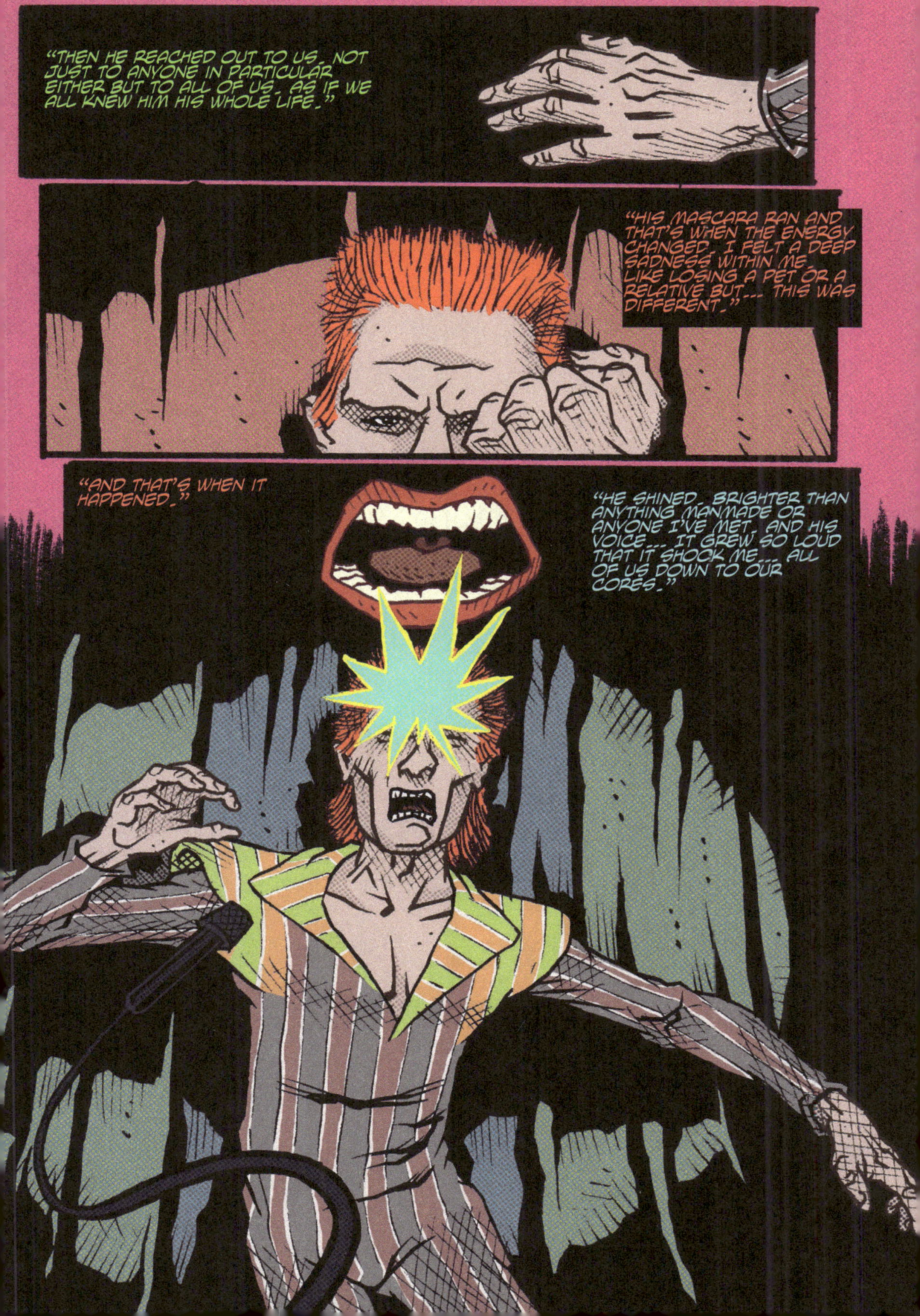
"THEN HE REACHED OUT TO US. NOT JUST TO ANYONE IN PARTICULAR EITHER BUT TO ALL OF US. AS IF WE ALL KNEW HIM HIS WHOLE LIFE."
"HIS MASCARA RAN AND THAT'S WHEN THE ENERGY CHANGED. I FELT A DEEP SADNESS WITHIN ME. LIKE LOSING A PET OR A RELATIVE BUT... THIS WAS DIFFERENT."
"AND THAT'S WHEN IT HAPPENED."
"HE SHINED. BRIGHTER THAN ANYTHING MANMADE OR ANYONE I'VE MET. AND HIS VOICE... IT GREW SO LOUD THAT IT SHOOK ME... ALL OF US DOWN TO OUR CORES."

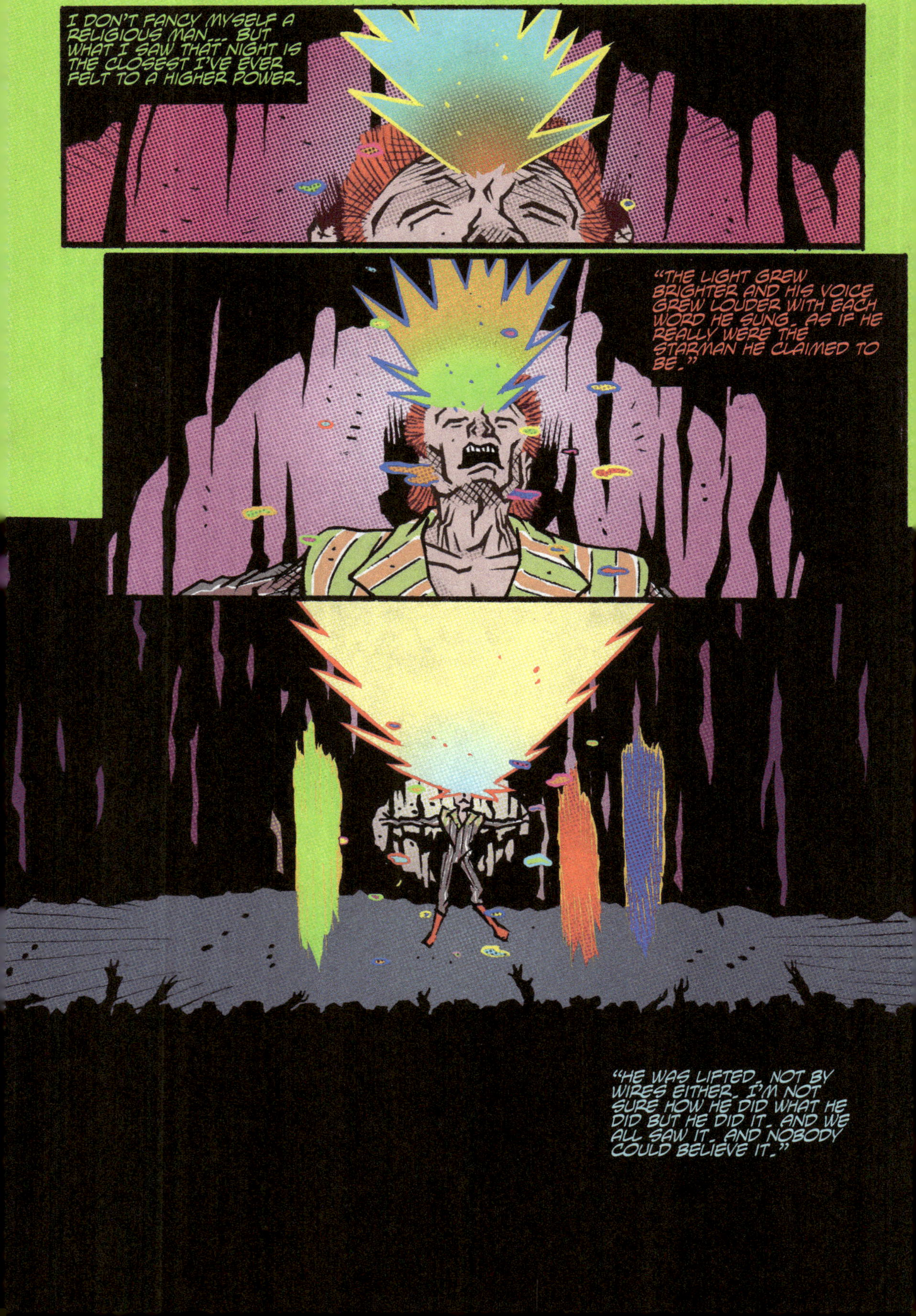
I DON'T FANCY MYSELF A RELIGIOUS MAN... BUT WHAT I SAW THAT NIGHT IS THE CLOSEST I'VE EVER FELT TO A HIGHER POWER.
"THE LIGHT GREW BRIGHTER AND HIS VOICE GREW LOUDER WITH EACH WORD HE SUNG. AS IF HE REALLY WERE THE STARMAN HE CLAIMED TO BE."
"HE WAS LIFTED. NOT BY WIRES EITHER. I'M NOT SURE HOW HE DID WHAT HE DID BUT HE DID IT. AND WE ALL SAW IT. AND NOBODY COULD BELIEVE IT."

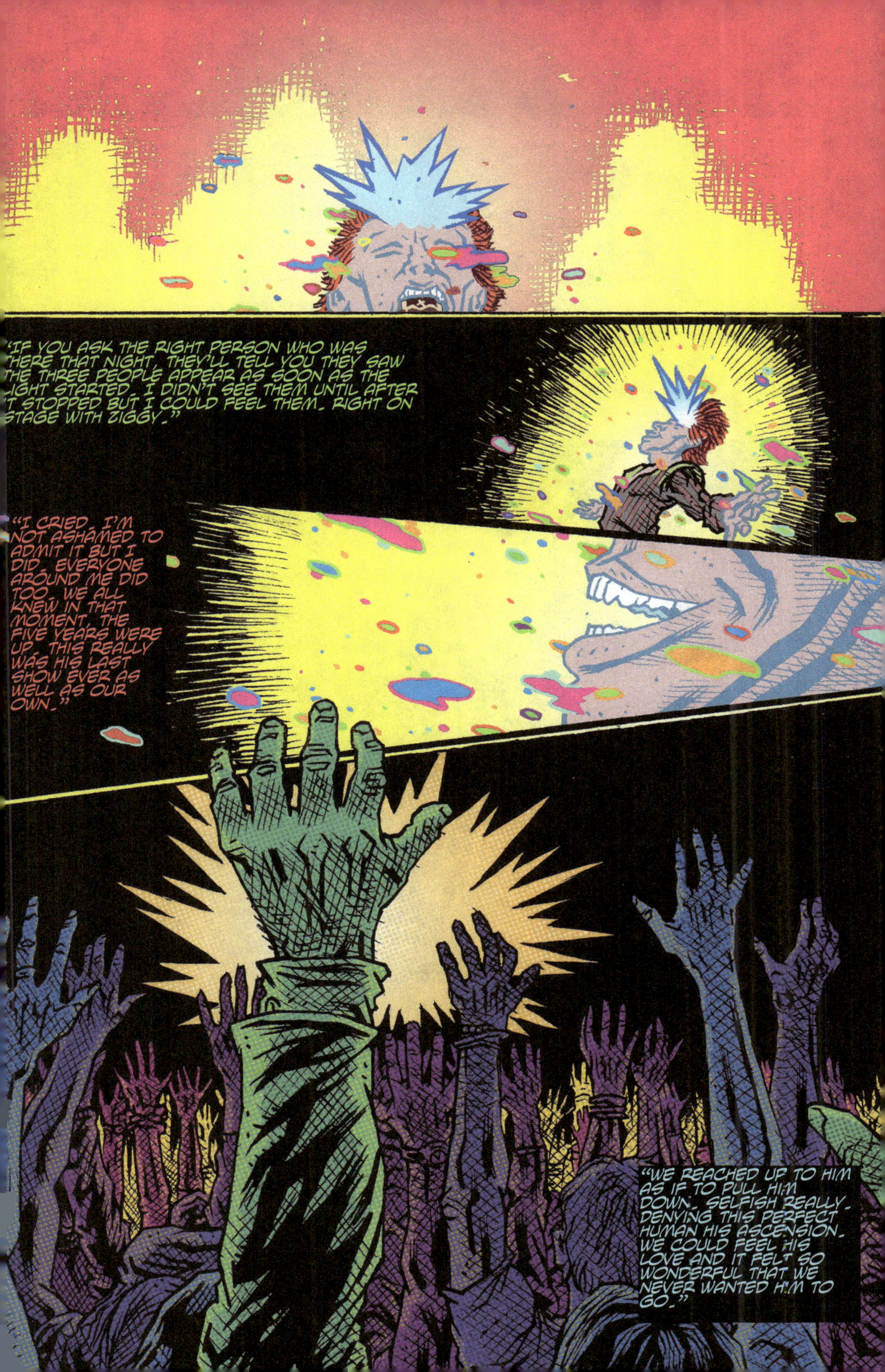
"IF YOU ASK THE RIGHT PERSON WHO WAS THERE THAT NIGHT, THEY'LL TELL YOU THEY SAW THE THREE PEOPLE APPEAR AS SOON AS THE LIGHT STARTED. I DIDN'T SEE THEM UNTIL AFTER IT STOPPED BUT I COULD FEEL THEM. RIGHT ON STAGE WITH ZIGGY."
"I CRIED. I'M NOT ASHAMED TO ADMIT IT BUT I DID. EVERYONE AROUND ME DID TOO. WE ALL KNEW IN THAT MOMENT, THE FIVE YEARS WERE UP. THIS REALLY WAS HIS LAST SHOW EVER AS WELL AS OUR OWN."
"WE REACHED UP TO HIM AS IF TO PULL HIM DOWN. SELFISH REALLY. DENYING THIS PERFECT HUMAN HIS ASCENSION. WE COULD FEEL HIS LOVE AND IT FELT SO WONDERFUL THAT WE NEVER WANTED HIM TO GO."

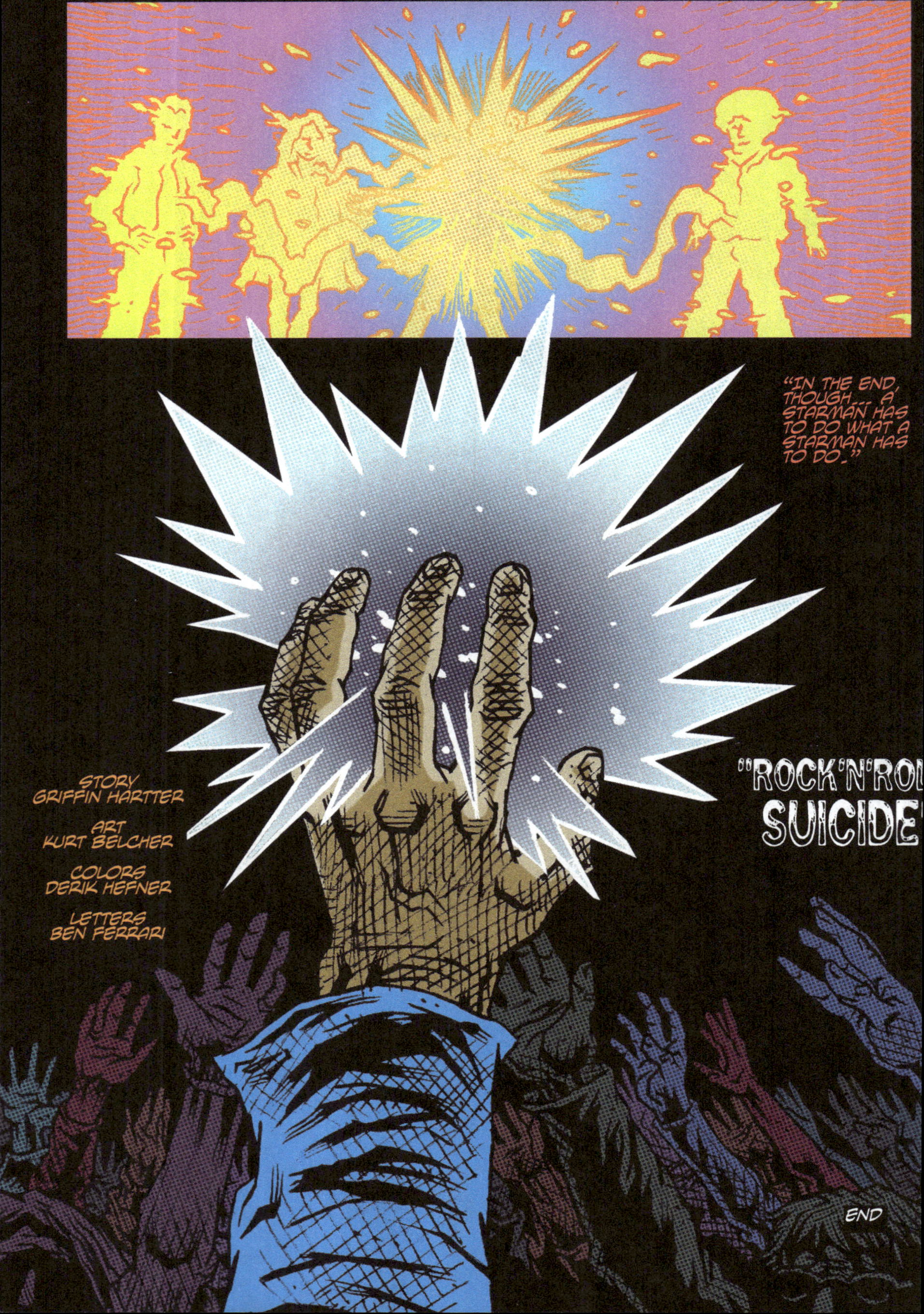
"IN THE END, THOUGH... A STARMAN HAS TO DO WHAT A STARMAN HAS TO DO."
STORY GRIFFIN HARTTER
ART KURT BELCHER
COLORS DERIK HEFNER
LETTERS BEN FERRARI
END

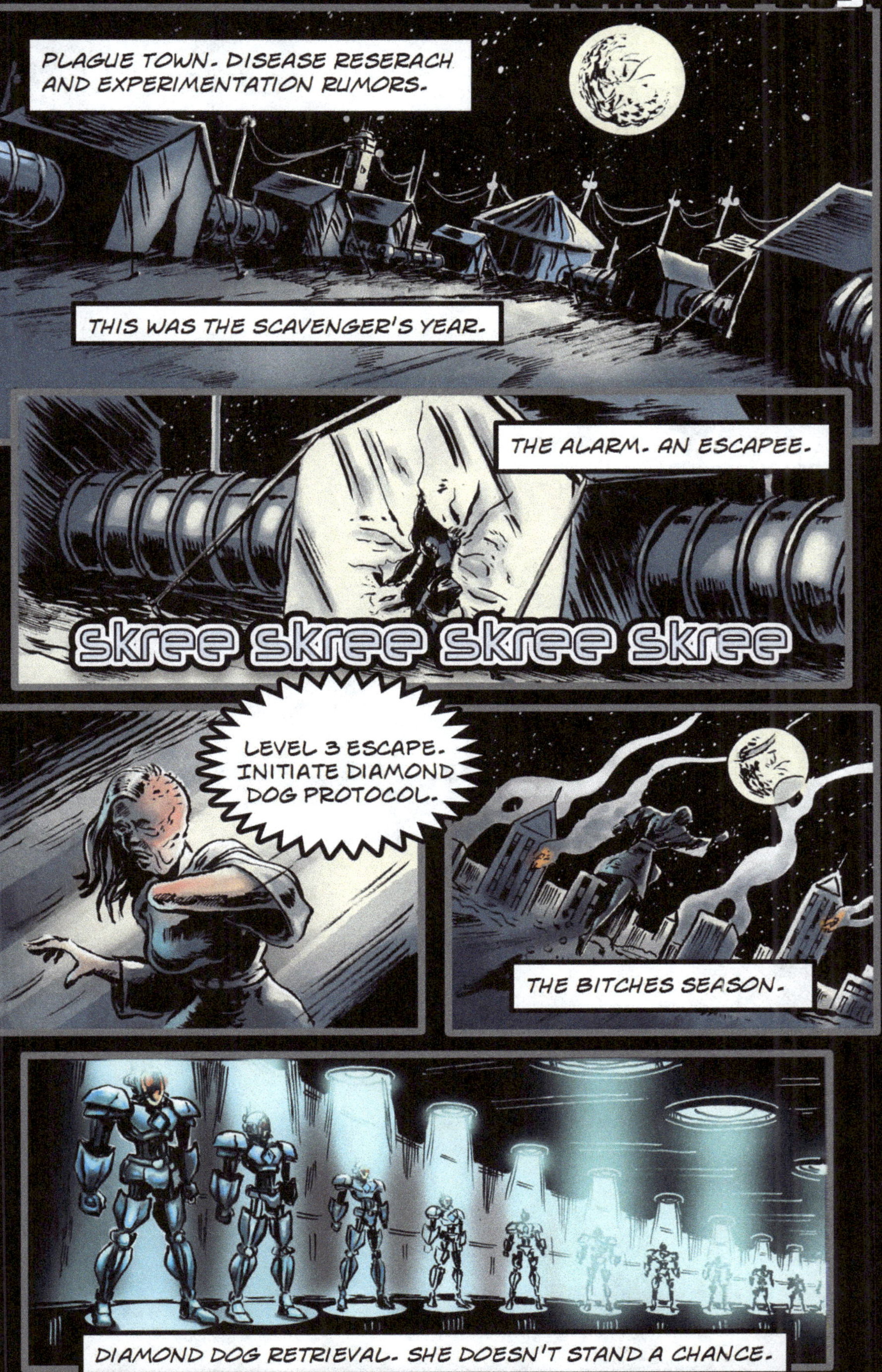
PLAGUE TOWN. DISEASE RESERACH AND EXPERIMENTATION RUMORS.
THIS WAS THE SCAVENGER'S YEAR.
THE ALARM. AN ESCAPEE.
skree skree skree skree
LEVEL 3 ESCAPE. INITIATE DIAMOND DOG PROTOCOL.
THE BITCHES SEASON.
DIAMOND DOG RETRIEVAL. SHE DOESN'T STAND A CHANCE.

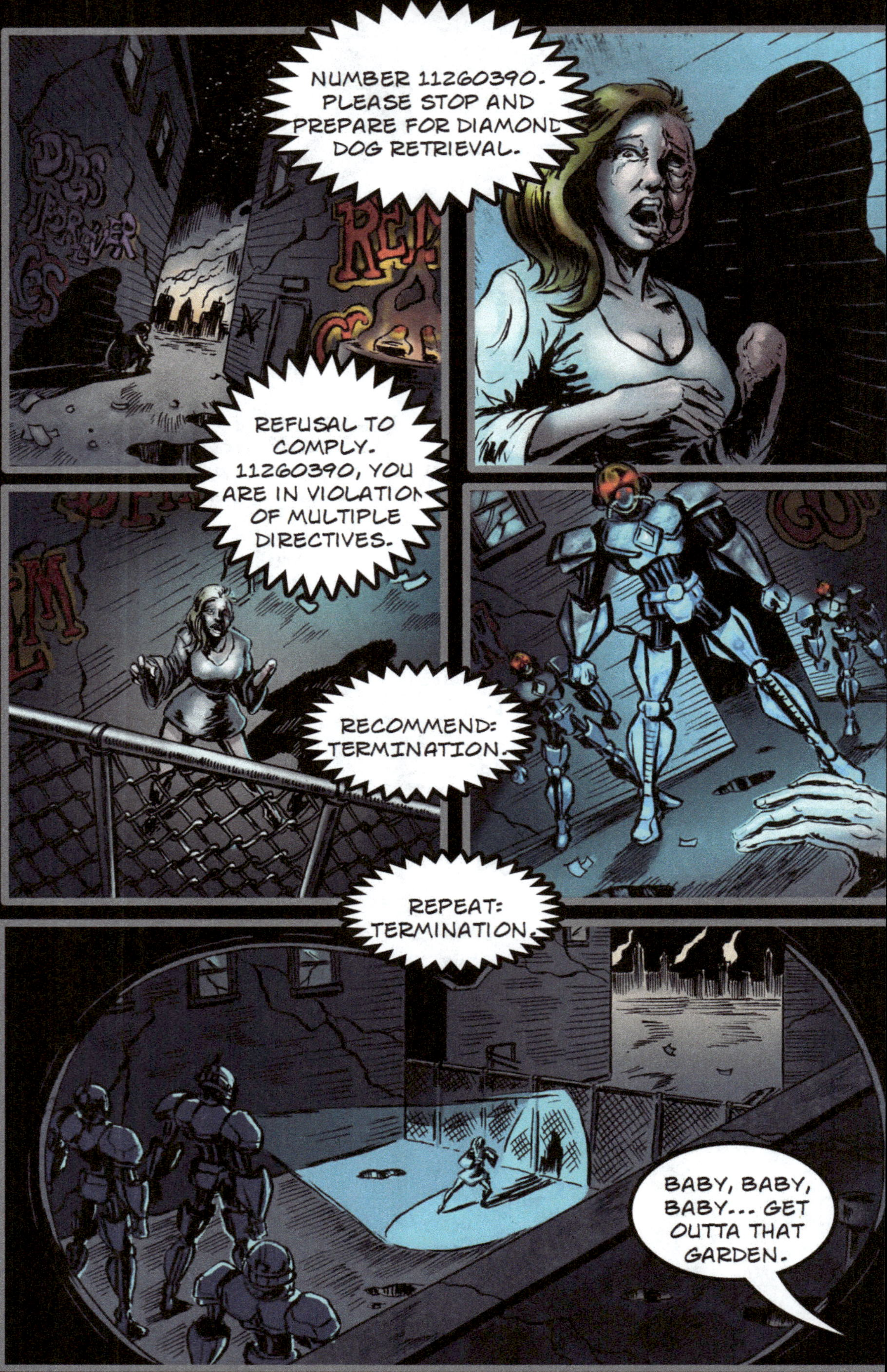
NUMBER 11260390. PLEASE STOP AND PREPARE FOR DIAMOND DOG RETRIEVAL.
DOGS FOREVER
REFUSAL TO COMPLY. 11260390, YOU ARE IN VIOLATION OF MULTIPLE DIRECTIVES.
RECOMMEND: TERMINATION.
REPEAT: TERMINATION.
BABY, BABY, BABY... GET OUTTA THAT GARDEN.

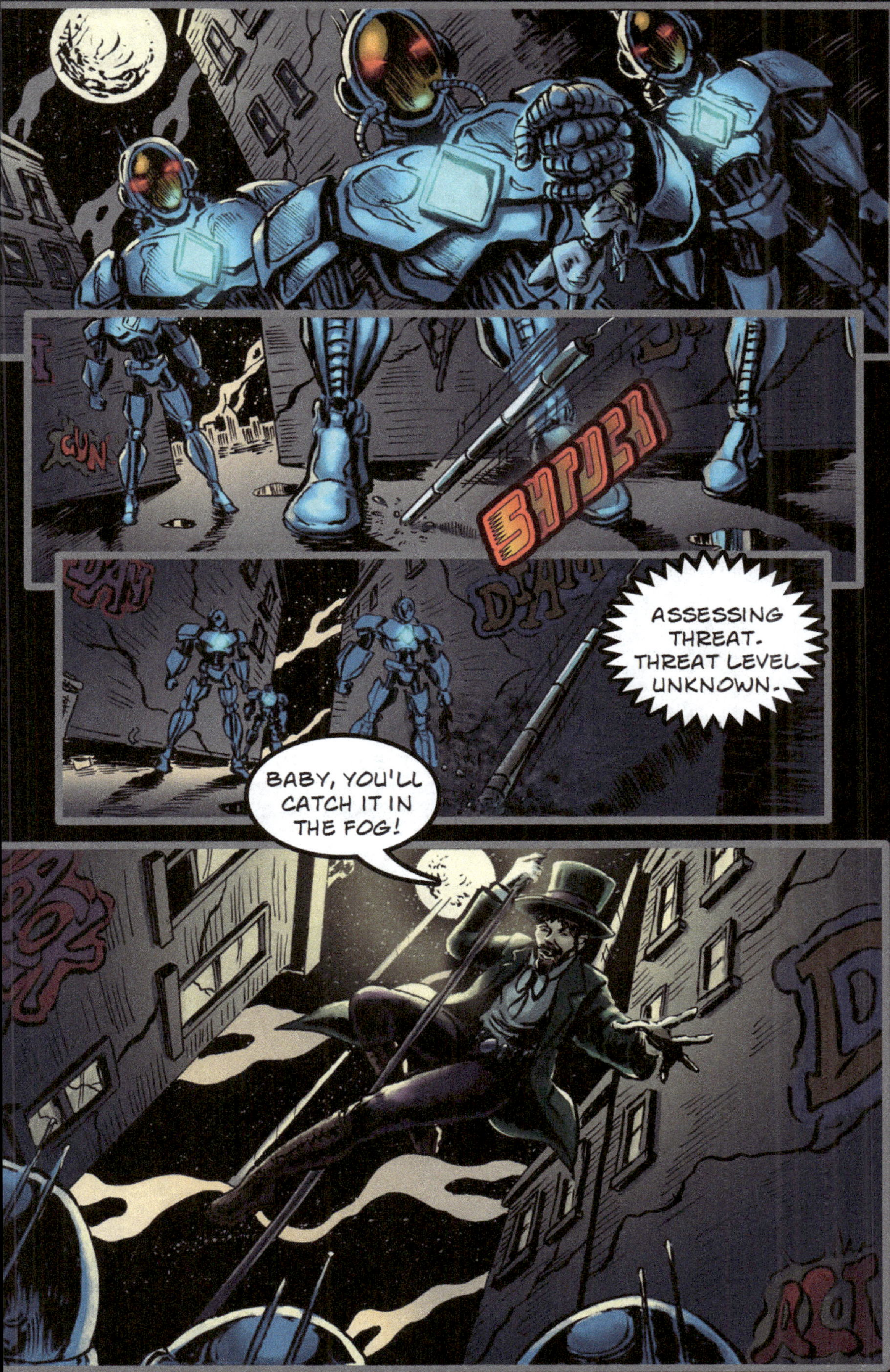
ASSESSING THREAT. THREAT LEVEL UNKNOWN.
BABY, YOU'LL CATCH IT IN THE FOG!

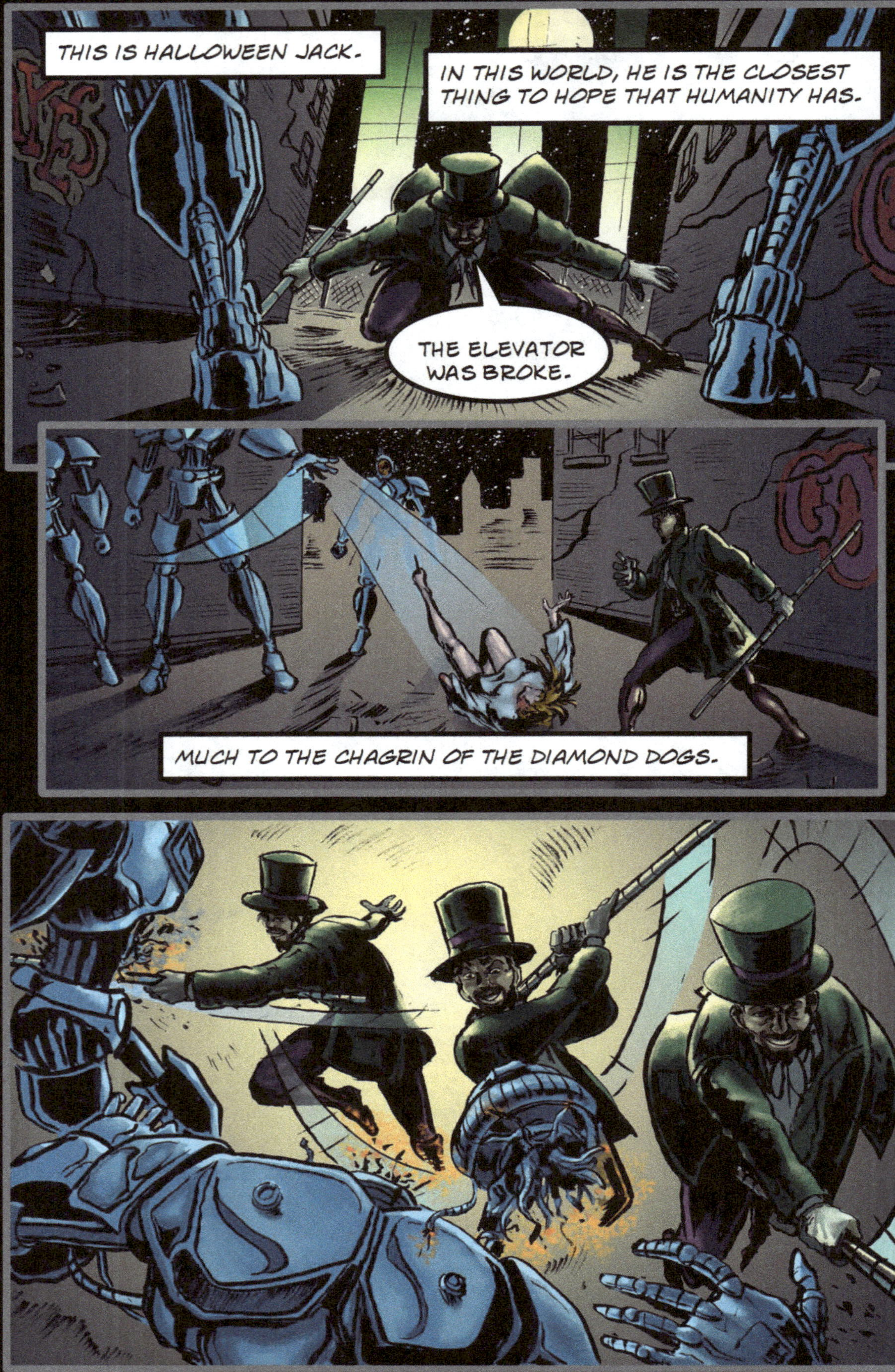
THIS IS HALLOWEEN JACK.
IN THIS WORLD, HE IS THE CLOSEST THING TO HOPE THAT HUMANITY HAS.
THE ELEVATOR WAS BROKE.
MUCH TO THE CHAGRIN OF THE DIAMOND DOGS.

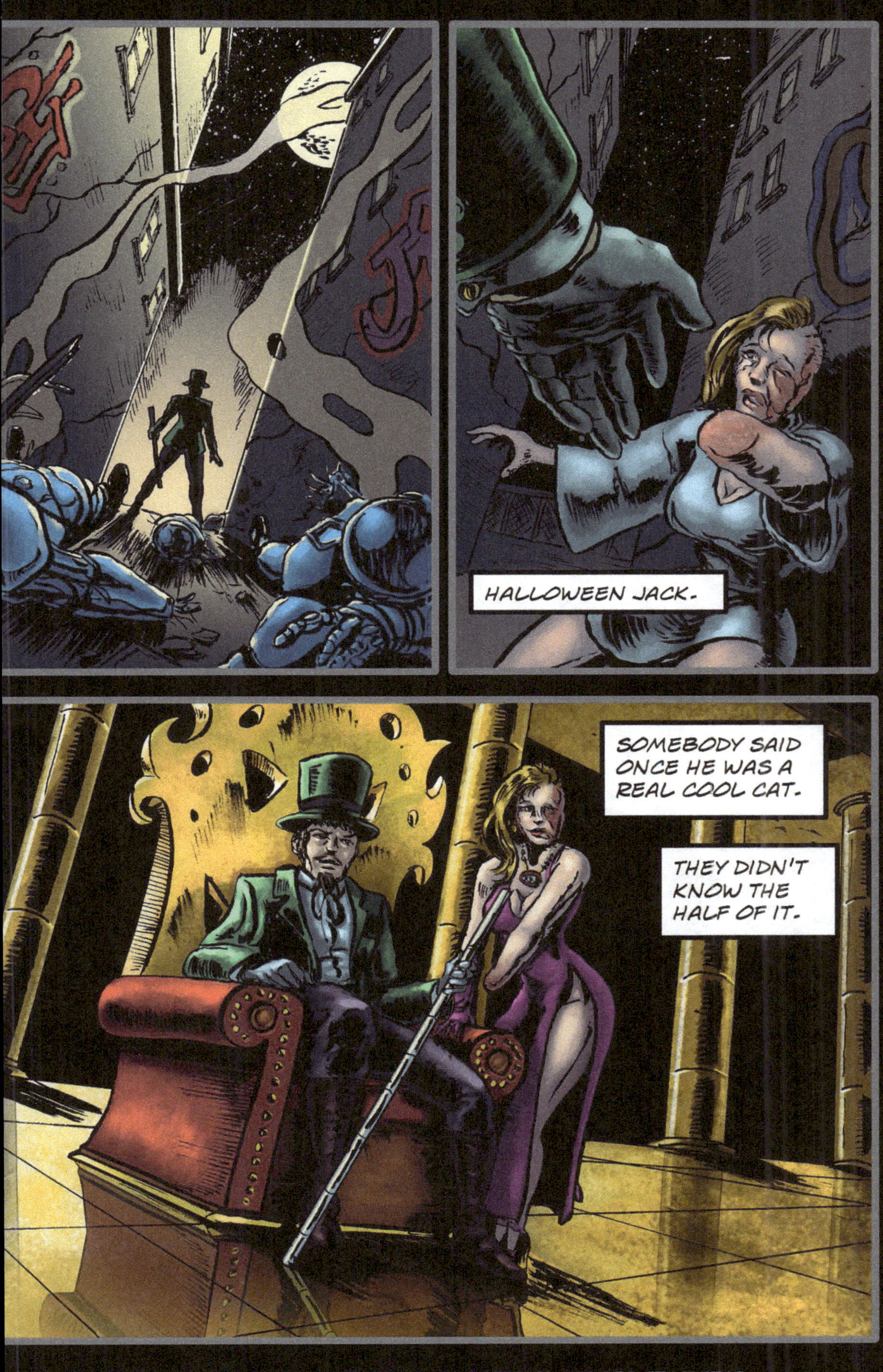
HALLOWEEN JACK.
SOMEBODY SAID ONCE HE WAS A REAL COOL CAT.
THEY DIDN'T KNOW THE HALF OF IT.

WORDS: DAVID C. HAYES, PICTURES: DAN GORMAN, COLORS: SEAN SEAL

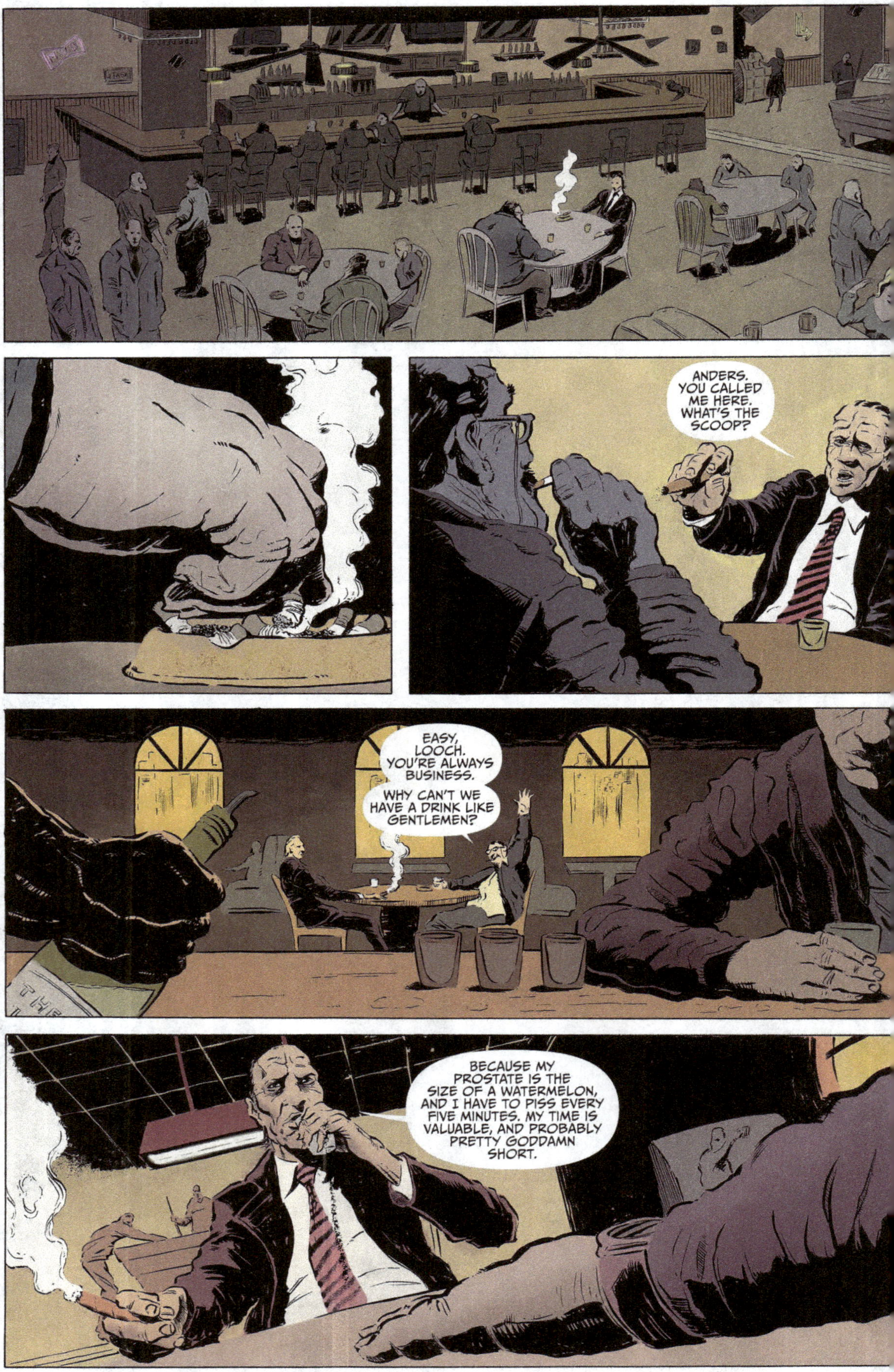
ANDERS. YOU CALLED ME HERE. WHAT'S THE SCOOP?
EASY, LOOCH. YOU'RE ALWAYS BUSINESS.
WHY CAN'T WE HAVE A DRINK LIKE GENTLEMEN?
BECAUSE MY PROSTATE IS THE SIZE OF A WATERMELON, AND I HAVE TO PISS EVERY FIVE MINUTES. MY TIME IS VALUABLE, AND PROBABLY PRETTY GODDAMN SHORT.

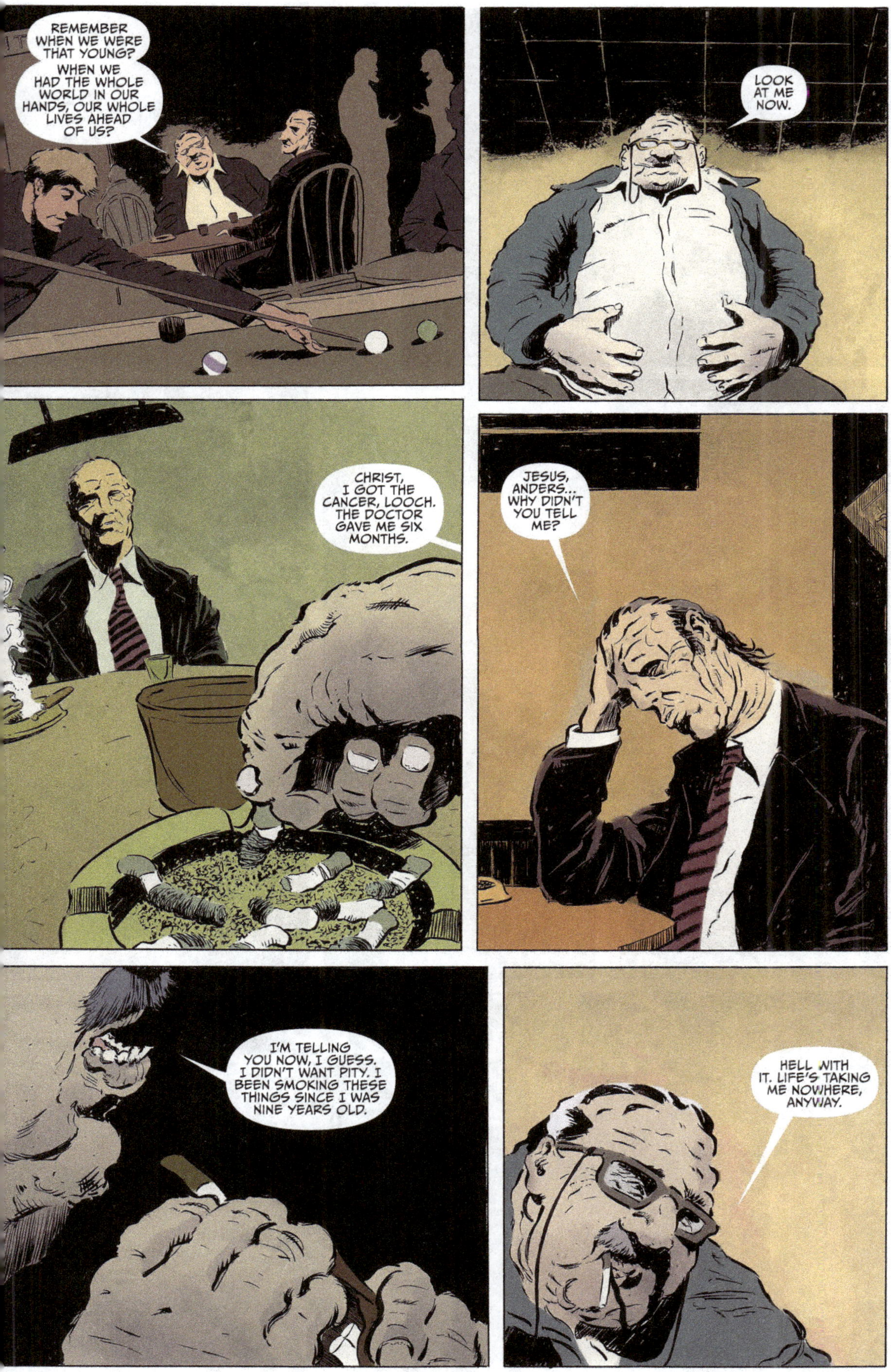
REMEMBER WHEN WE WERE THAT YOUNG?
WHEN WE HAD THE WHOLE WORLD IN OUR HANDS, OUR WHOLE LIVES AHEAD OF US?
LOOK AT ME NOW.
CHRIST, I GOT THE CANCER, LOOCH. THE DOCTOR GAVE ME SIX MONTHS.
JESUS, ANDERS... WHY DIDN'T YOU TELL ME?
I'M TELLING YOU NOW, I GUESS. I DIDN'T WANT PITY. I BEEN SMOKING THESE THINGS SINCE I WAS NINE YEARS OLD.
HELL WITH IT. LIFE'S TAKING ME NOWHERE, ANYWAY.

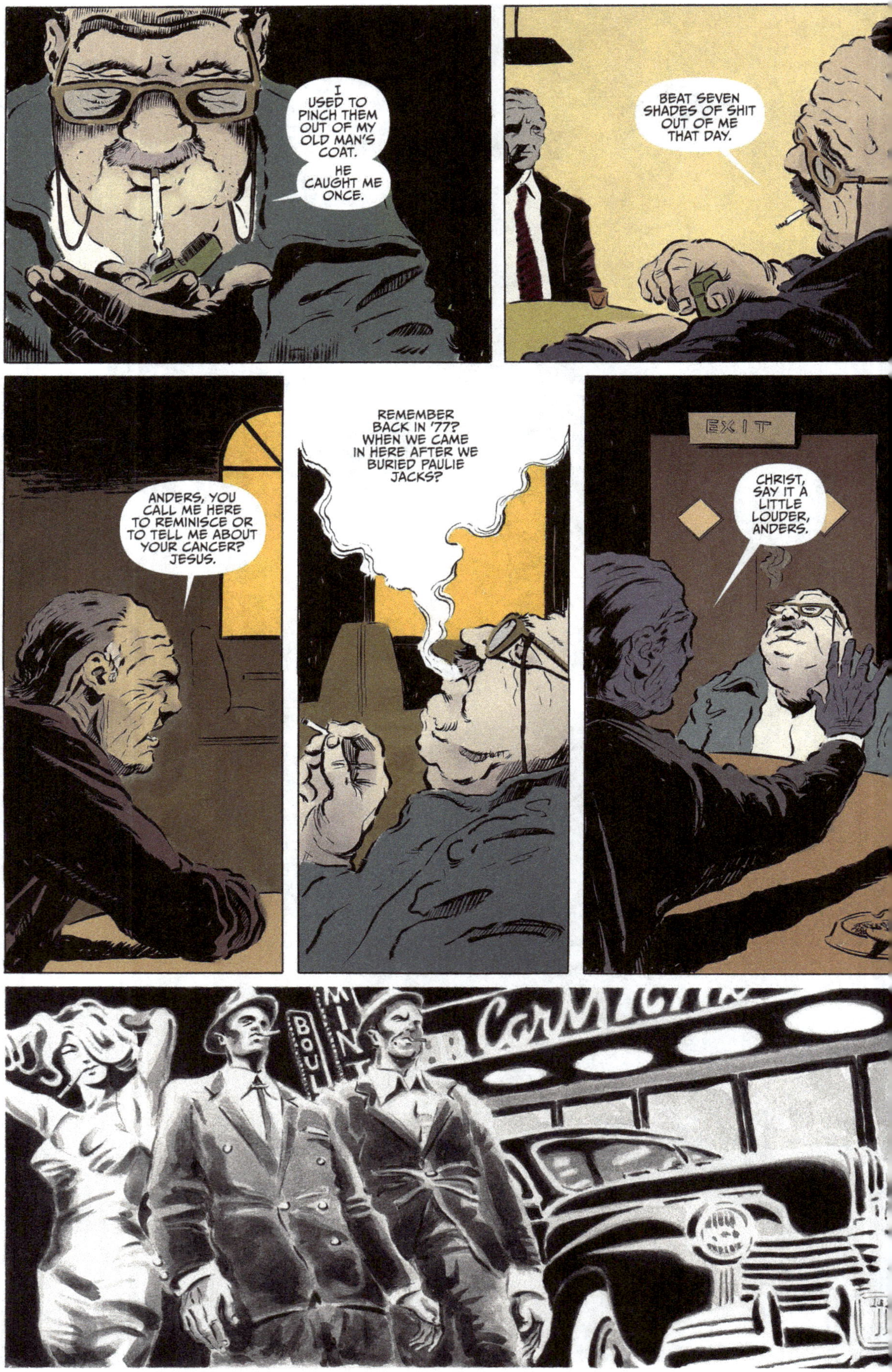
I USED TO PINCH THEM OUT OF MY OLD MAN'S COAT.
HE CAUGHT ME ONCE.
BEAT SEVEN SHADES OF SHIT OUT OF ME THAT DAY.
ANDERS, YOU CALL ME HERE TO REMINISCE OR TO TELL ME ABOUT YOUR CANCER? JESUS.
REMEMBER BACK IN '77? WHEN WE CAME IN HERE AFTER WE BURIED PAULIE JACKS?
EXIT
CHRIST, SAY IT A LITTLE LOUDER, ANDERS.

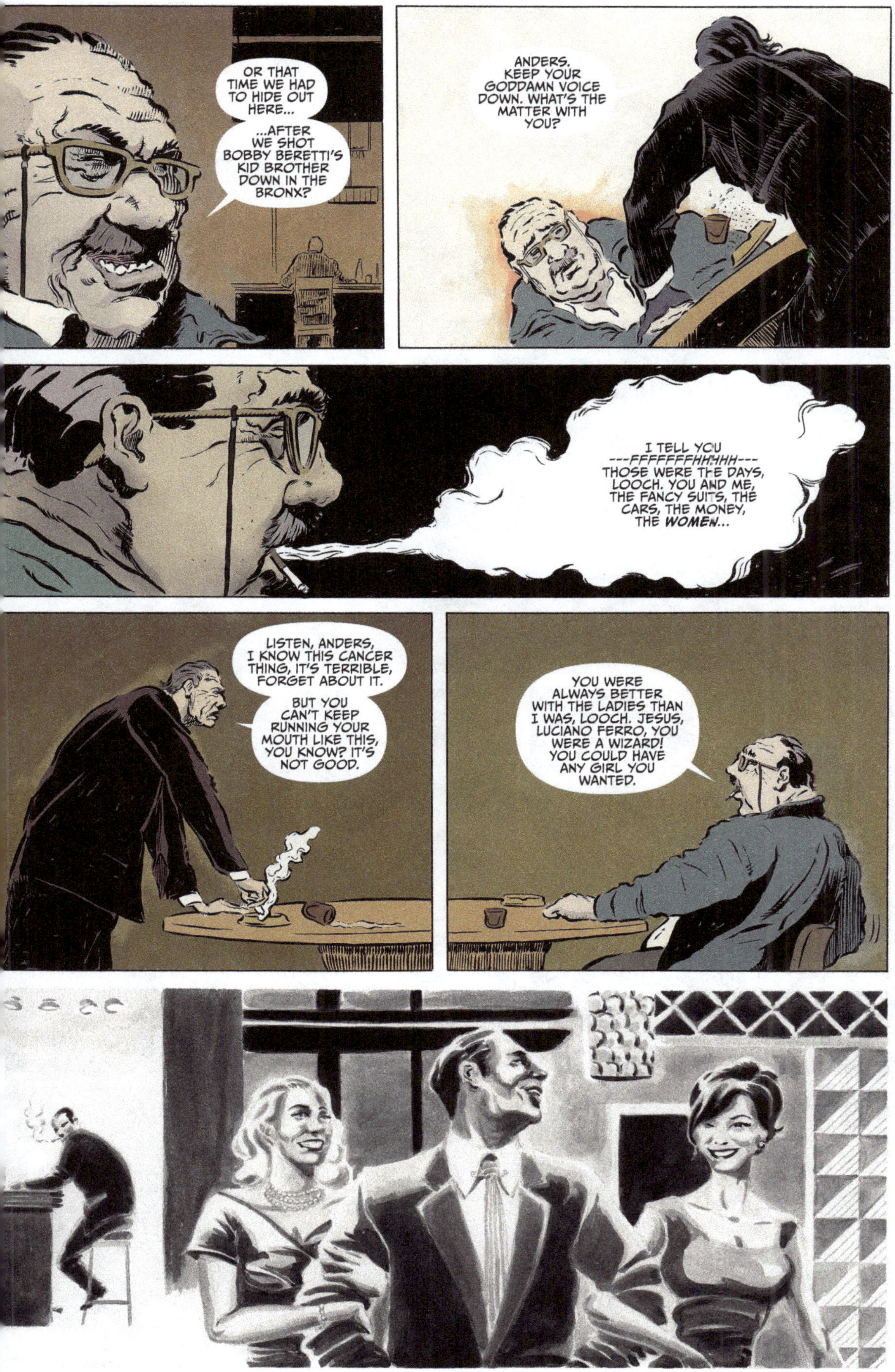
OR THAT TIME WE HAD TO HIDE OUT HERE...
...AFTER WE SHOT BOBBY BERETTI'S KID BROTHER DOWN IN THE BRONX?
ANDERS. KEEP YOUR GODDAMN VOICE DOWN. WHAT'S THE MATTER WITH YOU?
I TELL YOU ---FFFFFFFHHHHH--- THOSE WERE THE DAYS, LOOCH. YOU AND ME, THE FANCY SUITS, THE CARS, THE MONEY, THE WOMEN...
LISTEN, ANDERS, I KNOW THIS CANCER THING, IT'S TERRIBLE, FORGET ABOUT IT.
BUT YOU CAN'T KEEP RUNNING YOUR MOUTH LIKE THIS, YOU KNOW? IT'S NOT GOOD.
YOU WERE ALWAYS BETTER WITH THE LADIES THAN I WAS, LOOCH. JESUS, LUCIANO FERRO, YOU WERE A WIZARD! YOU COULD HAVE ANY GIRL YOU WANTED.

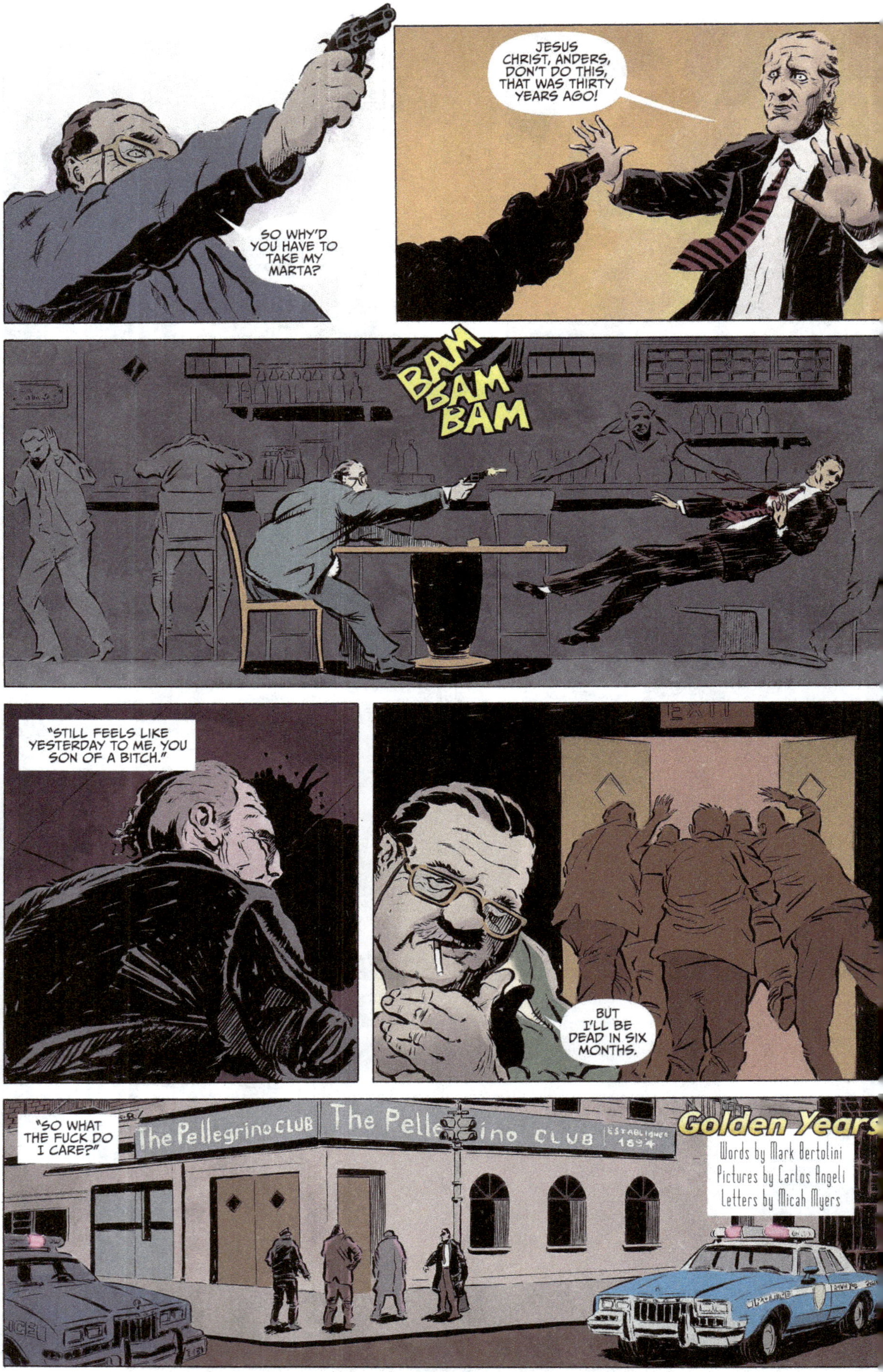
SO WHY'D YOU HAVE TO TAKE MY MARTA?
JESUS CHRIST, ANDERS, DON'T DO THIS, THAT WAS THIRTY YEARS AGO!
BAM BAM BAM
"STILL FEELS LIKE YESTERDAY TO ME, YOU SON OF A BITCH."
EXIT
BUT I'LL BE DEAD IN SIX MONTHS.
"SO WHAT THE FUCK DO I CARE?"
The Pellegrino CLUB
The Pellegrino CLUB
ESTABLISHED 1894
Golden Years
Words by Mark Bertolini
Pictures by Carlos Angeli
Letters by Micah Myers

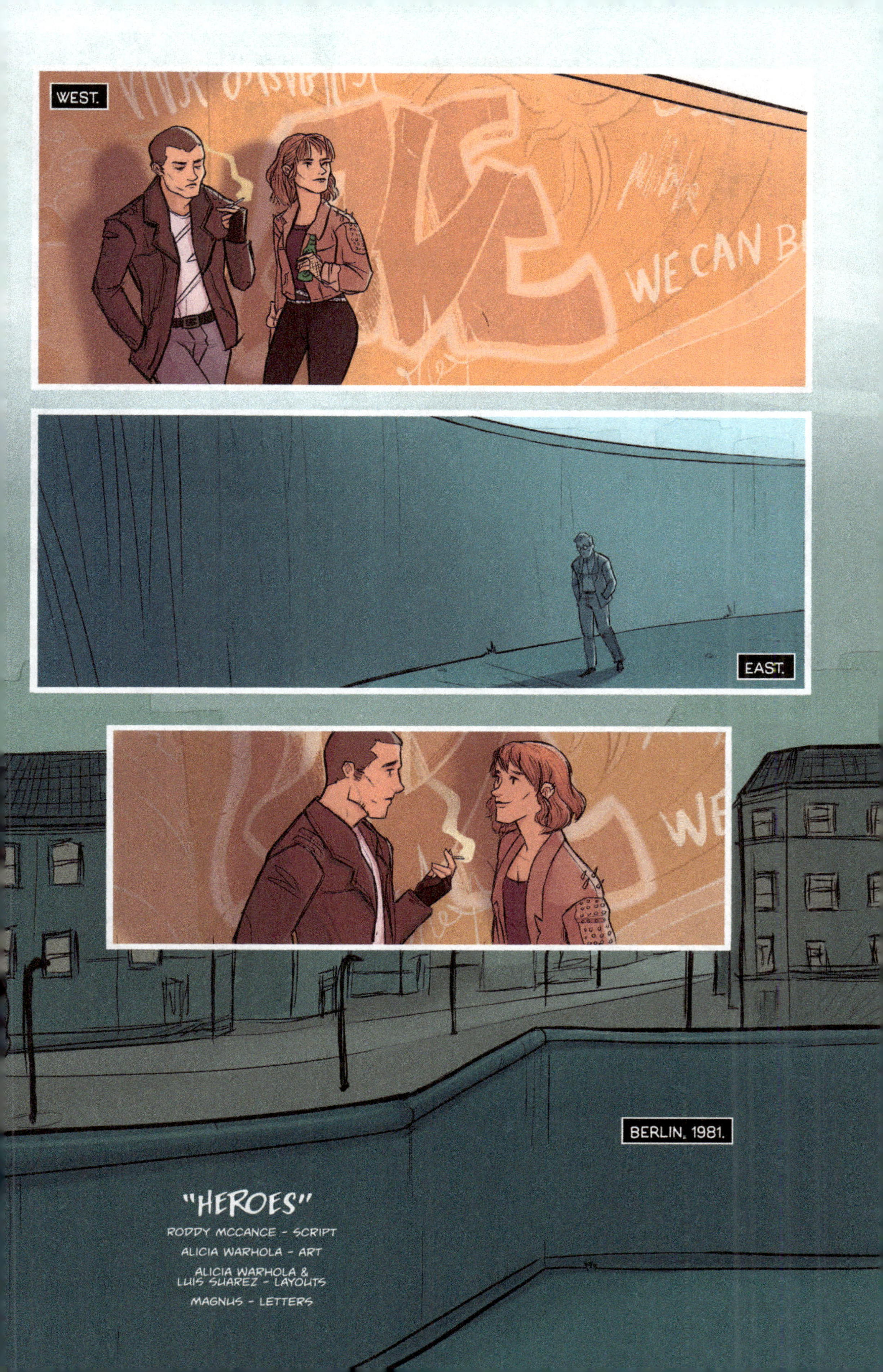
WEST.
EAST.
BERLIN, 1981.
"HEROES"
RODDY MCCANCE - SCRIPT
ALICIA WARHOLA - ART
ALICIA WARHOLA & LUIS SUAREZ - LAYOUTS
MAGNUS - LETTERS

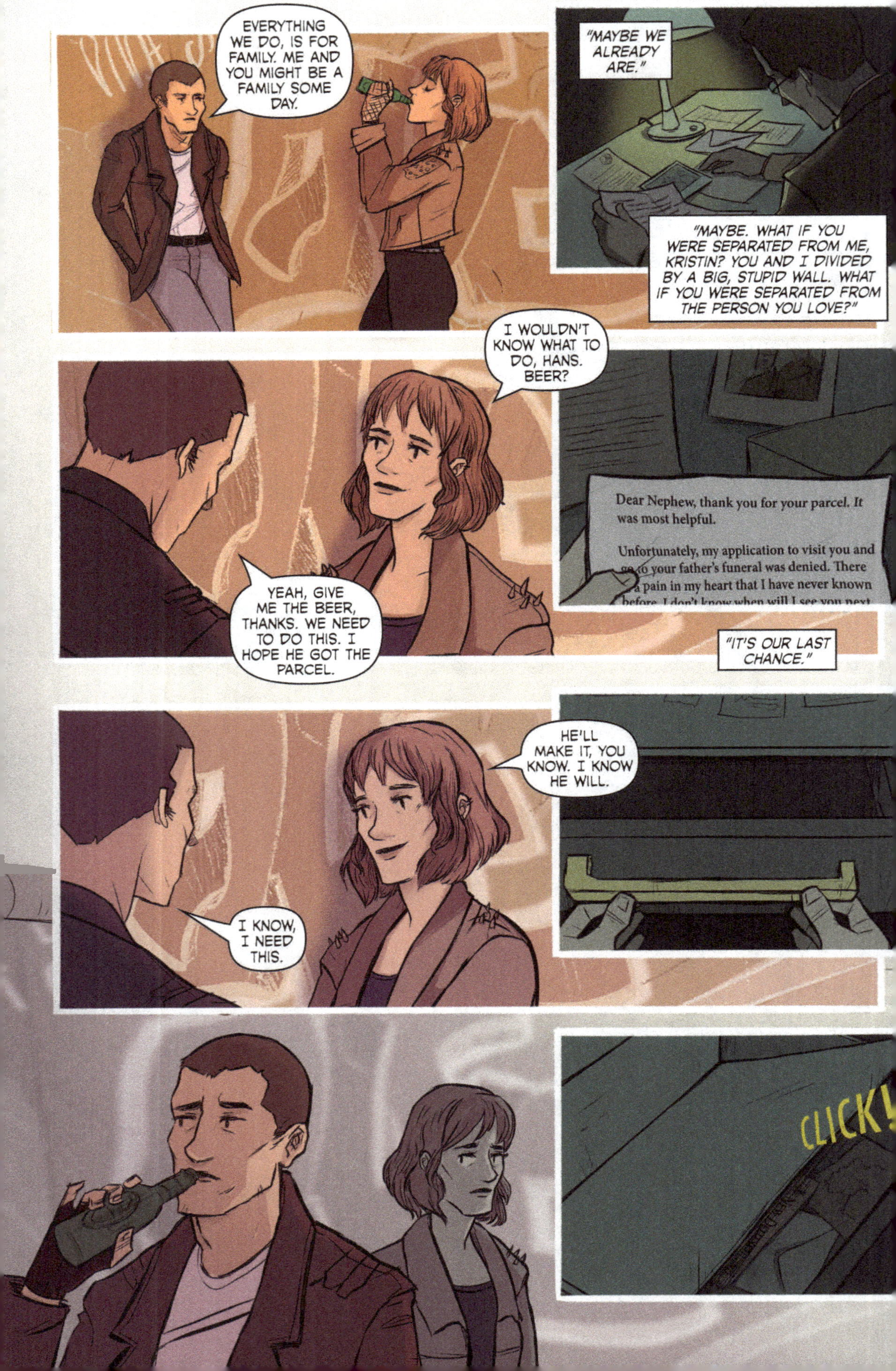

EVERYTHING WE DO, IS FOR FAMILY. ME AND YOU MIGHT BE A FAMILY SOME DAY.
"MAYBE WE ALREADY ARE."
"MAYBE. WHAT IF YOU WERE SEPARATED FROM ME, KRISTIN? YOU AND I DIVIDED BY A BIG, STUPID WALL. WHAT IF YOU WERE SEPARATED FROM THE PERSON YOU LOVE?"
I WOULDN'T KNOW WHAT TO DO, HANS. BEER?
YEAH, GIVE ME THE BEER, THANKS. WE NEED TO DO THIS. I HOPE HE GOT THE PARCEL.
Dear Nephew, thank you for your parcel. It was most helpful.
Unfortunately, my application to visit you and
to your father's funeral was denied. There
a pain in my heart that I have never known
"IT'S OUR LAST CHANCE."
HE'LL MAKE IT, YOU KNOW. I KNOW HE WILL.
I KNOW, I NEED THIS.
CLICK!

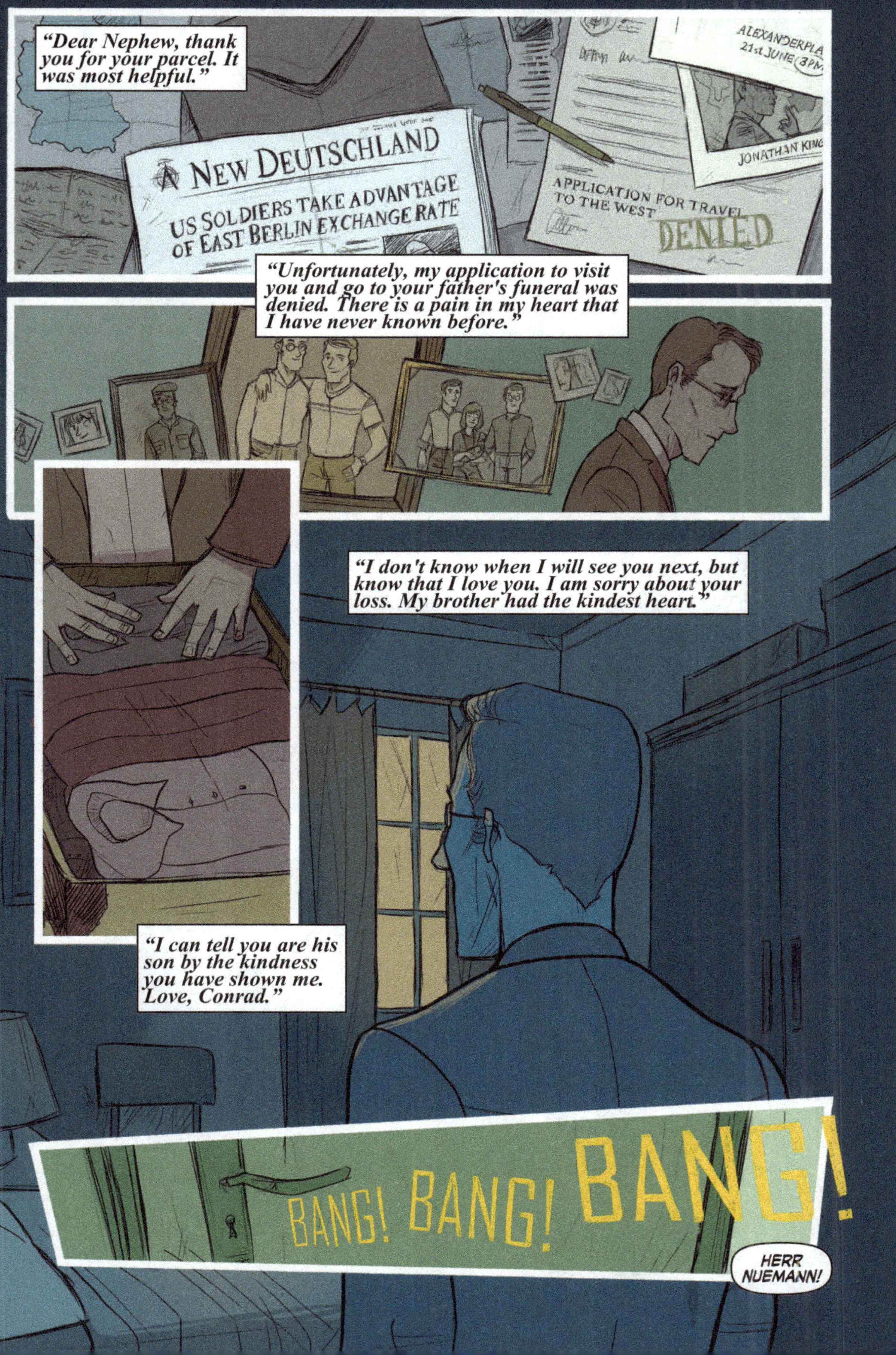

"Dear Nephew, thank you for your parcel. It was most helpful."
NEW DEUTSCHLAND
US SOLDIERS TAKE ADVANTAGE OF EAST BERLIN EXCHANGE RATE
ALEXANDERPLA
21st JUNE 3PM
JONATHAN KING
APPLICATION FOR TRAVEL TO THE WEST
DENIED
"Unfortunately, my application to visit you and go to your father's funeral was denied. There is a pain in my heart that I have never known before."
"I don't know when I will see you next, but know that I love you. I am sorry about your loss. My brother had the kindest heart."
"I can tell you are his son by the kindness you have shown me. Love, Conrad."
BANG! BANG! BANG!
HERR NUEMANN!

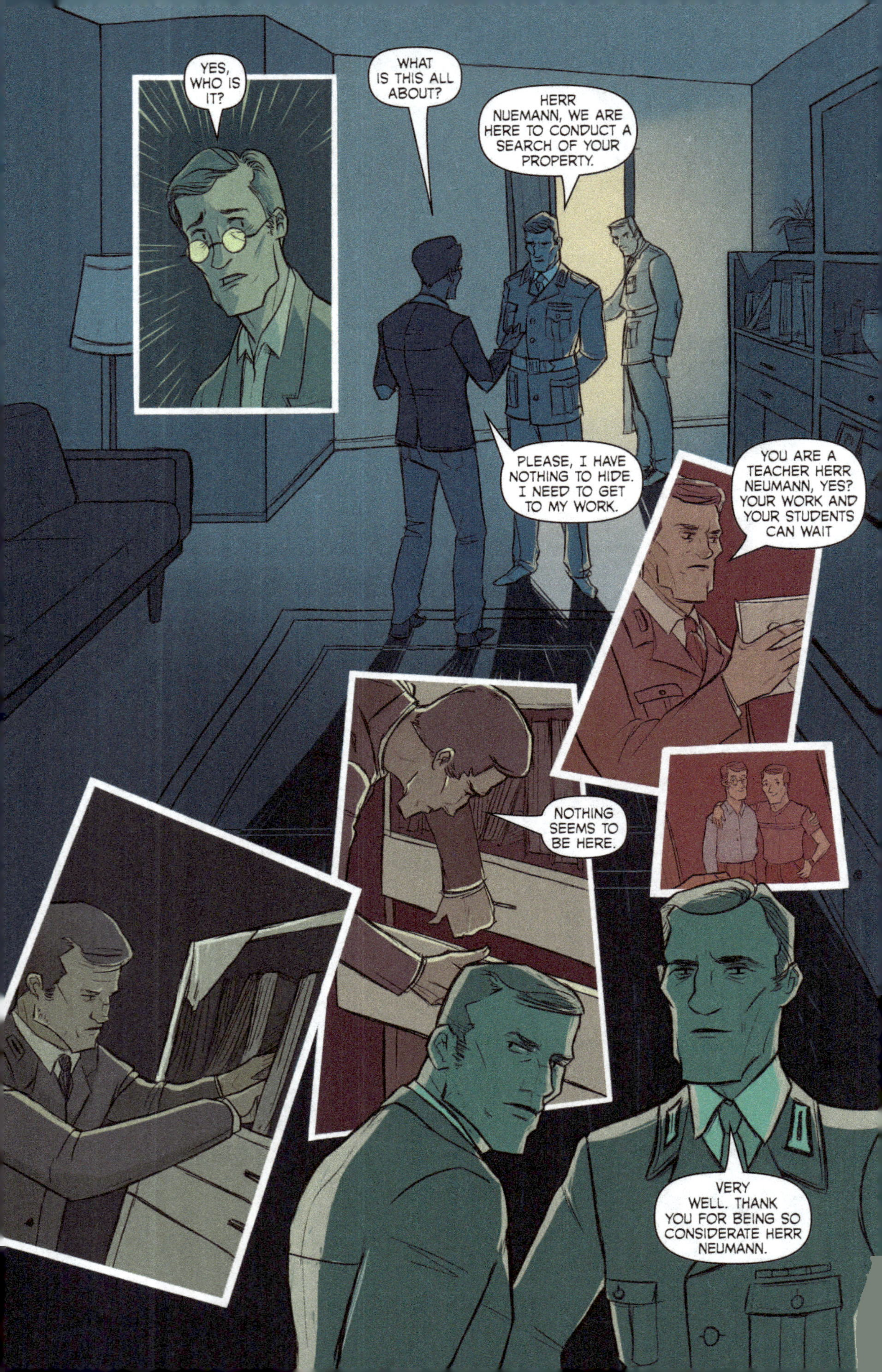

YES, WHO IS IT?
WHAT IS THIS ALL ABOUT?
HERR NUEMANN, WE ARE HERE TO CONDUCT A SEARCH OF YOUR PROPERTY.
PLEASE, I HAVE NOTHING TO HIDE. I NEED TO GET TO MY WORK.
YOU ARE A TEACHER HERR NEUMANN, YES? YOUR WORK AND YOUR STUDENTS CAN WAIT
NOTHING SEEMS TO BE HERE.
VERY WELL. THANK YOU FOR BEING SO CONSIDERATE HERR NEUMANN.

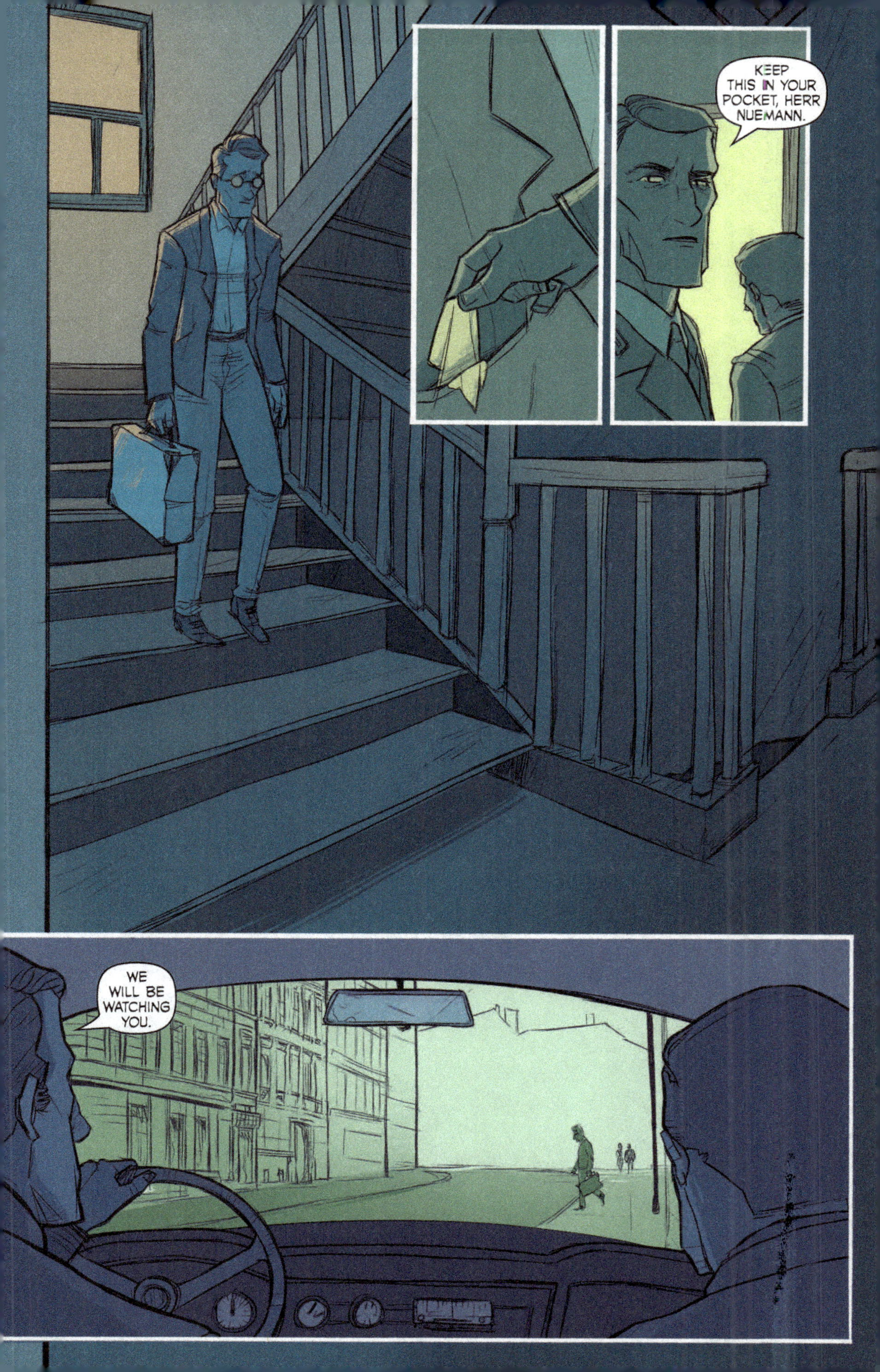
KEEP THIS IN YOUR POCKET, HERR NUEMANN.
WE WILL BE WATCHING YOU.

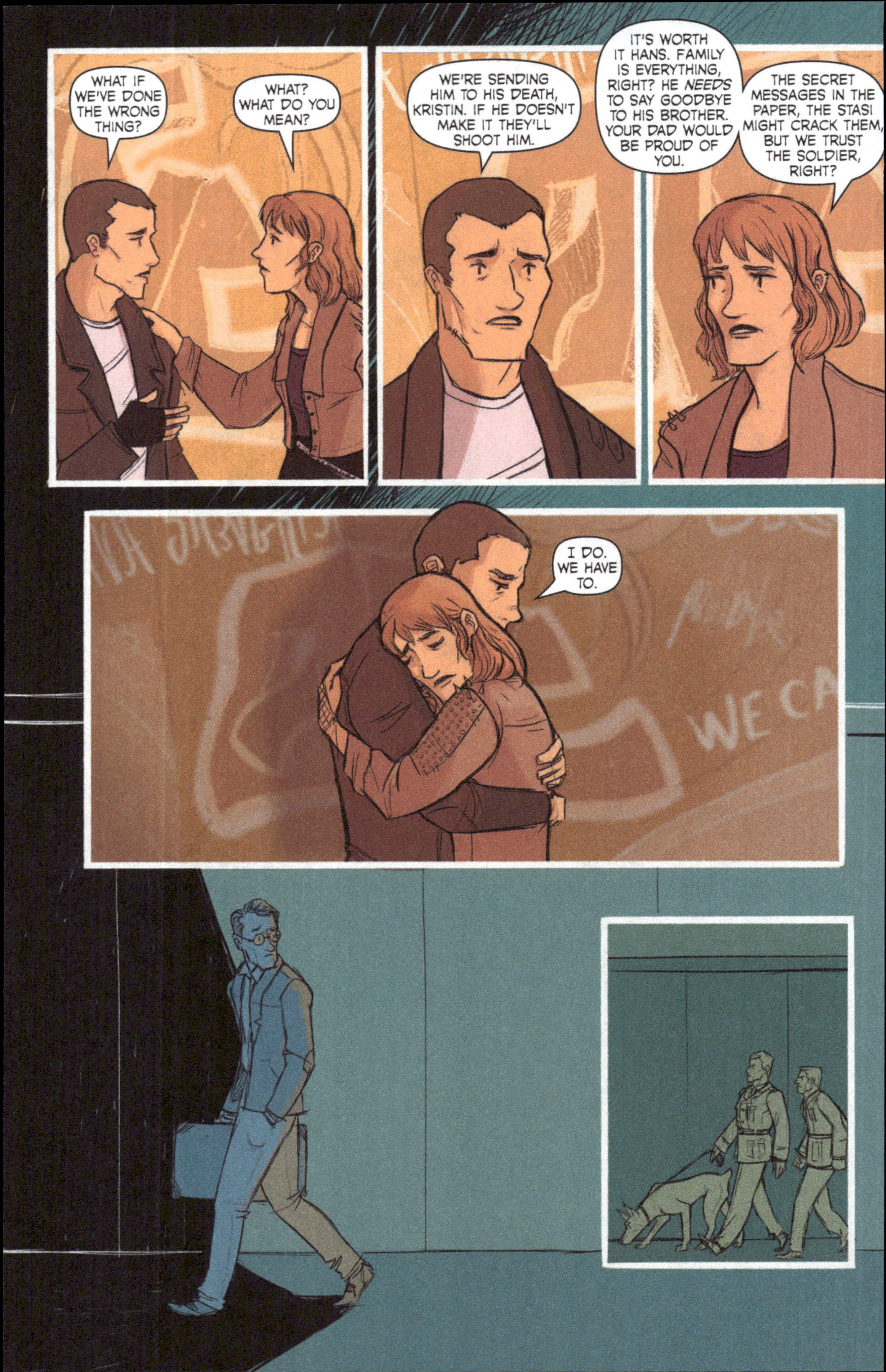
WHAT IF WE'VE DONE THE WRONG THING?
WHAT? WHAT DO YOU MEAN?
WE'RE SENDING HIM TO HIS DEATH, KRISTIN. IF HE DOESN'T MAKE IT THEY'LL SHOOT HIM.
IT'S WORTH IT HANS. FAMILY IS EVERYTHING, RIGHT? HE NEEDS TO SAY GOODBYE TO HIS BROTHER. YOUR DAD WOULD BE PROUD OF YOU.
THE SECRET MESSAGES IN THE PAPER, THE STASI MIGHT CRACK THEM, BUT WE TRUST THE SOLDIER, RIGHT?
I DO. WE HAVE TO.
WE CA

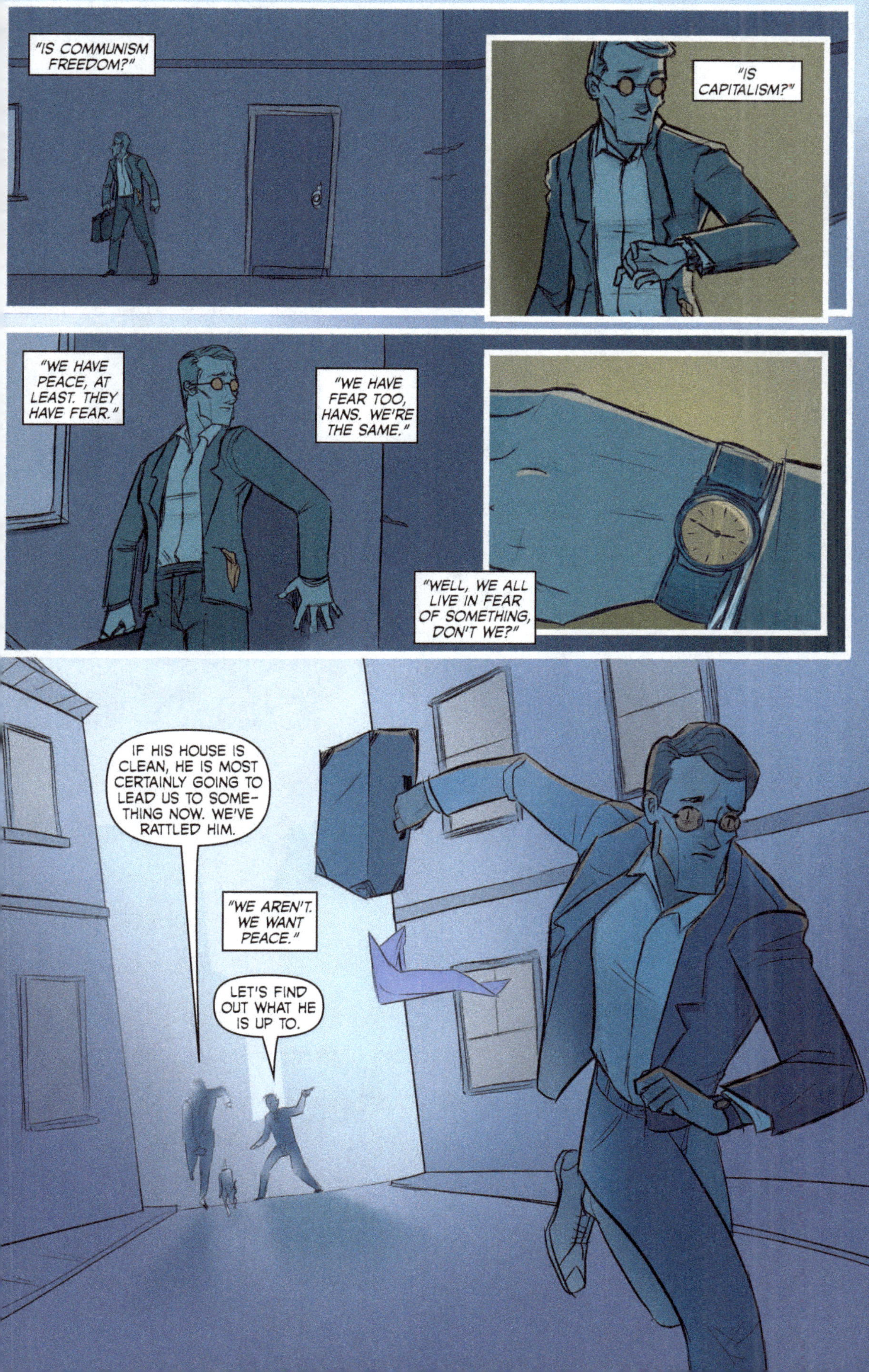
"IS COMMUNISM FREEDOM?"
"IS CAPITALISM?"
"WE HAVE PEACE, AT LEAST. THEY HAVE FEAR."
"WE HAVE FEAR TOO, HANS. WE'RE THE SAME."
"WELL, WE ALL LIVE IN FEAR OF SOMETHING, DON'T WE?"
IF HIS HOUSE IS CLEAN, HE IS MOST CERTAINLY GOING TO LEAD US TO SOME-THING NOW. WE'VE RATTLED HIM.
"WE AREN'T. WE WANT PEACE."
LET'S FIND OUT WHAT HE IS UP TO.

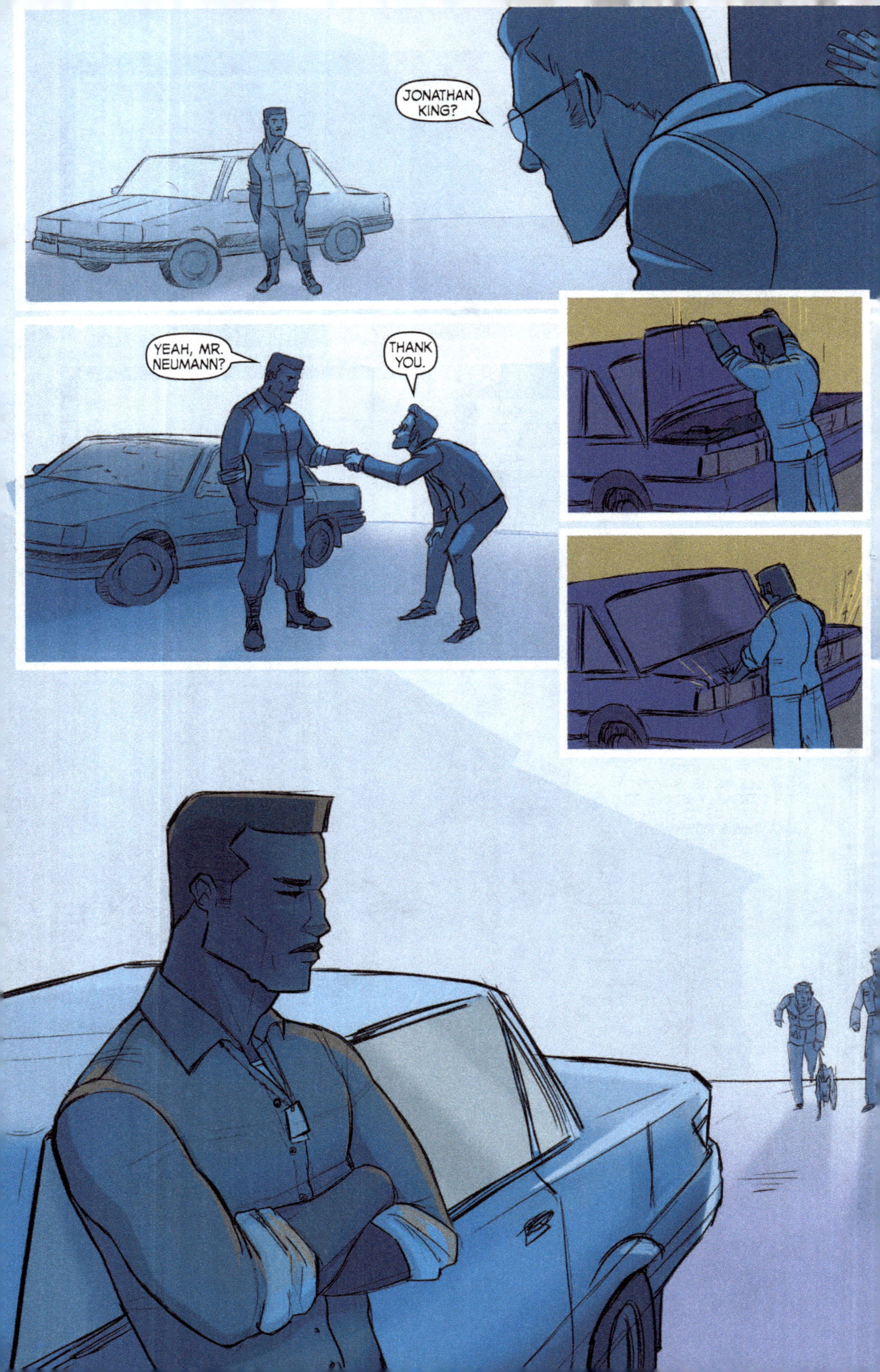
JONATHAN KING?
YEAH, MR. NEUMANN?
THANK YOU.

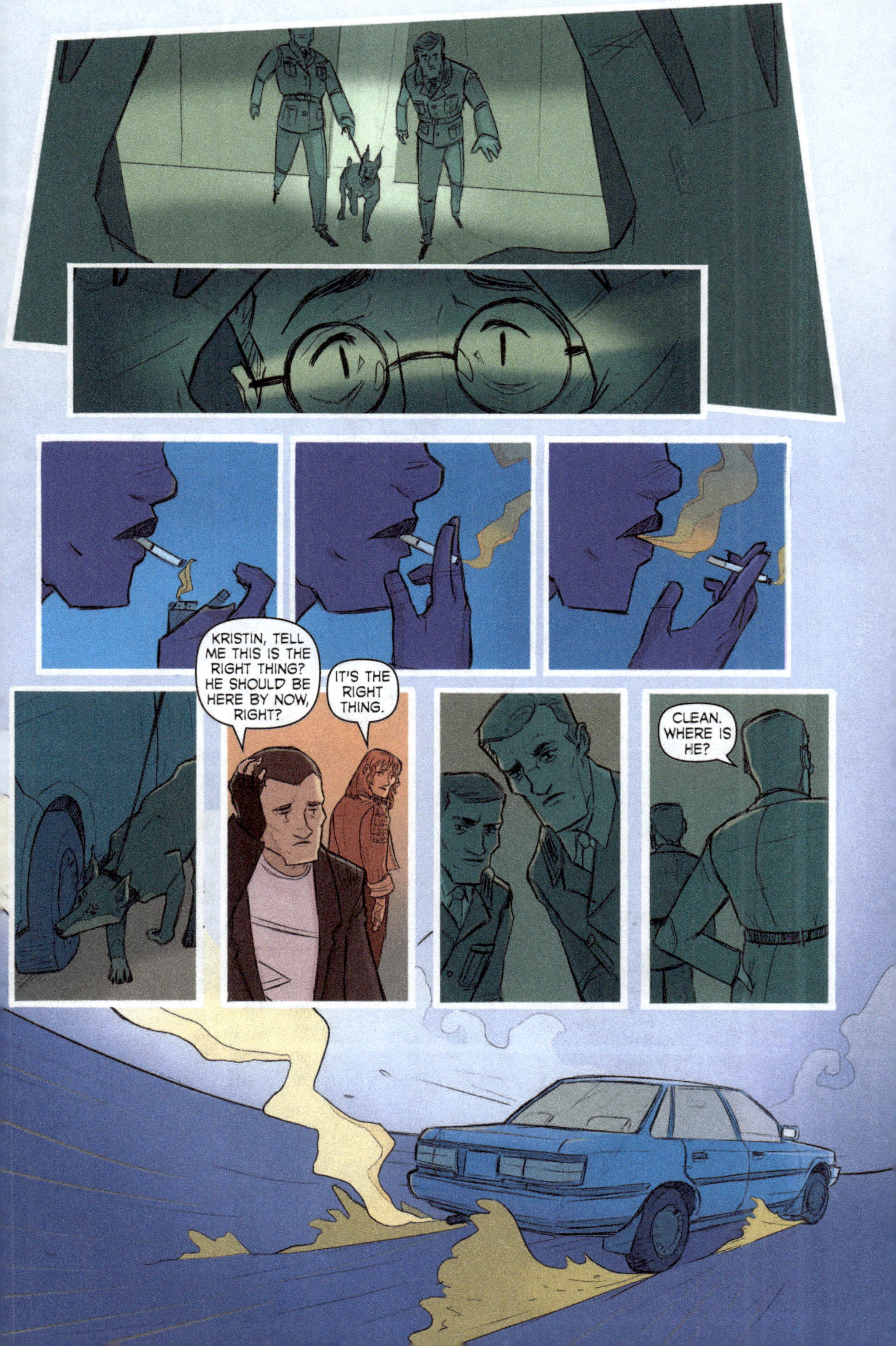
KRISTIN, TELL ME THIS IS THE RIGHT THING? HE SHOULD BE HERE BY NOW, RIGHT?
IT'S THE RIGHT THING.
CLEAN. WHERE IS HE?

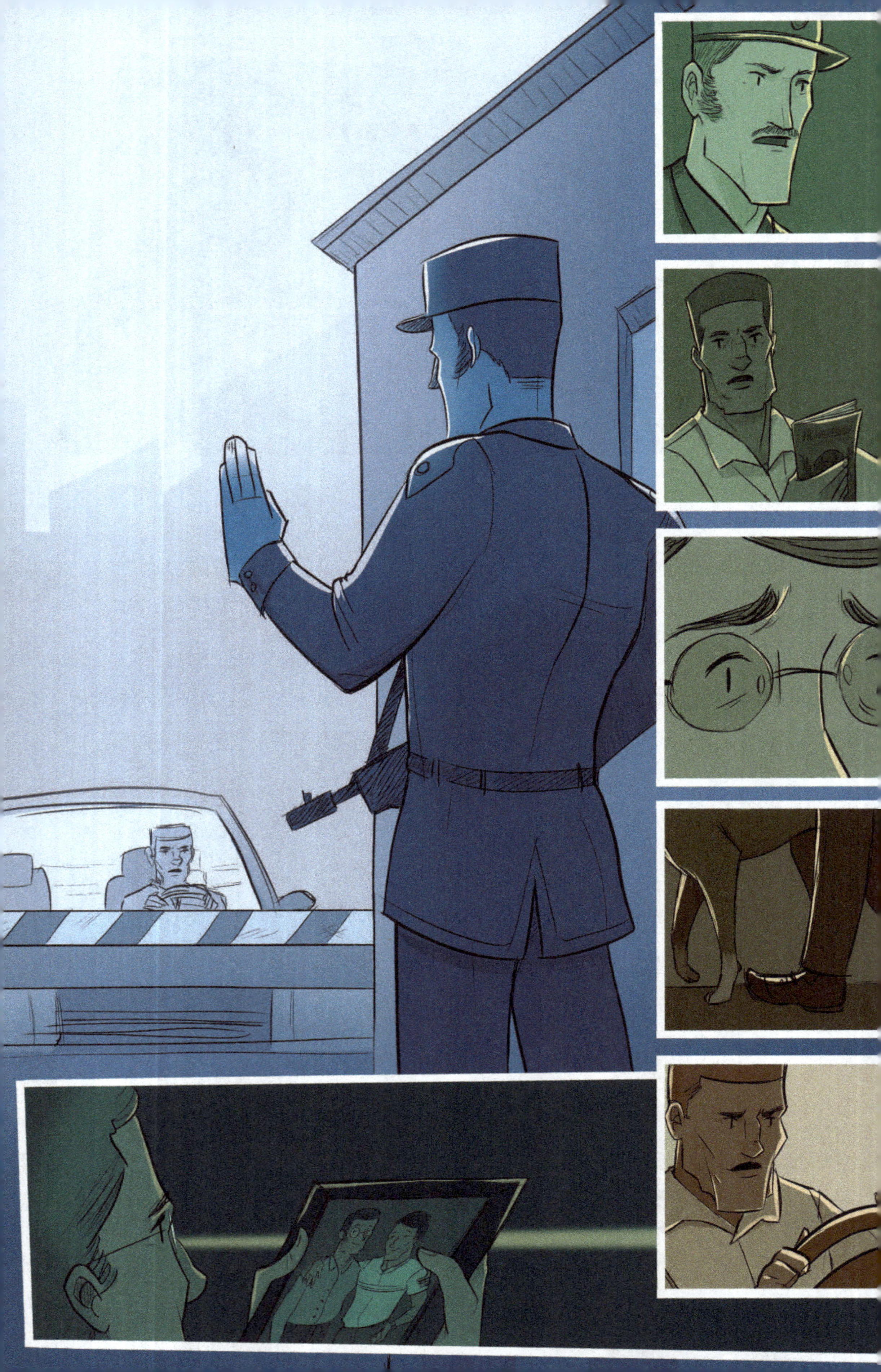

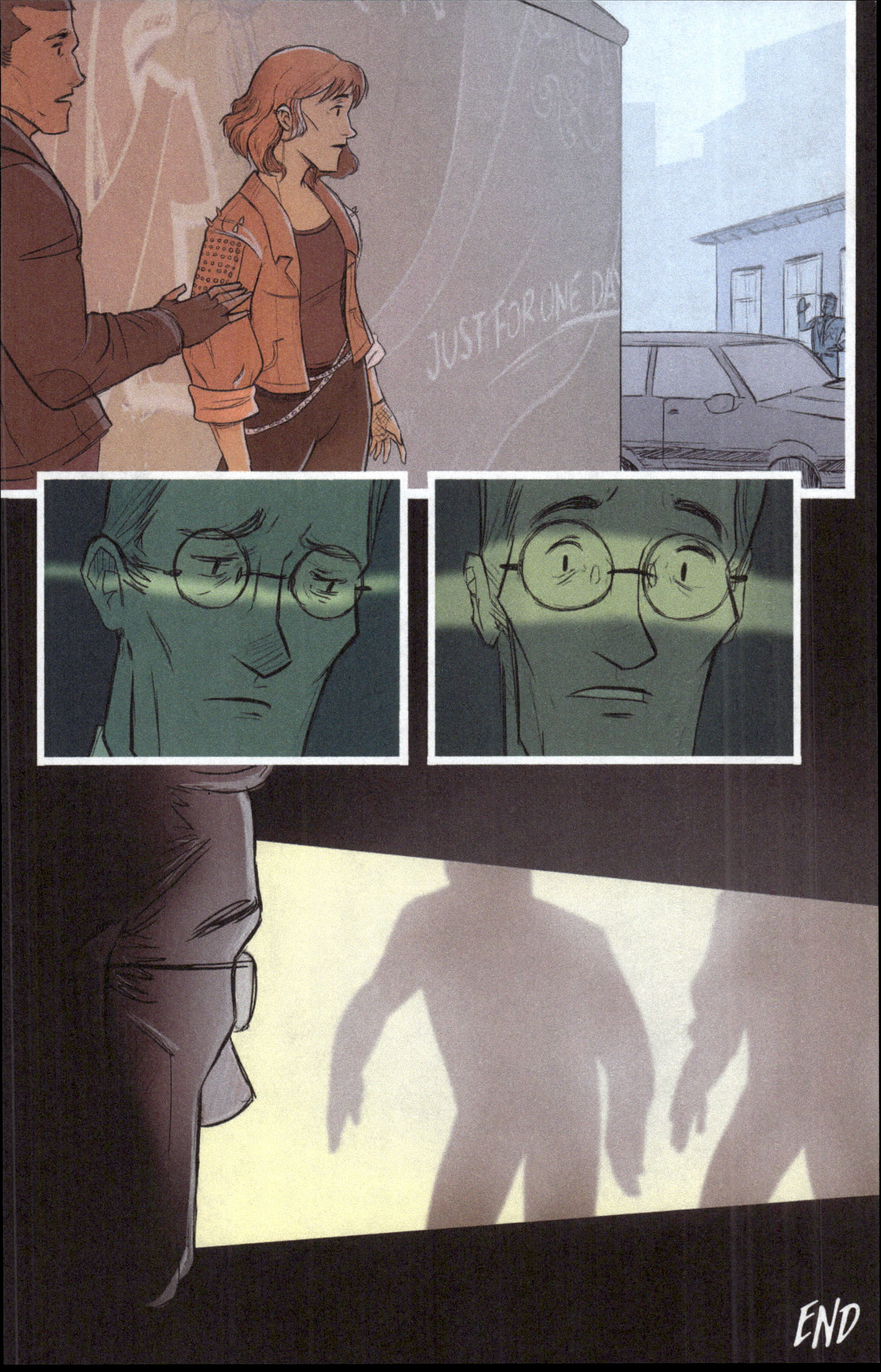
JUST FOR ONE DAY
END

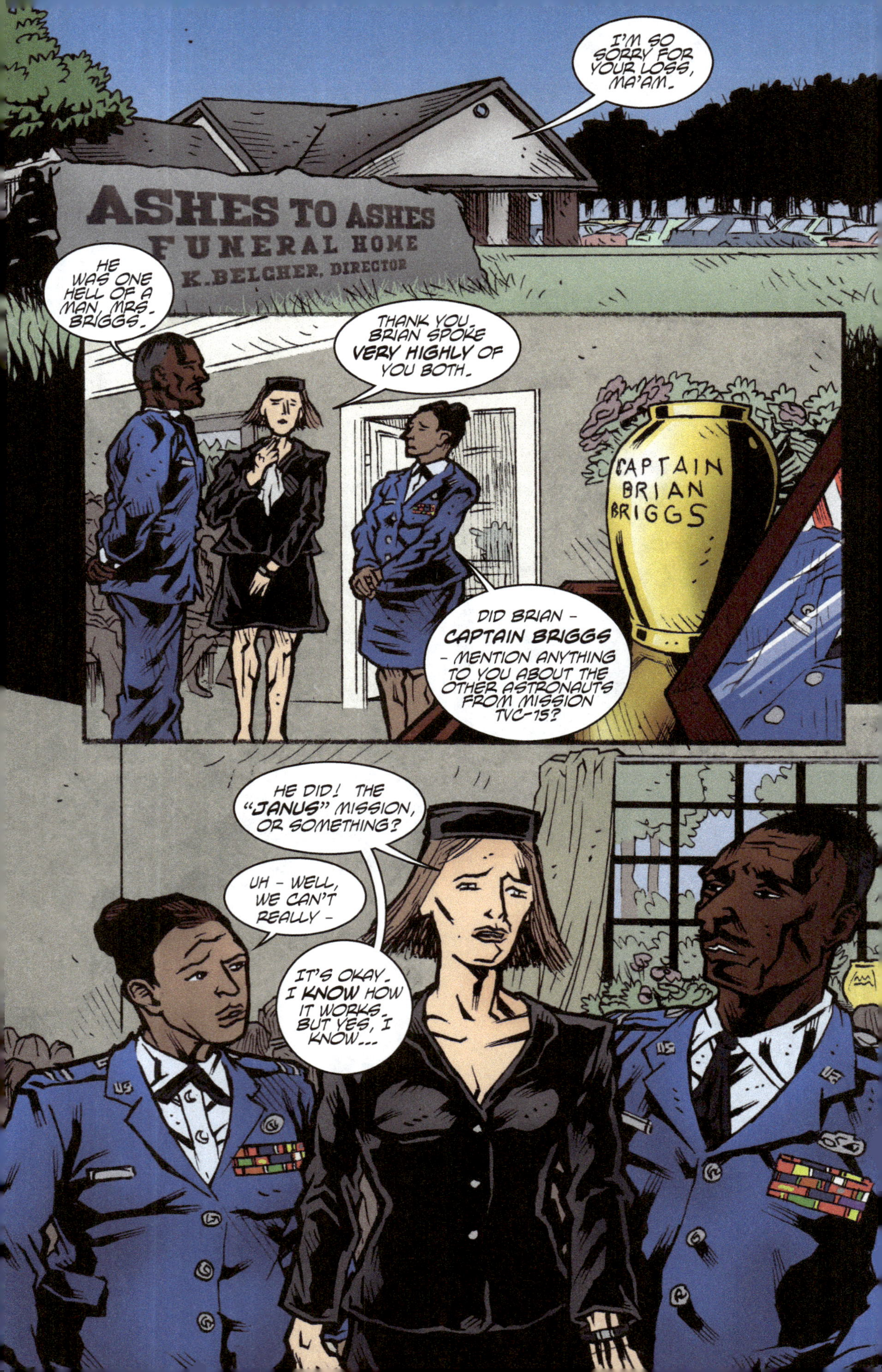
I'M SO SORRY FOR YOUR LOSS, MA'AM.
ASHES TO ASHES FUNERAL HOME K. BELCHER, DIRECTOR
HE WAS ONE HELL OF A MAN, MRS. BRIGGS.
THANK YOU. BRIAN SPOKE VERY HIGHLY OF YOU BOTH.
CAPTAIN BRIAN BRIGGS
DID BRIAN - CAPTAIN BRIGGS - MENTION ANYTHING TO YOU ABOUT THE OTHER ASTRONAUTS FROM MISSION TVC-15?
HE DID! THE "JANUS" MISSION, OR SOMETHING?
UH - WELL, WE CAN'T REALLY -
IT'S OKAY. I KNOW HOW IT WORKS. BUT YES, I KNOW...

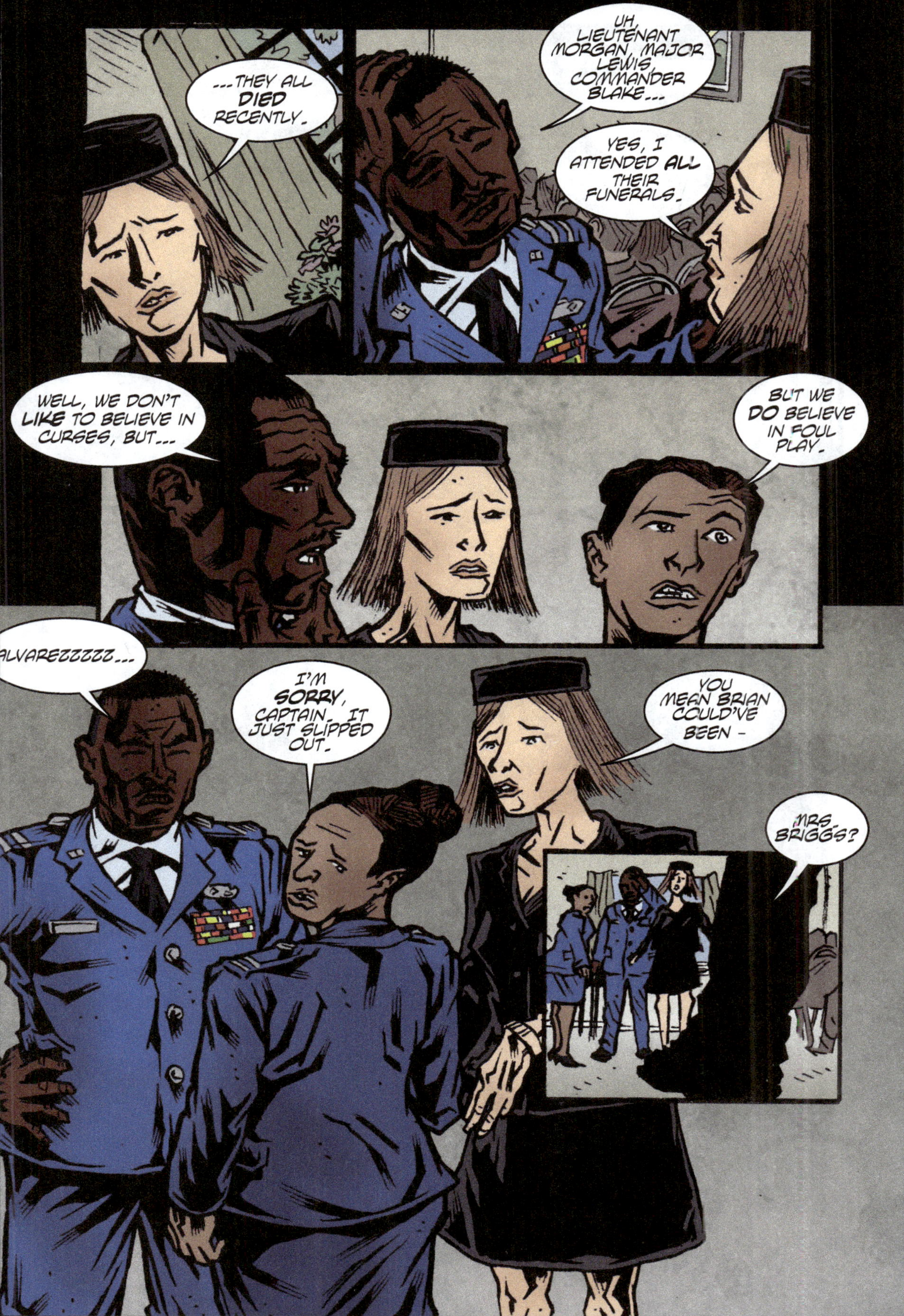
---THEY ALL DIED RECENTLY.
UH, LIEUTENANT MORGAN, MAJOR LEWIS COMMANDER BLAKE---
YES, I ATTENDED ALL THEIR FUNERALS.
WELL, WE DON'T LIKE TO BELIEVE IN CURSES, BUT---
BUT WE DO BELIEVE IN FOUL PLAY.
ALVAREZZZZZ---
I'M SORRY, CAPTAIN. IT JUST SLIPPED OUT.
YOU MEAN BRIAN COULD'VE BEEN -
MRS. BRIGGS?

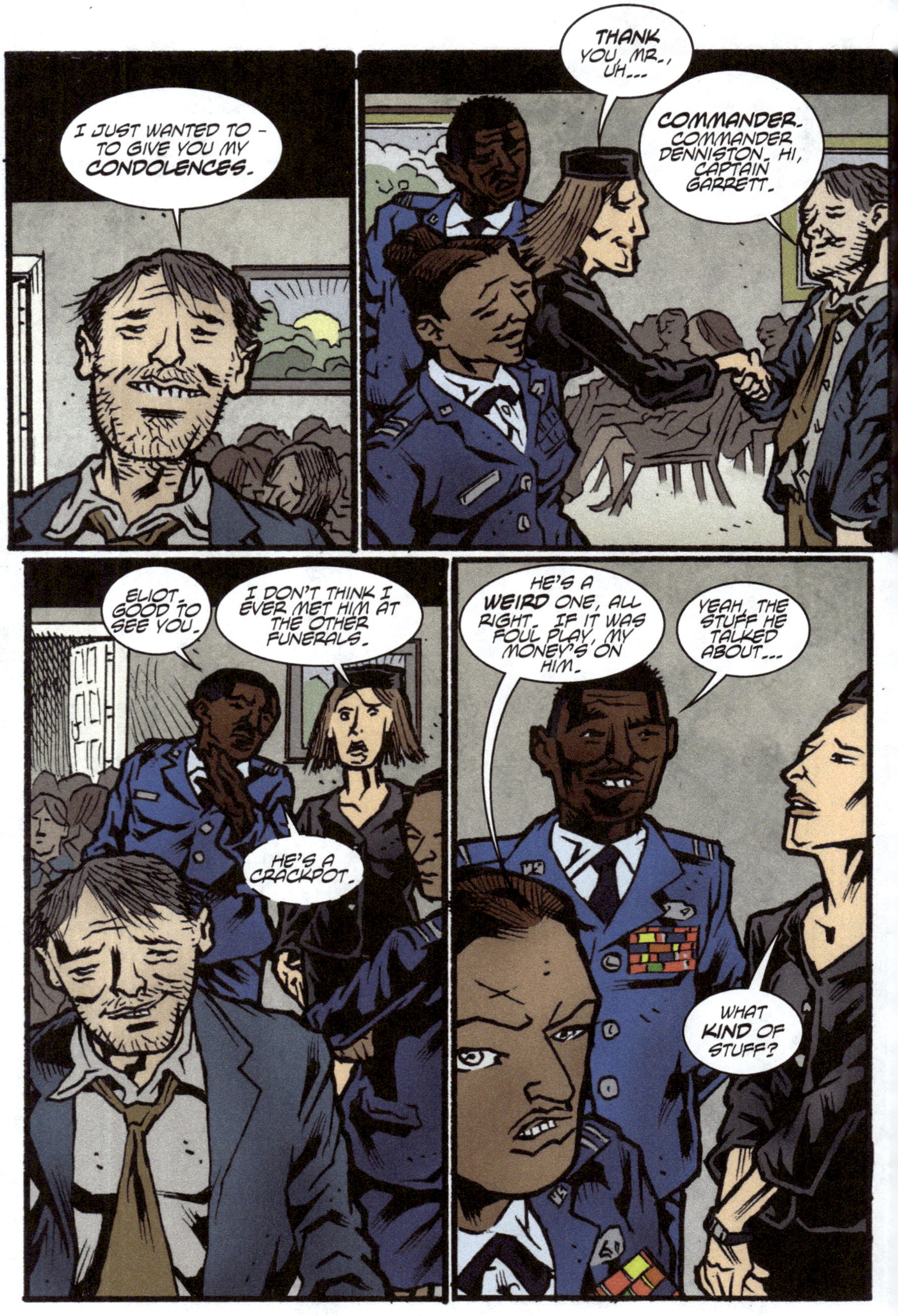
I JUST WANTED TO - TO GIVE YOU MY CONDOLENCES.
THANK YOU, MR., UH...
COMMANDER. COMMANDER DENNISTON. HI, CAPTAIN GARRETT.
ELIOT. GOOD TO SEE YOU.
I DON'T THINK I EVER MET HIM AT THE OTHER FUNERALS.
HE'S A CRACKPOT.
HE'S A WEIRD ONE, ALL RIGHT. IF IT WAS FOUL PLAY, MY MONEY'S ON HIM.
YEAH, THE STUFF HE TALKED ABOUT...
WHAT KIND OF STUFF?

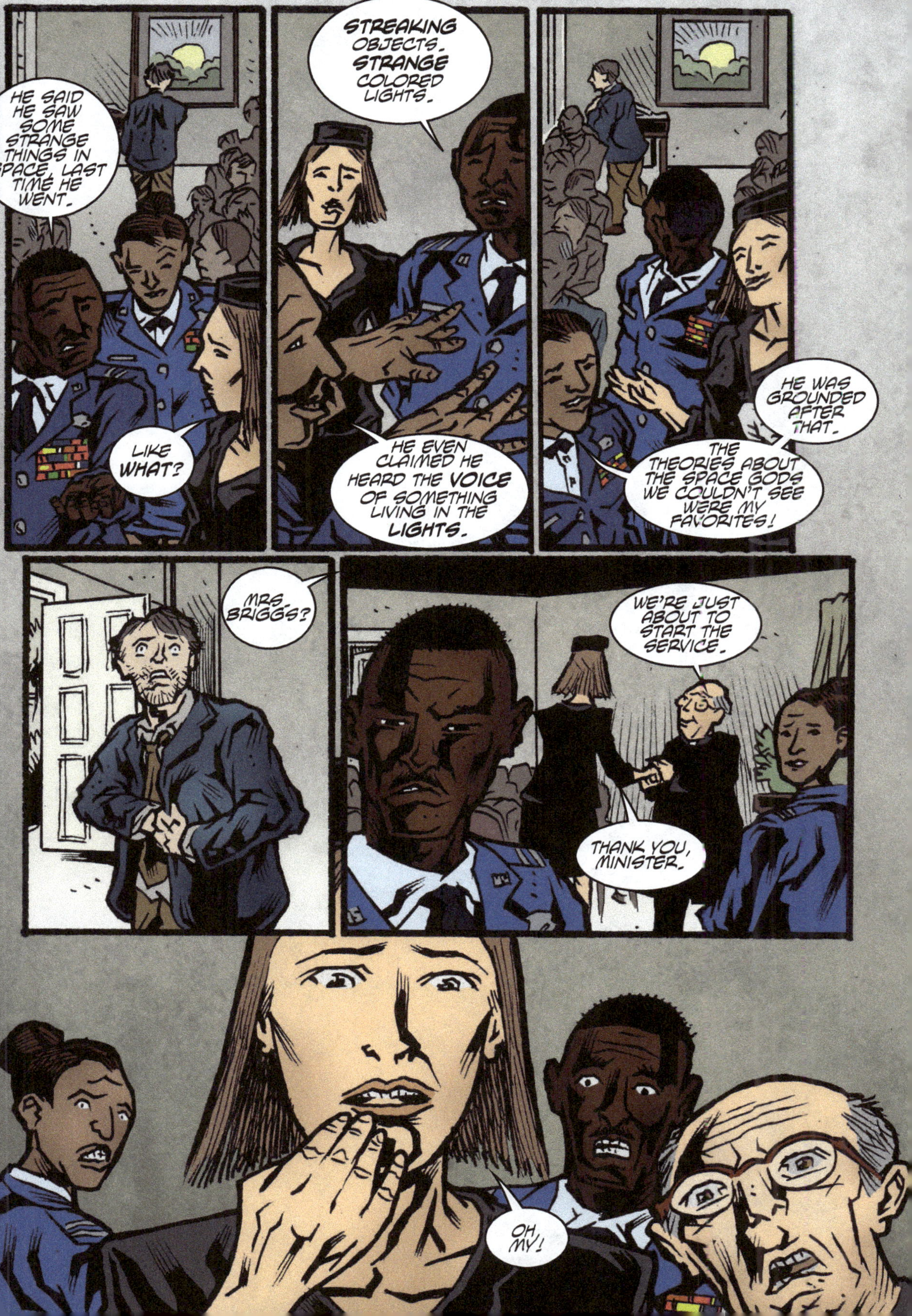
HE SAID HE SAW SOME STRANGE THINGS IN SPACE, LAST TIME HE WENT.
LIKE WHAT?
STREAKING OBJECTS. STRANGE COLORED LIGHTS.
HE EVEN CLAIMED HE HEARD THE VOICE OF SOMETHING LIVING IN THE LIGHTS.
HE WAS GROUNDED AFTER THAT.
THE THEORIES ABOUT THE SPACE GODS WE COULDN'T SEE WERE MY FAVORITES!
MRS. BRIGGS?
WE'RE JUST ABOUT TO START THE SERVICE.
THANK YOU, MINISTER.
OH MY!

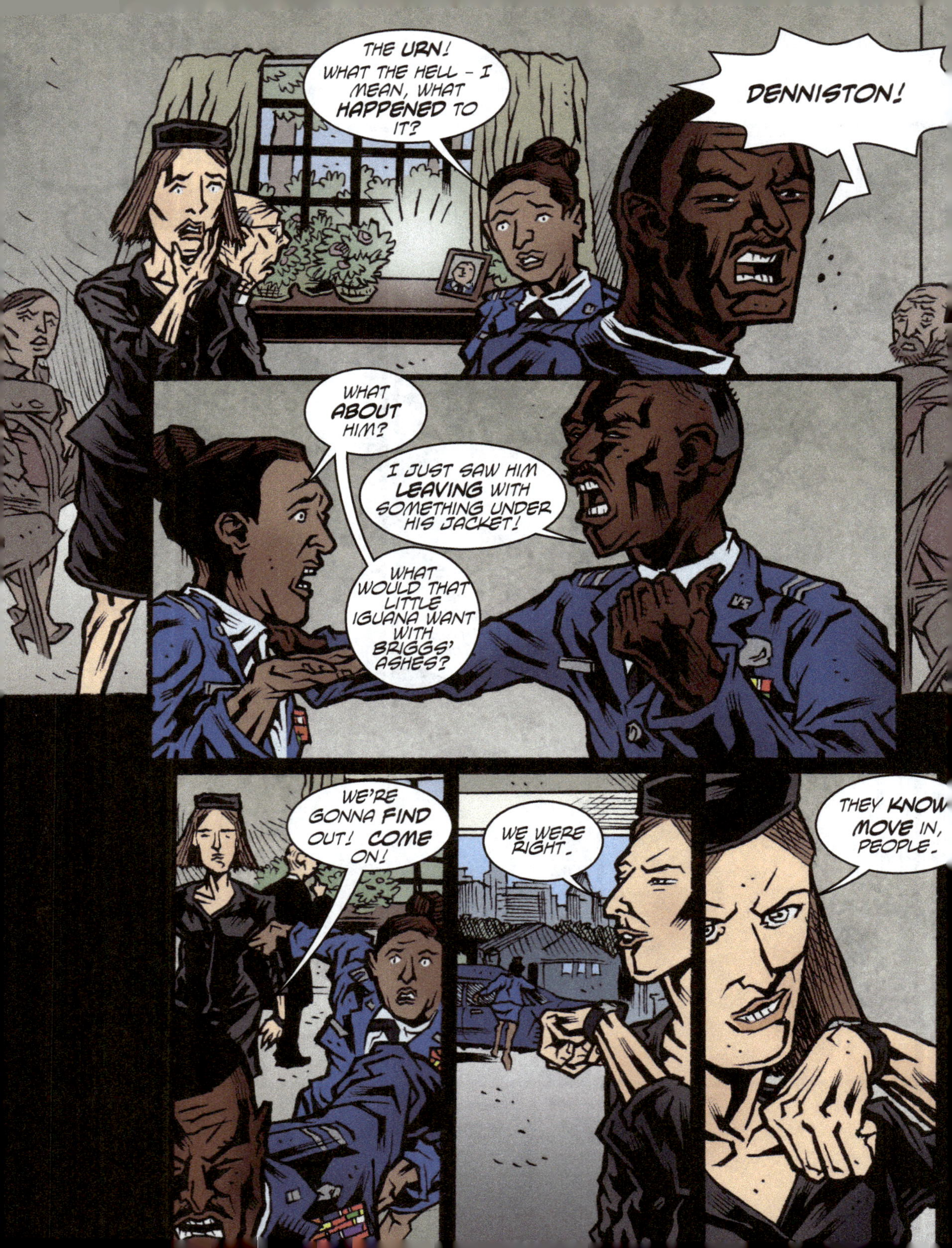
THE URN! WHAT THE HELL - I MEAN, WHAT HAPPENED TO IT?
DENNISTON!
WHAT ABOUT HIM?
I JUST SAW HIM LEAVING WITH SOMETHING UNDER HIS JACKET!
WHAT WOULD THAT LITTLE IGUANA WANT WITH BRIGGS' ASHES?
WE'RE GONNA FIND OUT! COME ON!
WE WERE RIGHT.
THEY KNOW
MOVE IN, PEOPLE.

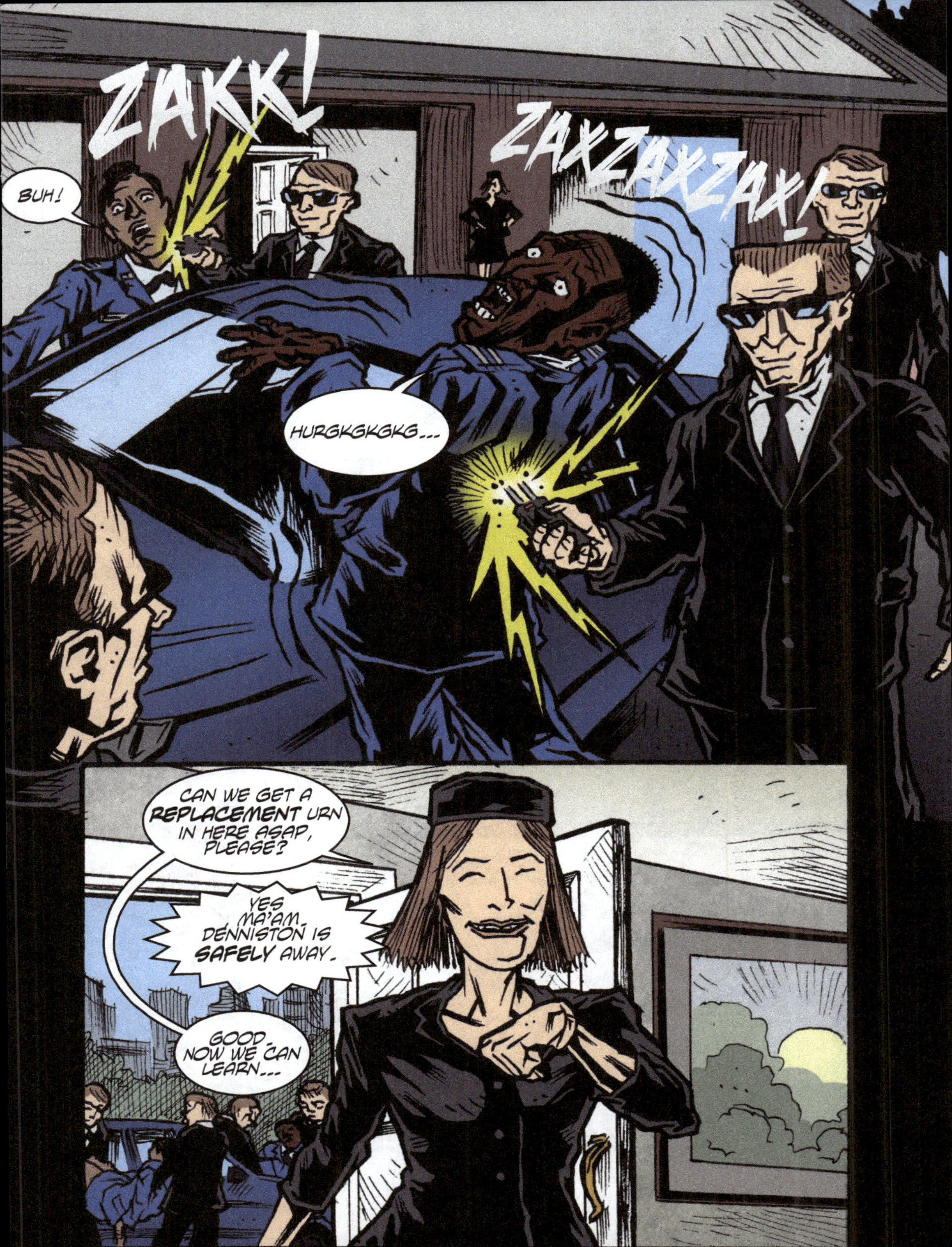
ZAKK!
BUH!
ZAXZAXZAX!
HURGKGKGKG...
CAN WE GET A REPLACEMENT URN IN HERE ASAP, PLEASE?
YES MA'AM. DENNISTON IS SAFELY AWAY.
GOOD. NOW WE CAN LEARN...

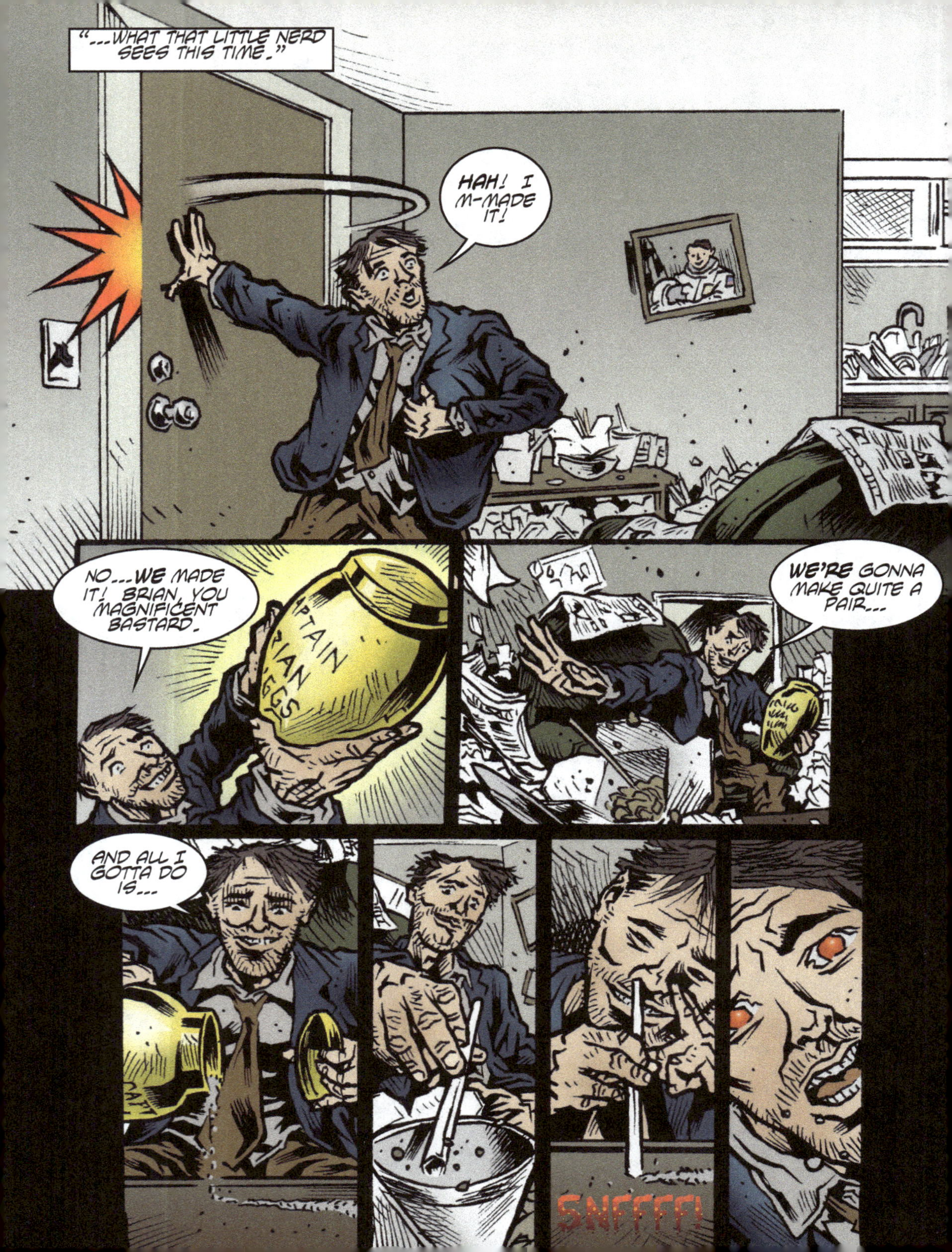
"...WHAT THAT LITTLE NERD SEES THIS TIME."
HAH! I M-MADE IT!
NO...WE MADE IT! BRIAN, YOU MAGNIFICENT BASTARD.
WE'RE GONNA MAKE QUITE A PAIR...
AND ALL I GOTTA DO IS...
SNFFFF!

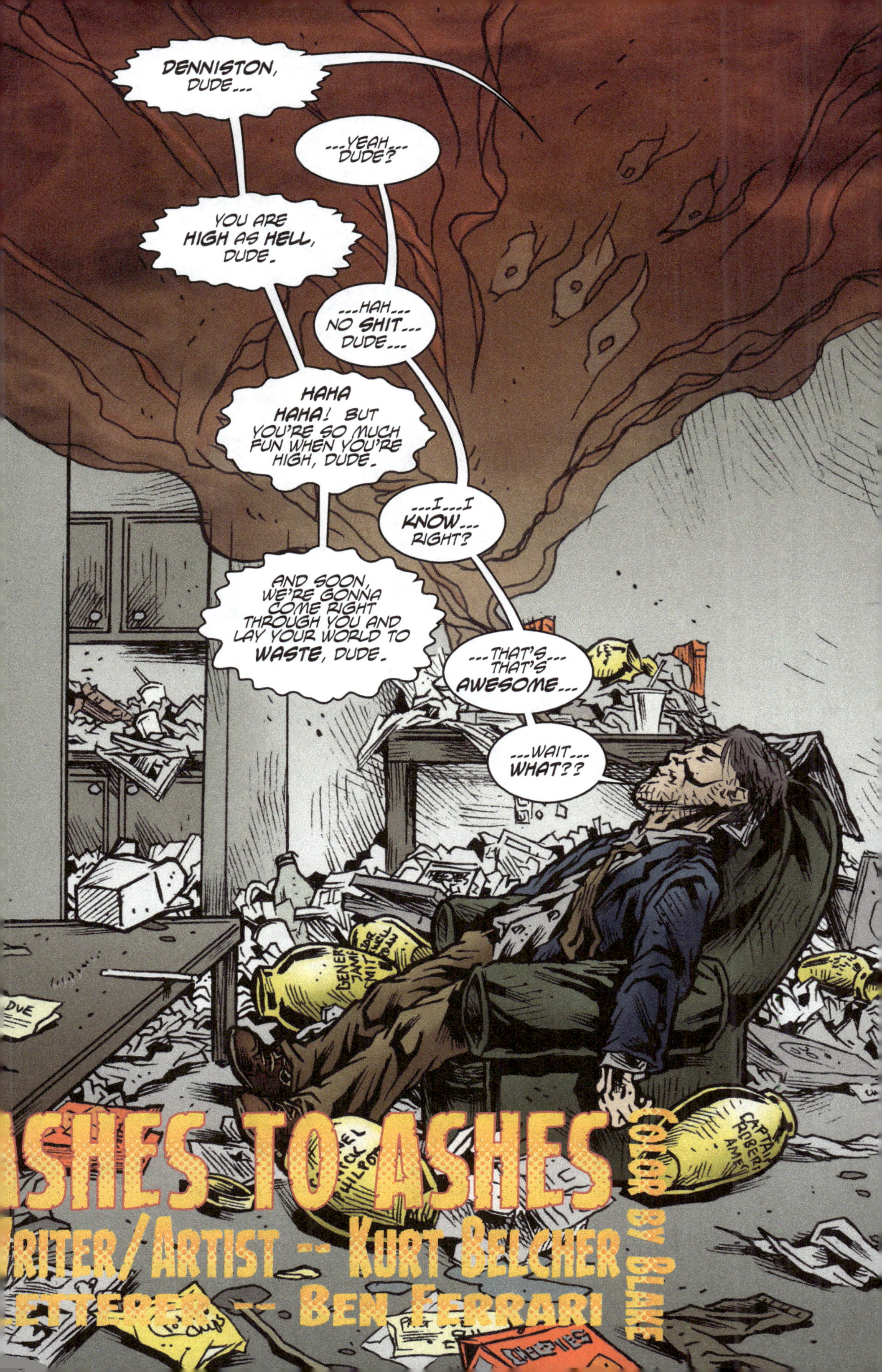
DENNISTON, DUDE...
...YEAH... DUDE?
YOU ARE HIGH AS HELL, DUDE.
...HAH... NO SHIT... DUDE...
HAHA HAHA! BUT YOU'RE SO MUCH FUN WHEN YOU'RE HIGH, DUDE.
...I...I KNOW... RIGHT?
AND SOON, WE'RE GONNA COME RIGHT THROUGH YOU AND LAY YOUR WORLD TO WASTE, DUDE.
...THAT'S... THAT'S AWESOME...
...WAIT... WHAT??
ASHES TO ASHES
RITER/ARTIST -- KURT BELCHER
ETTERED -- BEN FERRARI
COLOR BY BLAKE

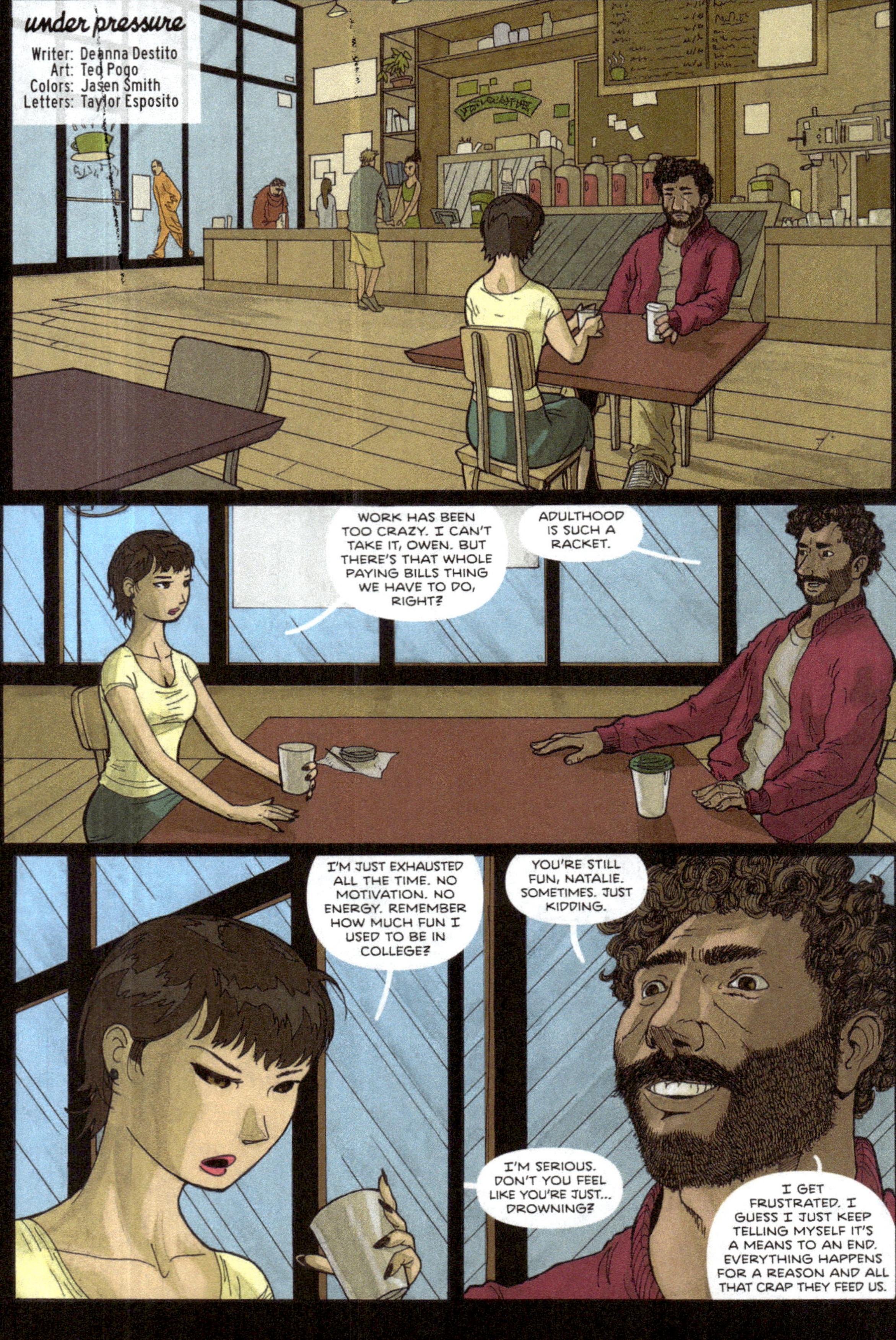

under pressure
Writer: Deanna Destito
Art: Ted Pogo
Colors: Jason Smith
Letters: Taylor Esposito
WORK HAS BEEN TOO CRAZY. I CAN'T TAKE IT, OWEN. BUT THERE'S THAT WHOLE PAYING BILLS THING WE HAVE TO DO, RIGHT?
ADULTHOOD IS SUCH A RACKET.
I'M JUST EXHAUSTED ALL THE TIME. NO MOTIVATION. NO ENERGY. REMEMBER HOW MUCH FUN I USED TO BE IN COLLEGE?
YOU'RE STILL FUN, NATALIE. SOMETIMES. JUST KIDDING.
I'M SERIOUS. DON'T YOU FEEL LIKE YOU'RE JUST... DROWNING?
I GET FRUSTRATED. I GUESS I JUST KEEP TELLING MYSELF IT'S A MEANS TO AN END. EVERYTHING HAPPENS FOR A REASON AND ALL THAT CRAP THEY FEED US.

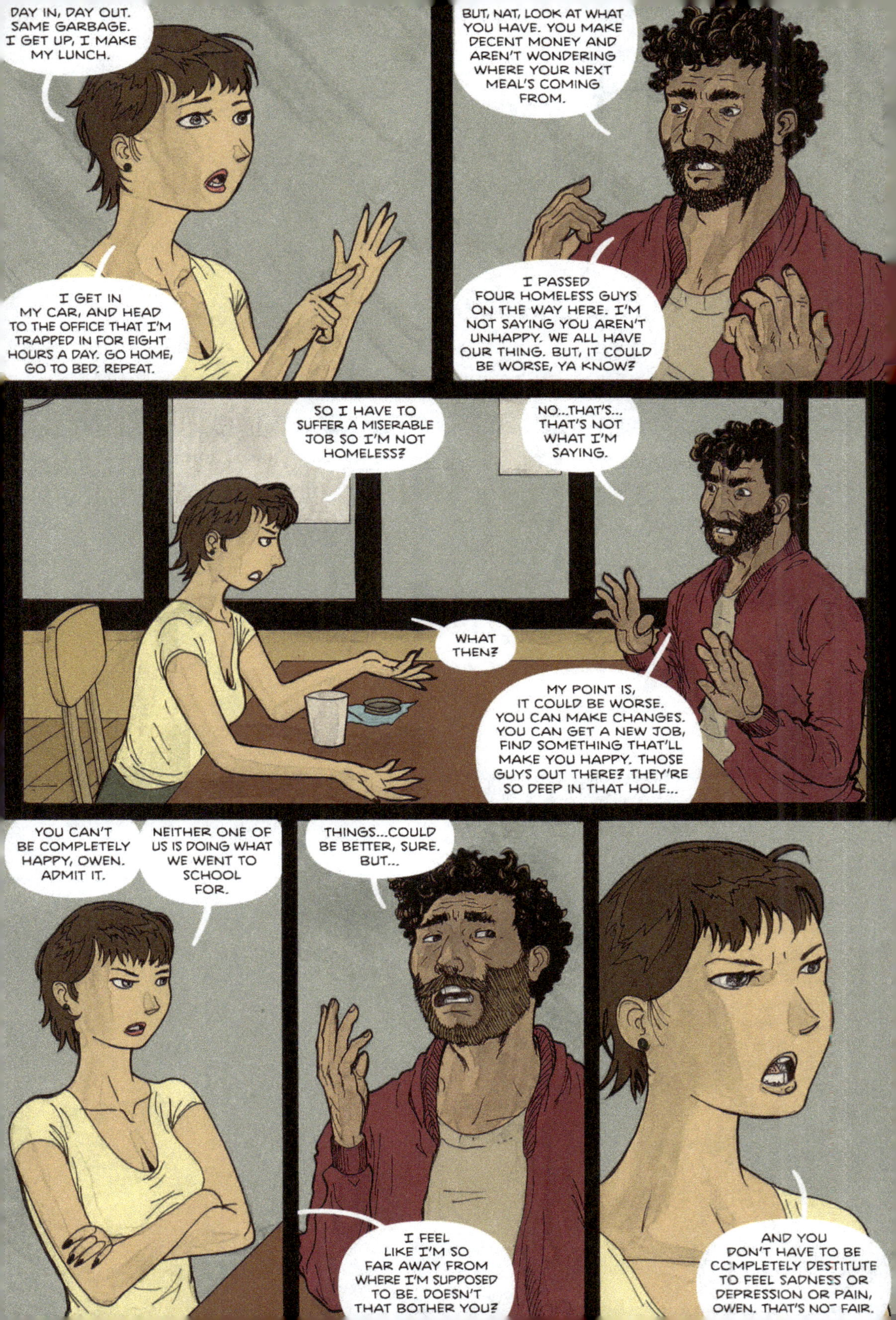
DAY IN, DAY OUT. SAME GARBAGE. I GET UP, I MAKE MY LUNCH.
I GET IN MY CAR, AND HEAD TO THE OFFICE THAT I'M TRAPPED IN FOR EIGHT HOURS A DAY. GO HOME, GO TO BED. REPEAT.
BUT, NAT, LOOK AT WHAT YOU HAVE. YOU MAKE DECENT MONEY AND AREN'T WONDERING WHERE YOUR NEXT MEAL'S COMING FROM.
I PASSED FOUR HOMELESS GUYS ON THE WAY HERE. I'M NOT SAYING YOU AREN'T UNHAPPY. WE ALL HAVE OUR THING. BUT, IT COULD BE WORSE, YA KNOW?
SO I HAVE TO SUFFER A MISERABLE JOB SO I'M NOT HOMELESS?
NO...THAT'S... THAT'S NOT WHAT I'M SAYING.
WHAT THEN?
MY POINT IS, IT COULD BE WORSE. YOU CAN MAKE CHANGES. YOU CAN GET A NEW JOB, FIND SOMETHING THAT'LL MAKE YOU HAPPY. THOSE GUYS OUT THERE? THEY'RE SO DEEP IN THAT HOLE...
YOU CAN'T BE COMPLETELY HAPPY, OWEN. ADMIT IT.
NEITHER ONE OF US IS DOING WHAT WE WENT TO SCHOOL FOR.
THINGS...COULD BE BETTER, SURE. BUT...
I FEEL LIKE I'M SO FAR AWAY FROM WHERE I'M SUPPOSED TO BE. DOESN'T THAT BOTHER YOU?
AND YOU DON'T HAVE TO BE COMPLETELY DESTITUTE TO FEEL SADNESS OR DEPRESSION OR PAIN, OWEN. THAT'S NOT FAIR.

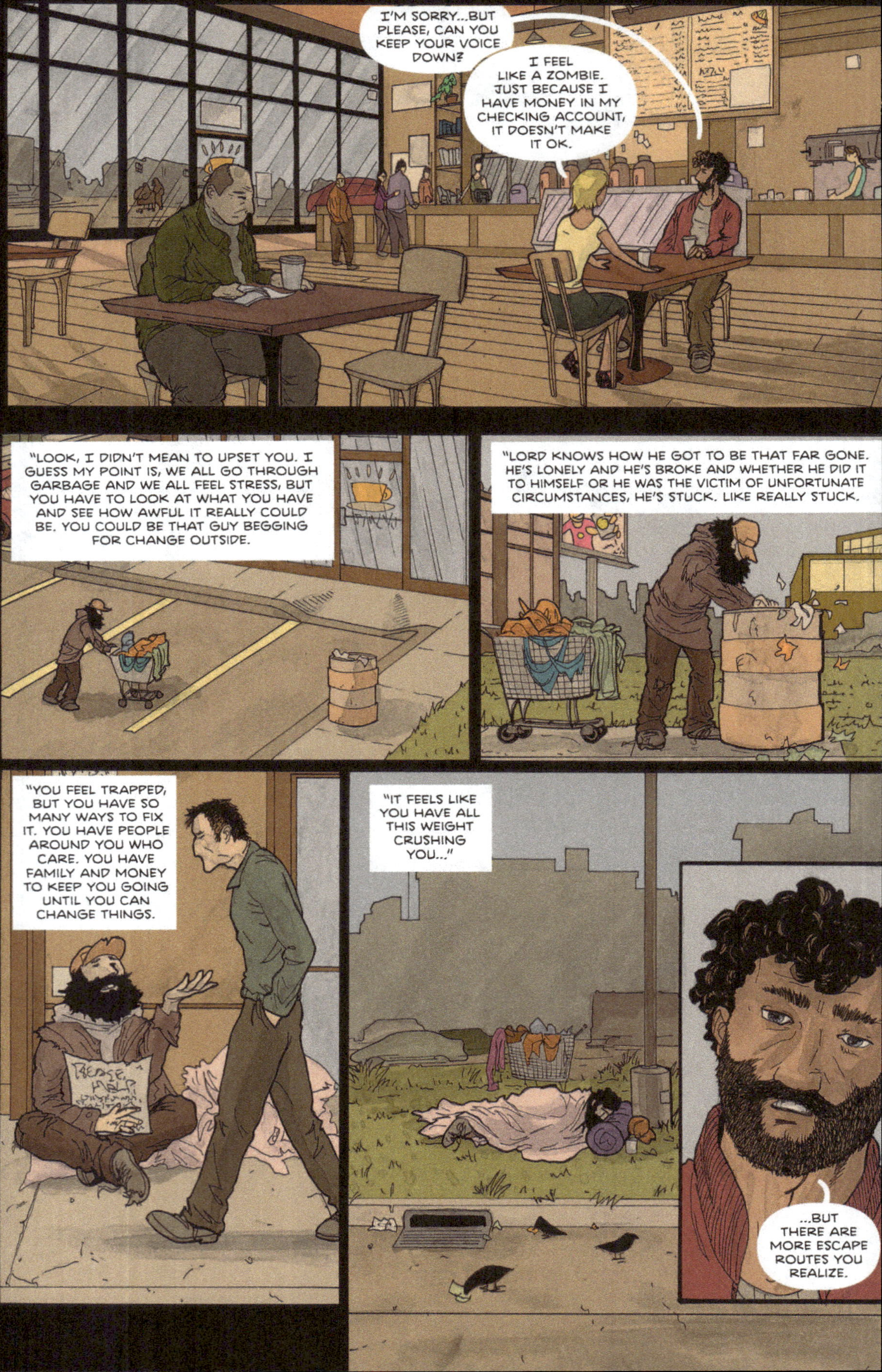
I'M SORRY...BUT PLEASE, CAN YOU KEEP YOUR VOICE DOWN?
I FEEL LIKE A ZOMBIE. JUST BECAUSE I HAVE MONEY IN MY CHECKING ACCOUNT, IT DOESN'T MAKE IT OK.
"LOOK, I DIDN'T MEAN TO UPSET YOU. I GUESS MY POINT IS, WE ALL GO THROUGH GARBAGE AND WE ALL FEEL STRESS, BUT YOU HAVE TO LOOK AT WHAT YOU HAVE AND SEE HOW AWFUL IT REALLY COULD BE. YOU COULD BE THAT GUY BEGGING FOR CHANGE OUTSIDE.
"LORD KNOWS HOW HE GOT TO BE THAT FAR GONE. HE'S LONELY AND HE'S BROKE AND WHETHER HE DID IT TO HIMSELF OR HE WAS THE VICTIM OF UNFORTUNATE CIRCUMSTANCES, HE'S STUCK. LIKE REALLY STUCK.
"YOU FEEL TRAPPED, BUT YOU HAVE SO MANY WAYS TO FIX IT. YOU HAVE PEOPLE AROUND YOU WHO CARE. YOU HAVE FAMILY AND MONEY TO KEEP YOU GOING UNTIL YOU CAN CHANGE THINGS.
"IT FEELS LIKE YOU HAVE ALL THIS WEIGHT CRUSHING YOU..."
...BUT THERE ARE MORE ESCAPE ROUTES YOU REALIZE.

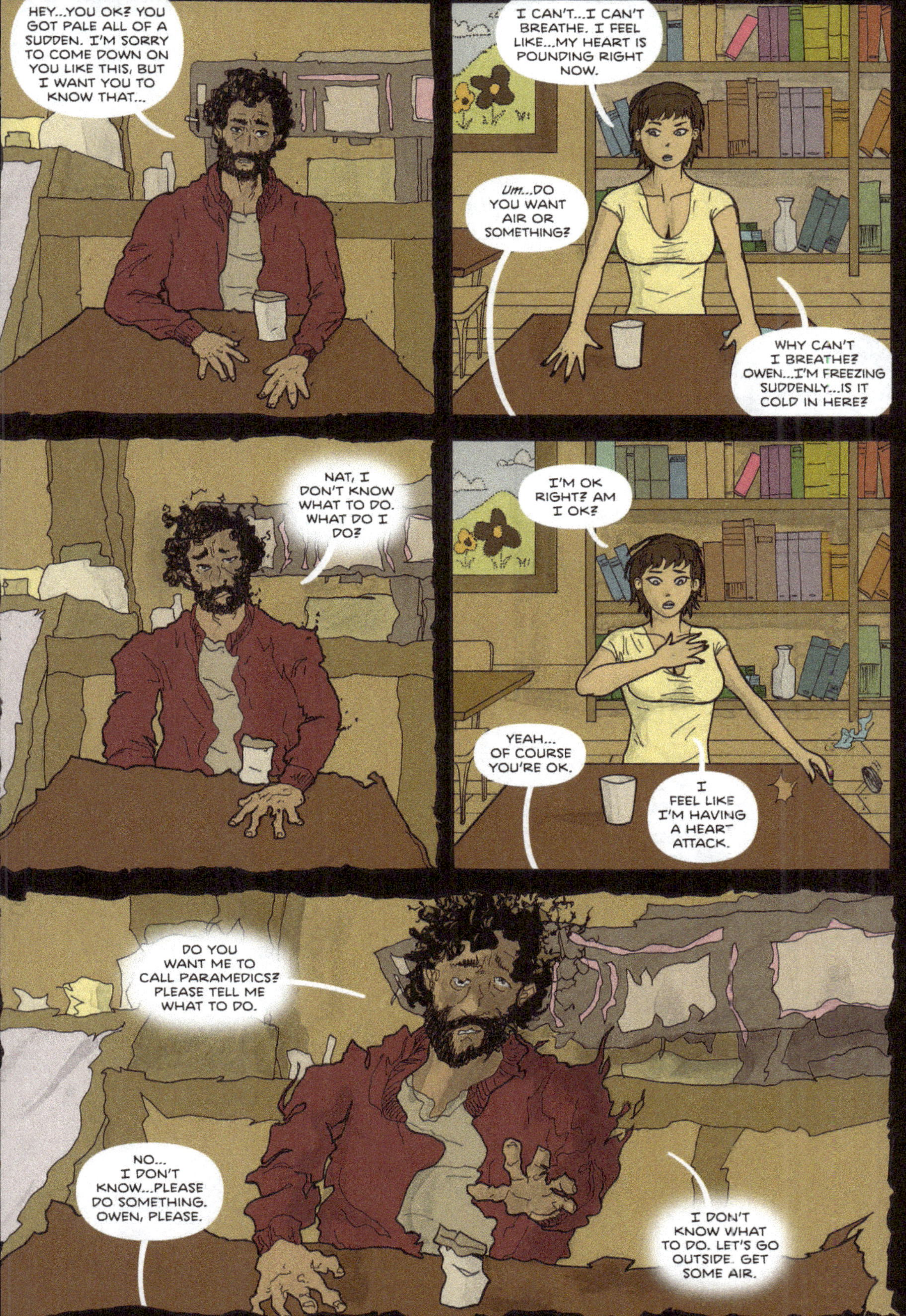
HEY...YOU OK? YOU GOT PALE ALL OF A SUDDEN. I'M SORRY TO COME DOWN ON YOU LIKE THIS, BUT I WANT YOU TO KNOW THAT...
I CAN'T...I CAN'T BREATHE. I FEEL LIKE...MY HEART IS POUNDING RIGHT NOW.
Um...DO YOU WANT AIR OR SOMETHING?
WHY CAN'T I BREATHE? OWEN...I'M FREEZING SUDDENLY...IS IT COLD IN HERE?
NAT, I DON'T KNOW WHAT TO DO. WHAT DO I DO?
I'M OK RIGHT? AM I OK?
YEAH... OF COURSE YOU'RE OK.
I FEEL LIKE I'M HAVING A HEART ATTACK.
DO YOU WANT ME TO CALL PARAMEDICS? PLEASE TELL ME WHAT TO DO.
NO... I DON'T KNOW...PLEASE DO SOMETHING. OWEN, PLEASE.
I DON'T KNOW WHAT TO DO. LET'S GO OUTSIDE. GET SOME AIR.

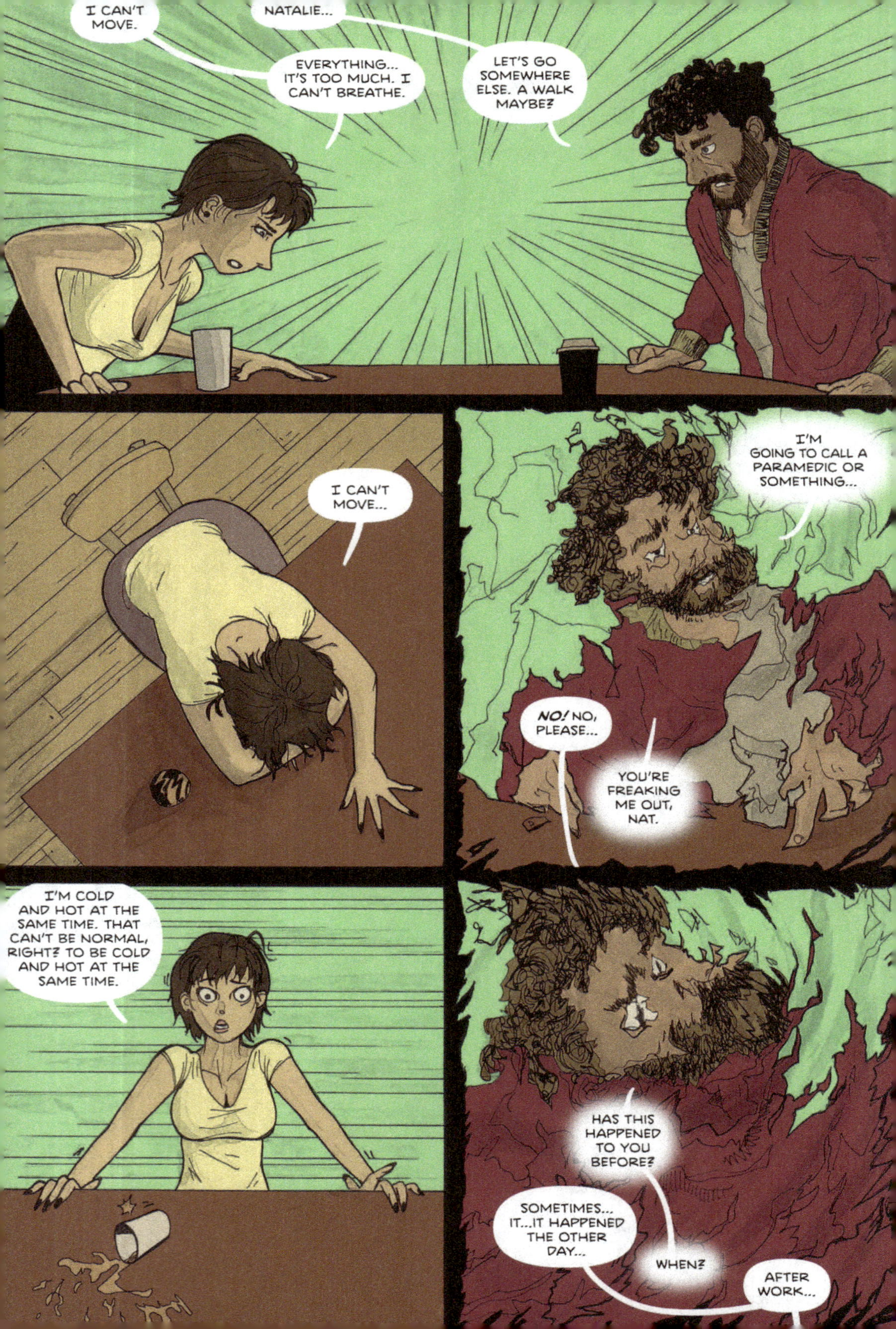
I CAN'T MOVE.
NATALIE...
EVERYTHING... IT'S TOO MUCH. I CAN'T BREATHE.
LET'S GO SOMEWHERE ELSE. A WALK MAYBE?
I CAN'T MOVE...
I'M GOING TO CALL A PARAMEDIC OR SOMETHING...
NO! NO, PLEASE...
YOU'RE FREAKING ME OUT, NAT.
I'M COLD AND HOT AT THE SAME TIME. THAT CAN'T BE NORMAL, RIGHT? TO BE COLD AND HOT AT THE SAME TIME.
HAS THIS HAPPENED TO YOU BEFORE?
SOMETIMES... IT...IT HAPPENED THE OTHER DAY...
WHEN?
AFTER WORK...

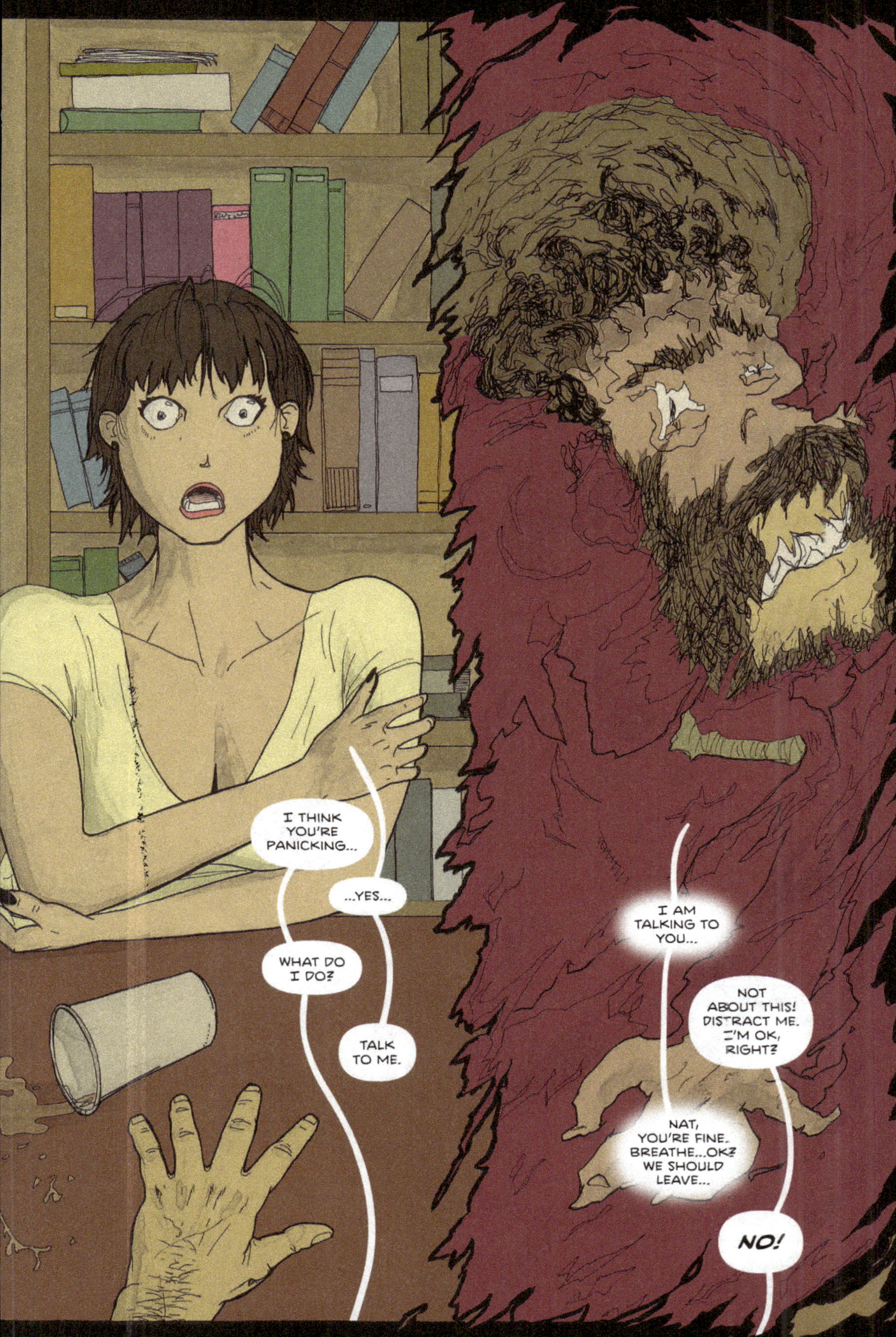
I THINK YOU'RE PANICKING...
...YES...
WHAT DO I DO?
TALK TO ME.
I AM TALKING TO YOU...
NOT ABOUT THIS! DISTRACT ME. I'M OK, RIGHT?
NAT, YOU'RE FINE. BREATHE...OK? WE SHOULD LEAVE...
NO!

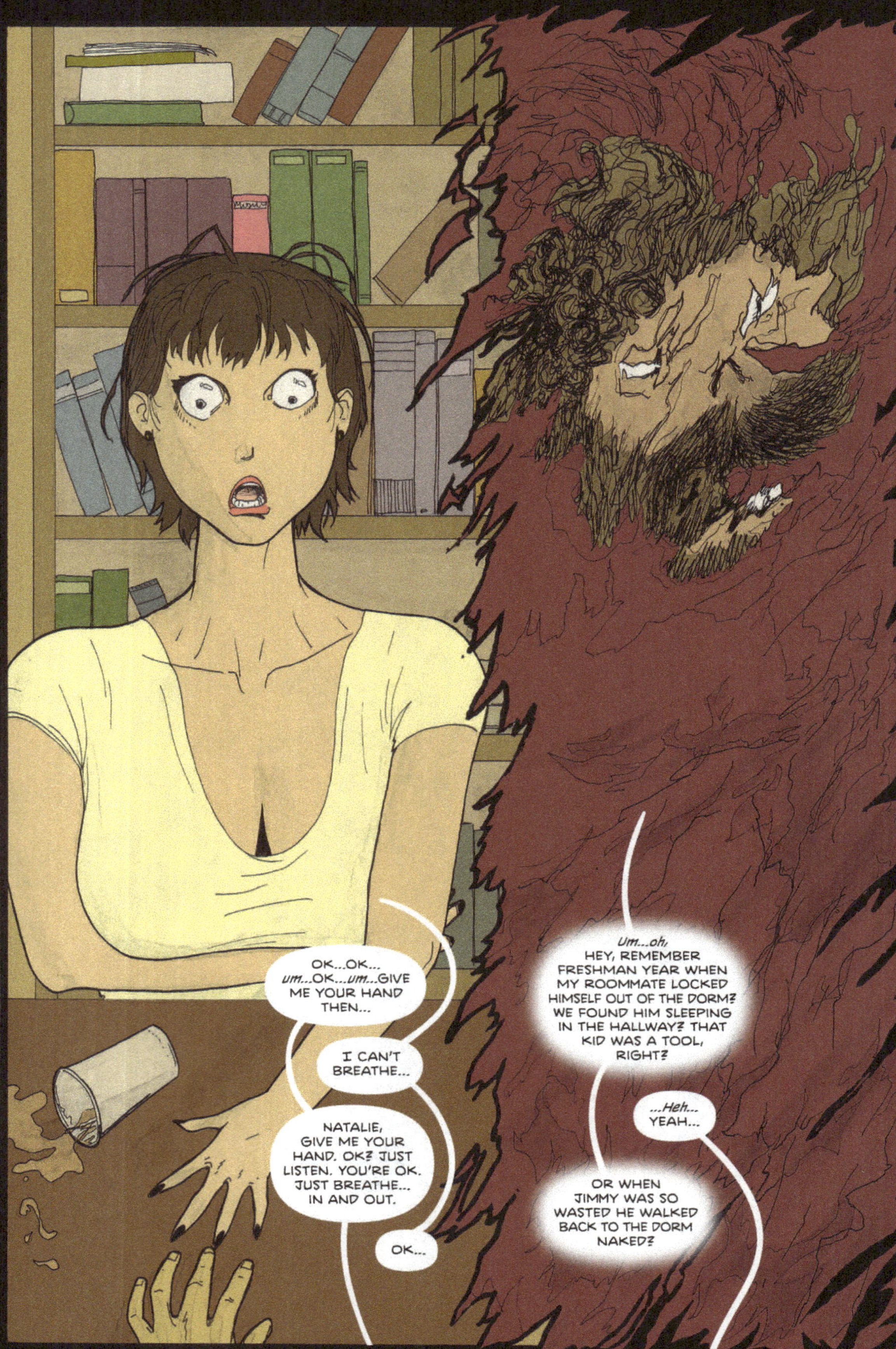
OK...OK... um...OK...um...GIVE ME YOUR HAND THEN...
I CAN'T BREATHE...
NATALIE, GIVE ME YOUR HAND. OK? JUST LISTEN. YOU'RE OK. JUST BREATHE... IN AND OUT.
OK...
Um...oh, HEY, REMEMBER FRESHMAN YEAR WHEN MY ROOMMATE LOCKED HIMSELF OUT OF THE DORM? WE FOUND HIM SLEEPING IN THE HALLWAY? THAT KID WAS A TOOL, RIGHT?
...Heh... YEAH...
OR WHEN JIMMY WAS SO WASTED HE WALKED BACK TO THE DORM NAKED?

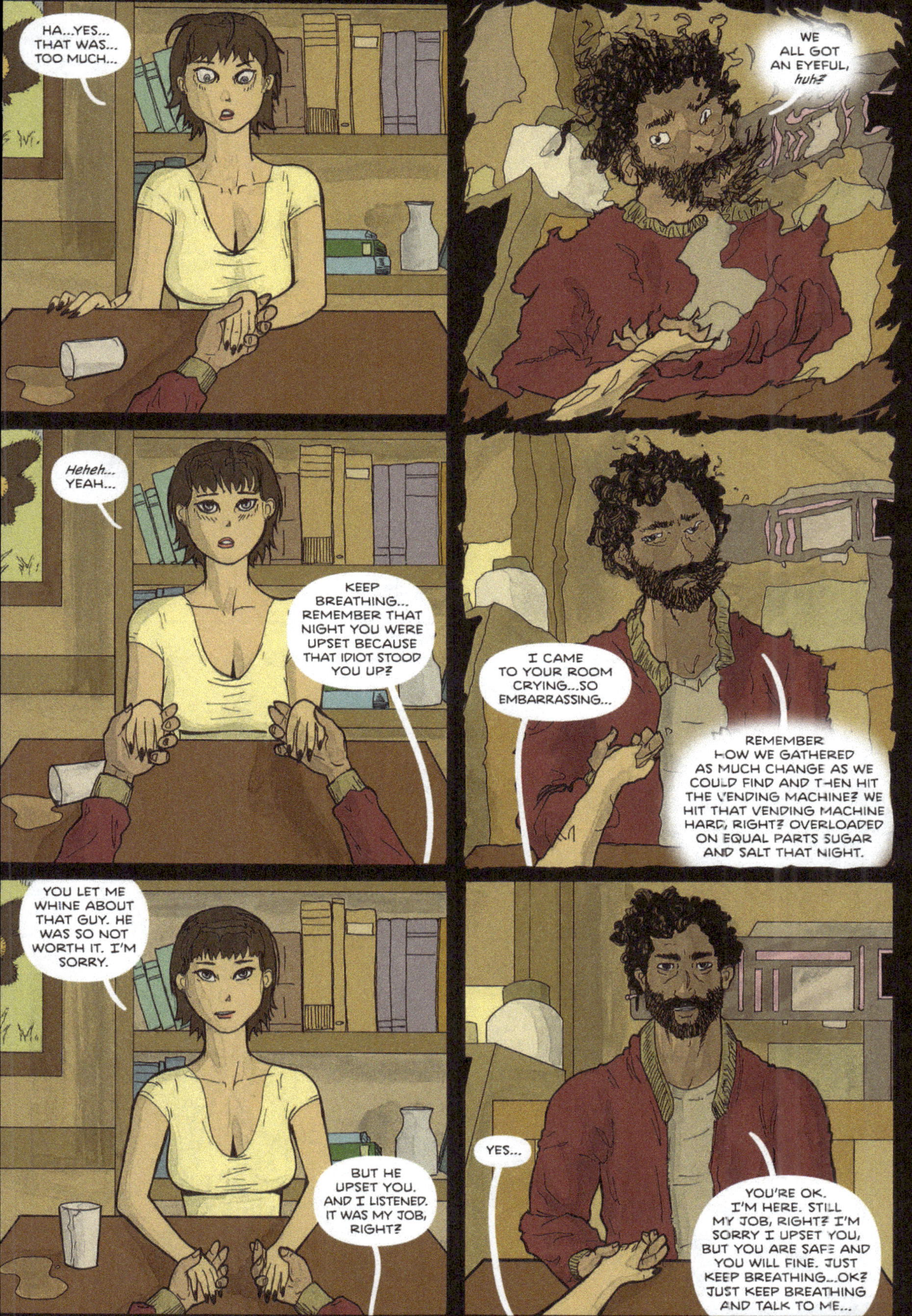
HA...YES... THAT WAS... TOO MUCH...
WE ALL GOT AN EYEFUL, huh?
Heheh... YEAH...
KEEP BREATHING... REMEMBER THAT NIGHT YOU WERE UPSET BECAUSE THAT IDIOT STOOD YOU UP?
I CAME TO YOUR ROOM CRYING...SO EMBARRASSING...
REMEMBER HOW WE GATHERED AS MUCH CHANGE AS WE COULD FIND AND THEN HIT THE VENDING MACHINE? WE HIT THAT VENDING MACHINE HARD, RIGHT? OVERLOADED ON EQUAL PARTS SUGAR AND SALT THAT NIGHT.
YOU LET ME WHINE ABOUT THAT GUY. HE WAS SO NOT WORTH IT. I'M SORRY.
BUT HE UPSET YOU. AND I LISTENED. IT WAS MY JOB, RIGHT?
YES...
YOU'RE OK. I'M HERE. STILL MY JOB, RIGHT? I'M SORRY I UPSET YOU, BUT YOU ARE SAFE AND YOU WILL FINE. JUST KEEP BREATHING...OK? JUST KEEP BREATHING AND TALK TO ME...

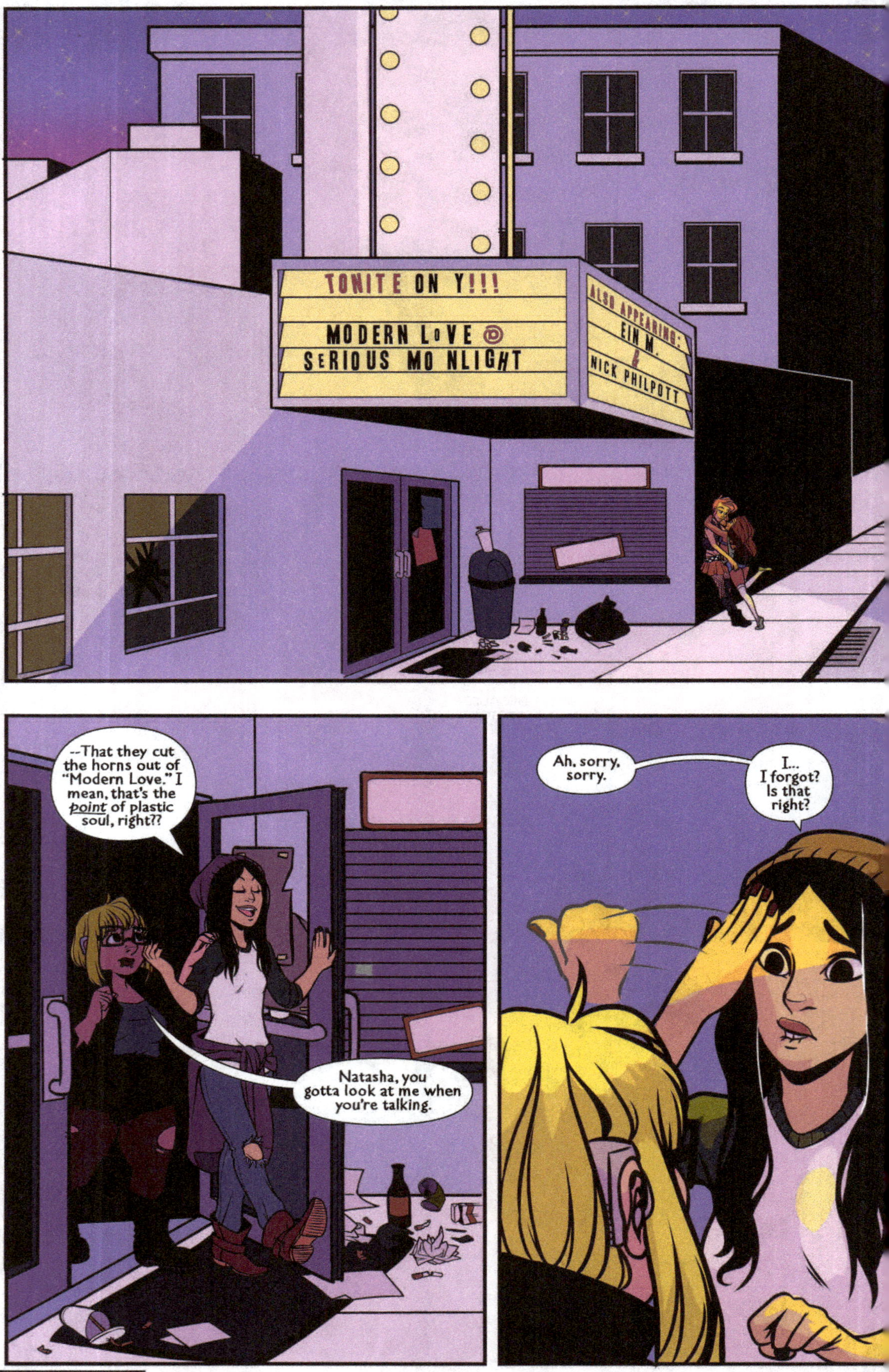
TONITE ON Y!!!
MODERN LOVE @
SERIOUS MO NLIGHT
ALSO APPEARING:
EIN M.
&
NICK PHILPOTT
--That they cut the horns out of "Modern Love." I mean, that's the *point* of plastic soul, right??
Natasha, you gotta look at me when you're talking.
Ah, sorry, sorry.
I... I forgot? Is that right?

"The Sweetest Chill"

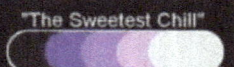

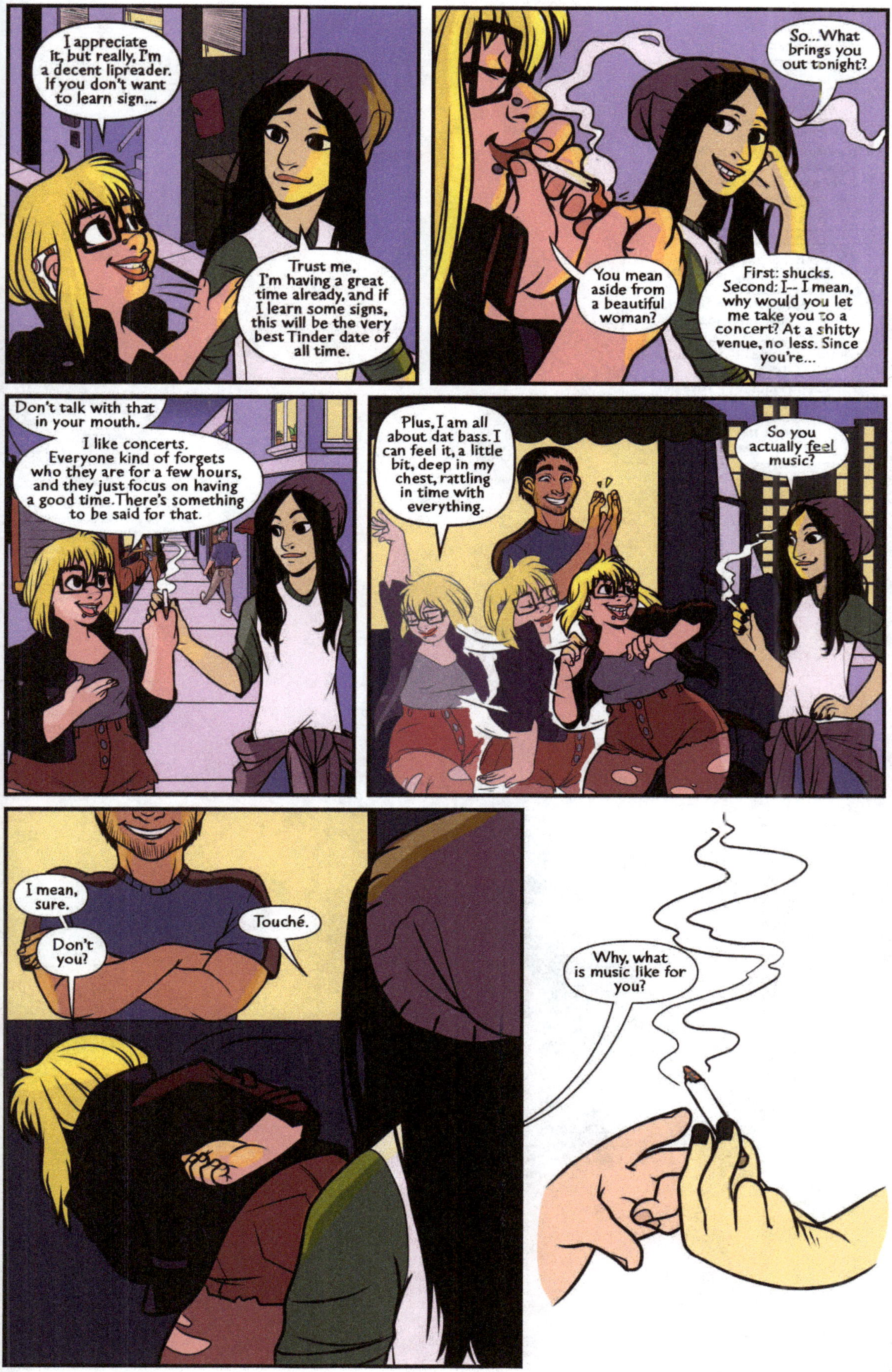
I appreciate it, but really, I'm a decent lipreader. If you don't want to learn sign...
Trust me, I'm having a great time already, and if I learn some signs, this will be the very best Tinder date of all time.
So...What brings you out tonight?
You mean aside from a beautiful woman?
First: shucks. Second: I-- I mean, why would you let me take you to a concert? At a shitty venue, no less. Since you're...
Don't talk with that in your mouth.
I like concerts. Everyone kind of forgets who they are for a few hours, and they just focus on having a good time. There's something to be said for that.
Plus, I am all about dat bass. I can feel it, a little bit, deep in my chest, rattling in time with everything.
So you actually feel music?
I mean, sure.
Don't you?
Touché.
Why, what is music like for you?

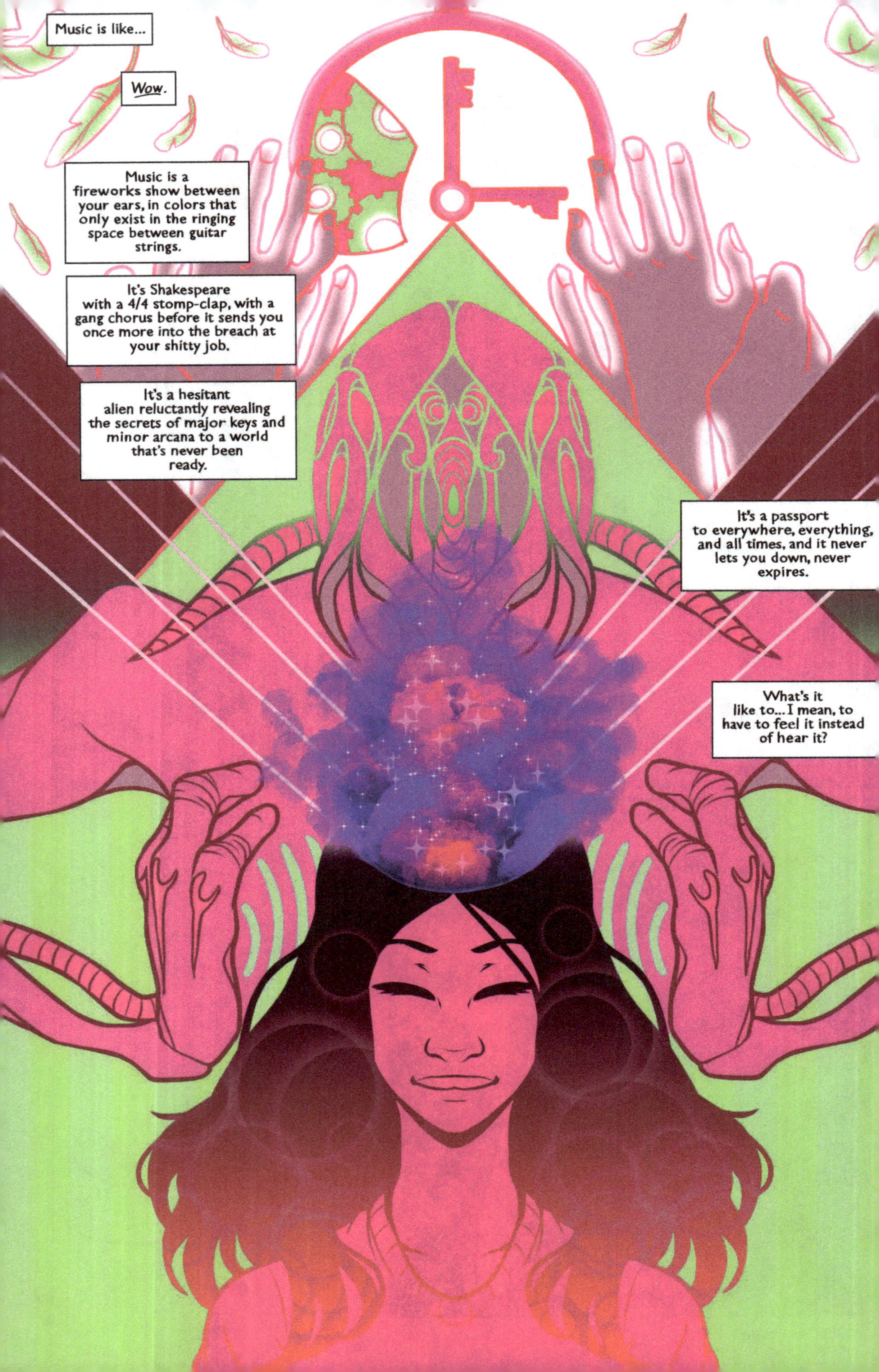
Music is like...
Wow.
Music is a fireworks show between your ears, in colors that only exist in the ringing space between guitar strings.
It's Shakespeare with a 4/4 stomp-clap, with a gang chorus before it sends you once more into the breach at your shitty job.
It's a hesitant alien reluctantly revealing the secrets of major keys and minor arcana to a world that's never been ready.
It's a passport to everywhere, everything, and all times, and it never lets you down, never expires.
What's it like to... I mean, to have to feel it instead of hear it?

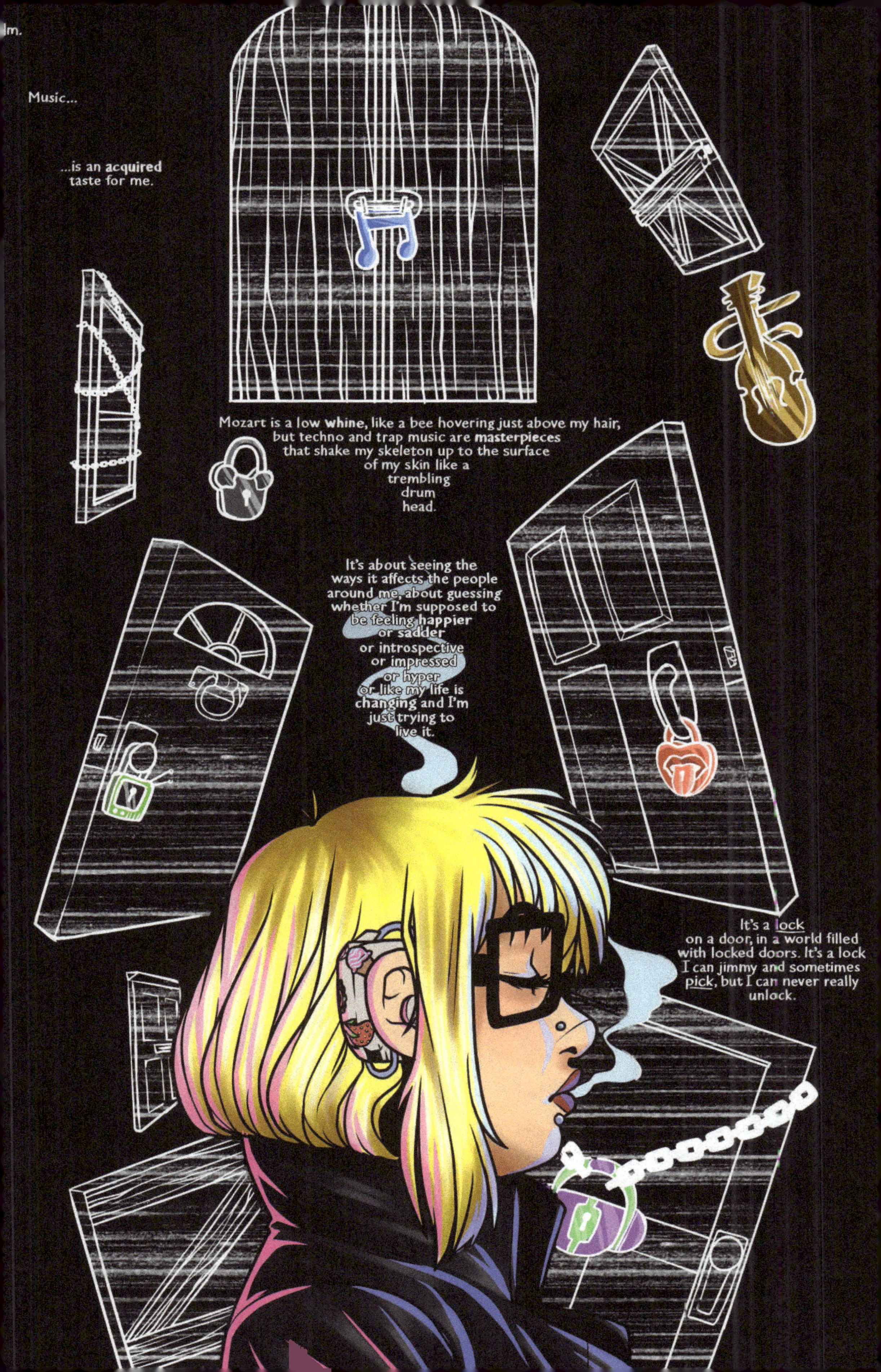
lm.
Music...
...is an **acquired** taste for me.
Mozart is a low **whine**, like a bee hovering just above my hair, but techno and trap music are **masterpieces** that shake my skeleton up to the surface of my skin like a trembling drum head.
It's about seeing the ways it affects the people around me, about guessing whether I'm supposed to be feeling **happier** or sadder or introspective or impressed or hyper or like my life is changing and I'm just trying to live it.
It's a lock on a door, in a world filled with locked doors. It's a lock I can jimmy and sometimes pick, but I can never really unlock.

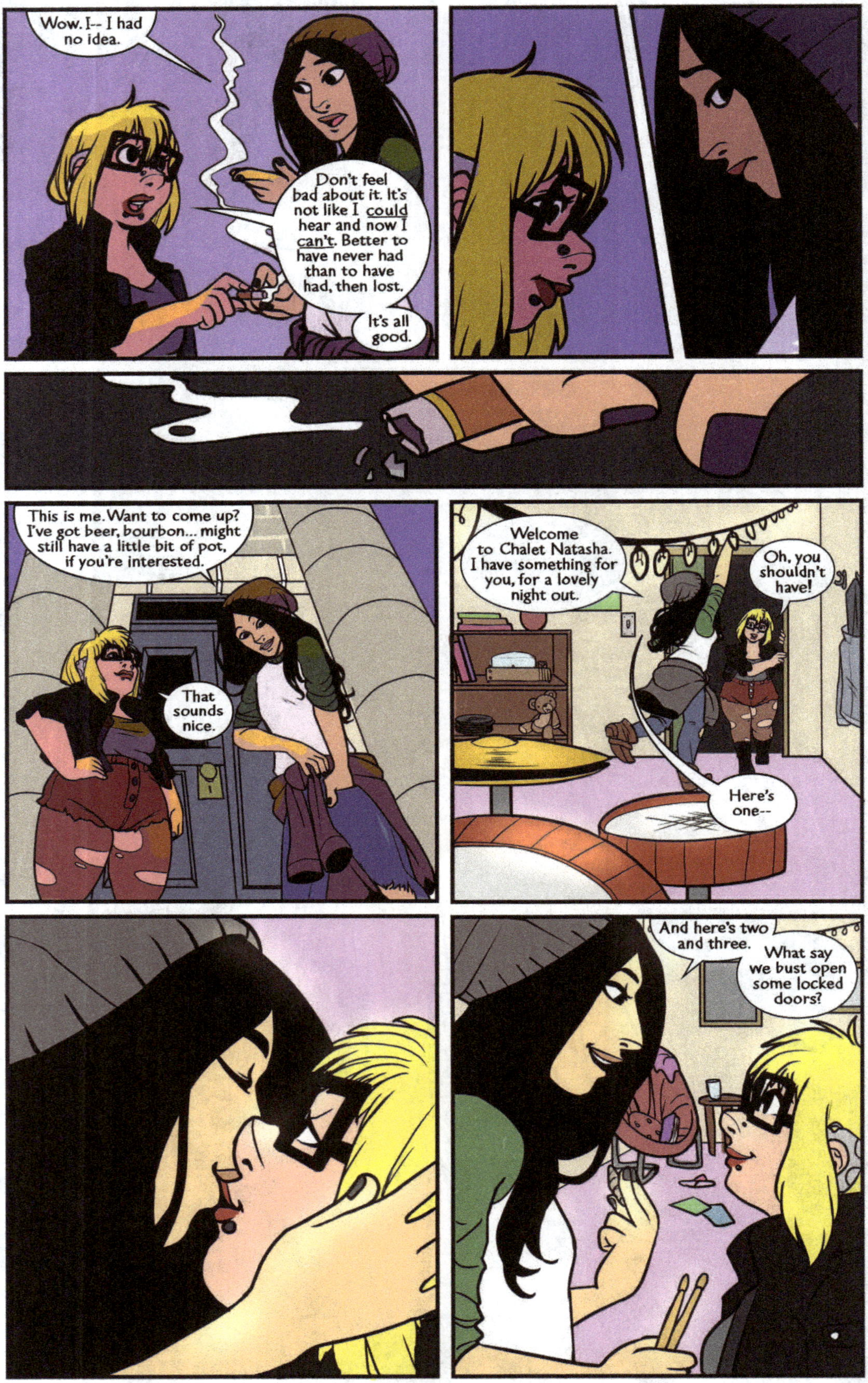
Wow. I-- I had no idea.
Don't feel bad about it. It's not like I could hear and now I can't. Better to have never had than to have had, then lost.
It's all good.
This is me. Want to come up? I've got beer, bourbon... might still have a little bit of pot, if you're interested.
That sounds nice.
Welcome to Chalet Natasha. I have something for you, for a lovely night out.
Oh, you shouldn't have!
Here's one--
And here's two and three.
What say we bust open some locked doors?

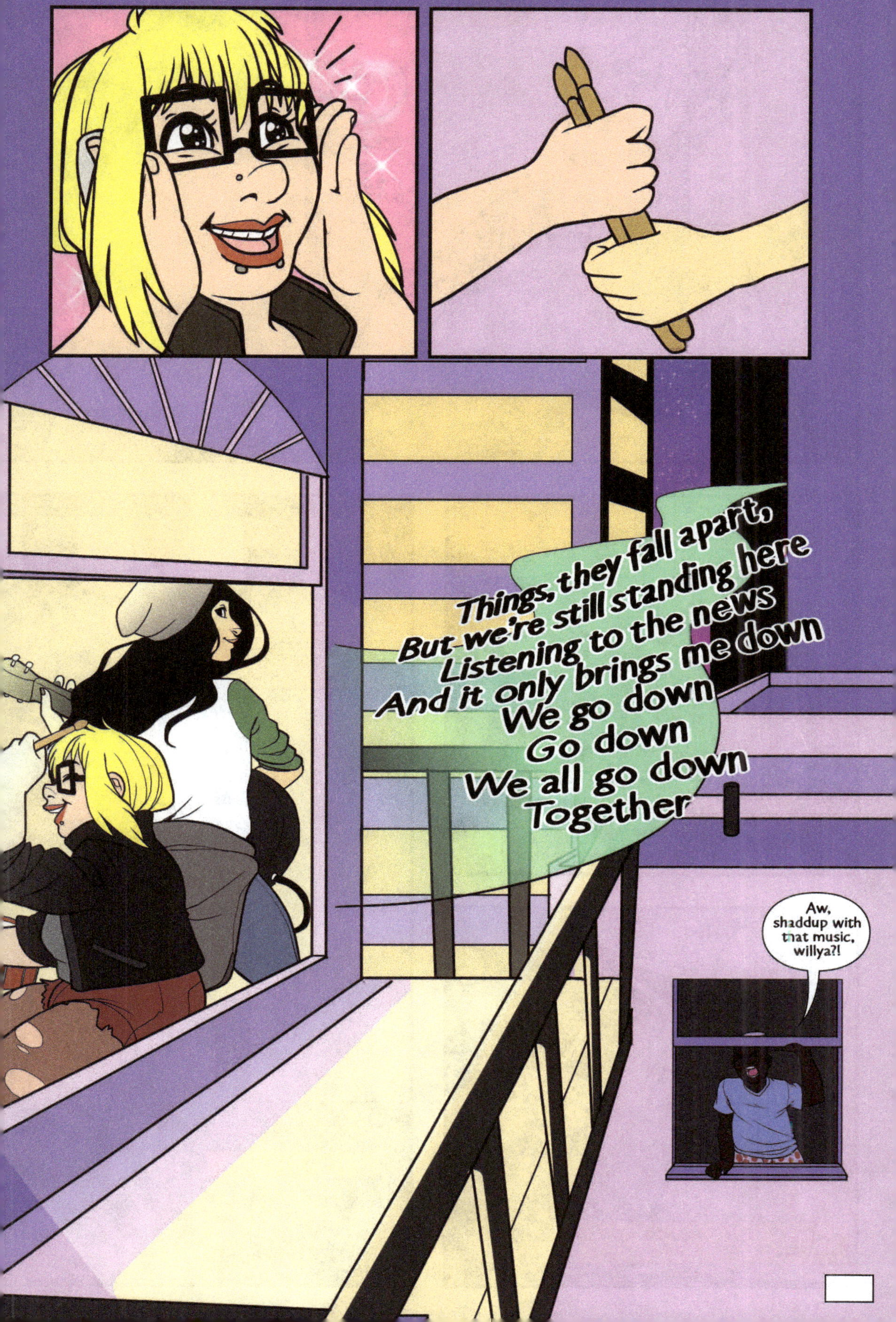
Things, they fall apart,
But we're still standing here
Listening to the news
And it only brings me down
We go down
Go down
We all go down
Together
Aw, shaddup with that music, willya?!

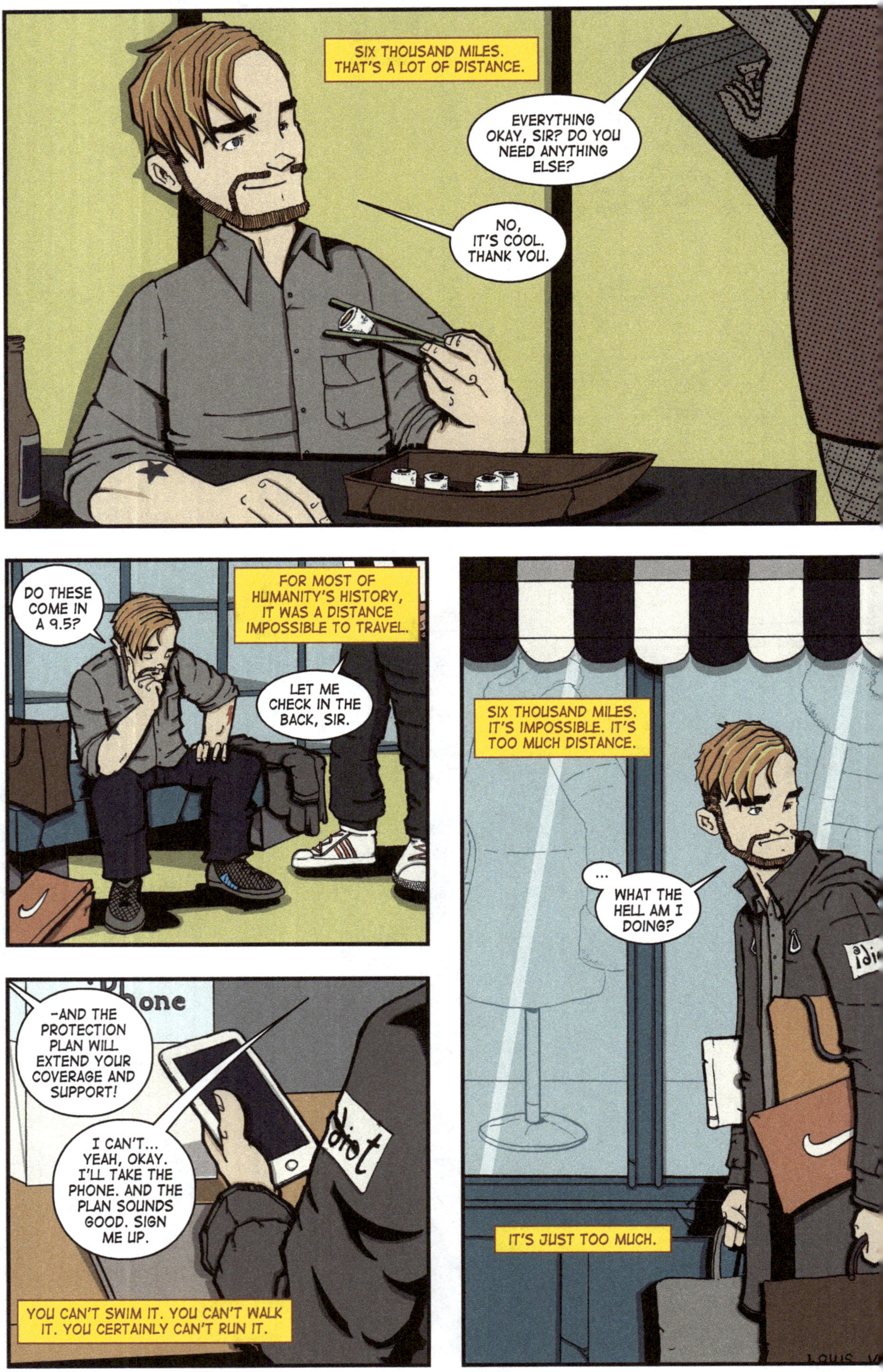
SIX THOUSAND MILES. THAT'S A LOT OF DISTANCE.
EVERYTHING OKAY, SIR? DO YOU NEED ANYTHING ELSE?
NO, IT'S COOL. THANK YOU.
FOR MOST OF HUMANITY'S HISTORY, IT WAS A DISTANCE IMPOSSIBLE TO TRAVEL.
DO THESE COME IN A 9.5?
LET ME CHECK IN THE BACK, SIR.
-AND THE PROTECTION PLAN WILL EXTEND YOUR COVERAGE AND SUPPORT!
I CAN'T... YEAH, OKAY. I'LL TAKE THE PHONE. AND THE PLAN SOUNDS GOOD. SIGN ME UP.
YOU CAN'T SWIM IT. YOU CAN'T WALK IT. YOU CERTAINLY CAN'T RUN IT.
SIX THOUSAND MILES. IT'S IMPOSSIBLE. IT'S TOO MUCH DISTANCE.
...
WHAT THE HELL AM I DOING?
IT'S JUST TOO MUCH.

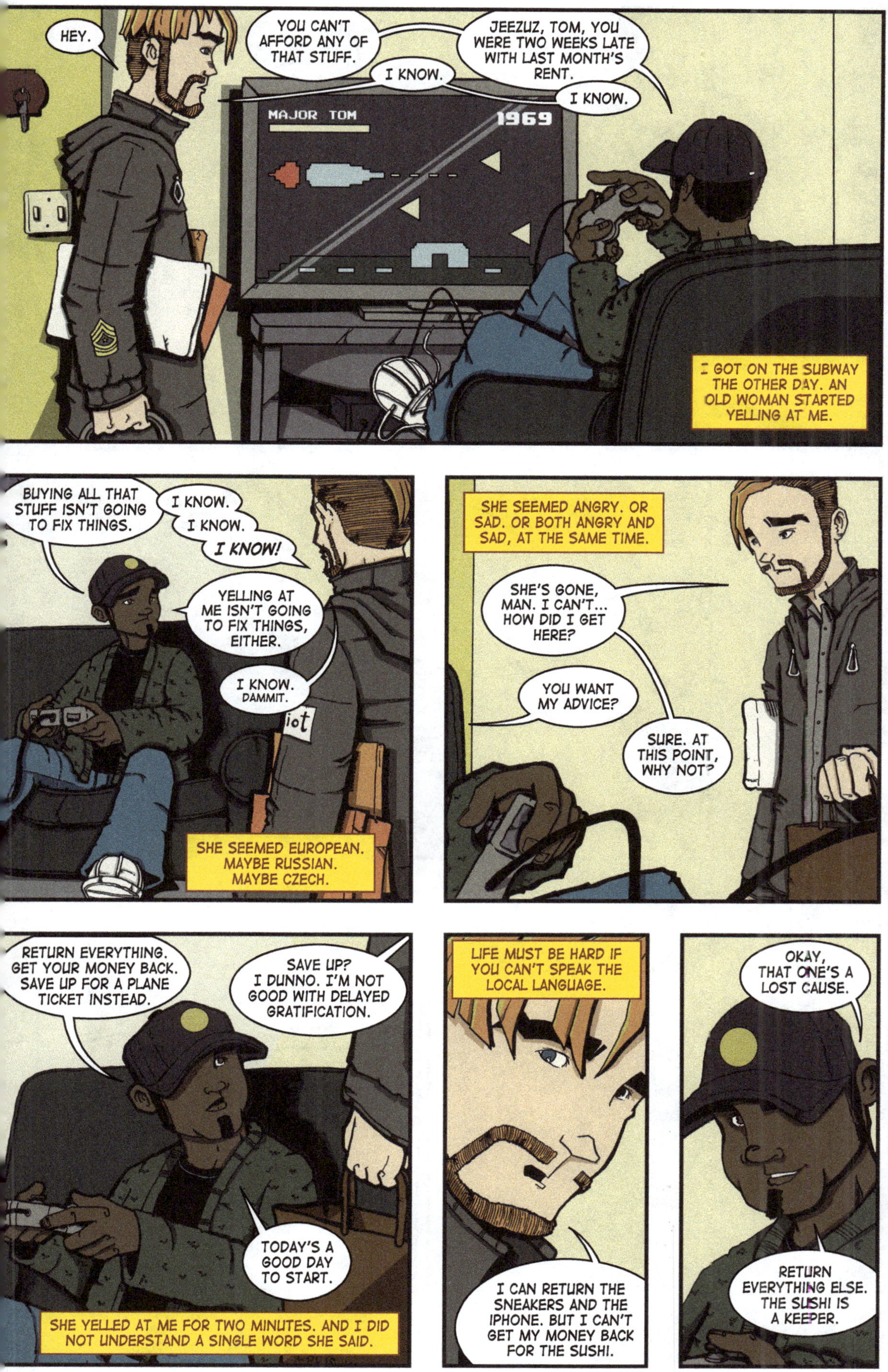
HEY.
YOU CAN'T AFFORD ANY OF THAT STUFF.
I KNOW.
JEEZUZ, TOM, YOU WERE TWO WEEKS LATE WITH LAST MONTH'S RENT.
I KNOW.
MAJOR TOM
1969
I GOT ON THE SUBWAY THE OTHER DAY. AN OLD WOMAN STARTED YELLING AT ME.
BUYING ALL THAT STUFF ISN'T GOING TO FIX THINGS.
I KNOW.
I KNOW.
I KNOW!
YELLING AT ME ISN'T GOING TO FIX THINGS, EITHER.
I KNOW. DAMMIT.
SHE SEEMED EUROPEAN. MAYBE RUSSIAN. MAYBE CZECH.
SHE SEEMED ANGRY. OR SAD. OR BOTH ANGRY AND SAD, AT THE SAME TIME.
SHE'S GONE, MAN. I CAN'T... HOW DID I GET HERE?
YOU WANT MY ADVICE?
SURE. AT THIS POINT, WHY NOT?
RETURN EVERYTHING. GET YOUR MONEY BACK. SAVE UP FOR A PLANE TICKET INSTEAD.
SAVE UP? I DUNNO. I'M NOT GOOD WITH DELAYED GRATIFICATION.
TODAY'S A GOOD DAY TO START.
SHE YELLED AT ME FOR TWO MINUTES. AND I DID NOT UNDERSTAND A SINGLE WORD SHE SAID.
LIFE MUST BE HARD IF YOU CAN'T SPEAK THE LOCAL LANGUAGE.
I CAN RETURN THE SNEAKERS AND THE IPHONE. BUT I CAN'T GET MY MONEY BACK FOR THE SUSHI.
OKAY, THAT ONE'S A LOST CAUSE.
RETURN EVERYTHING ELSE. THE SUSHI IS A KEEPER.

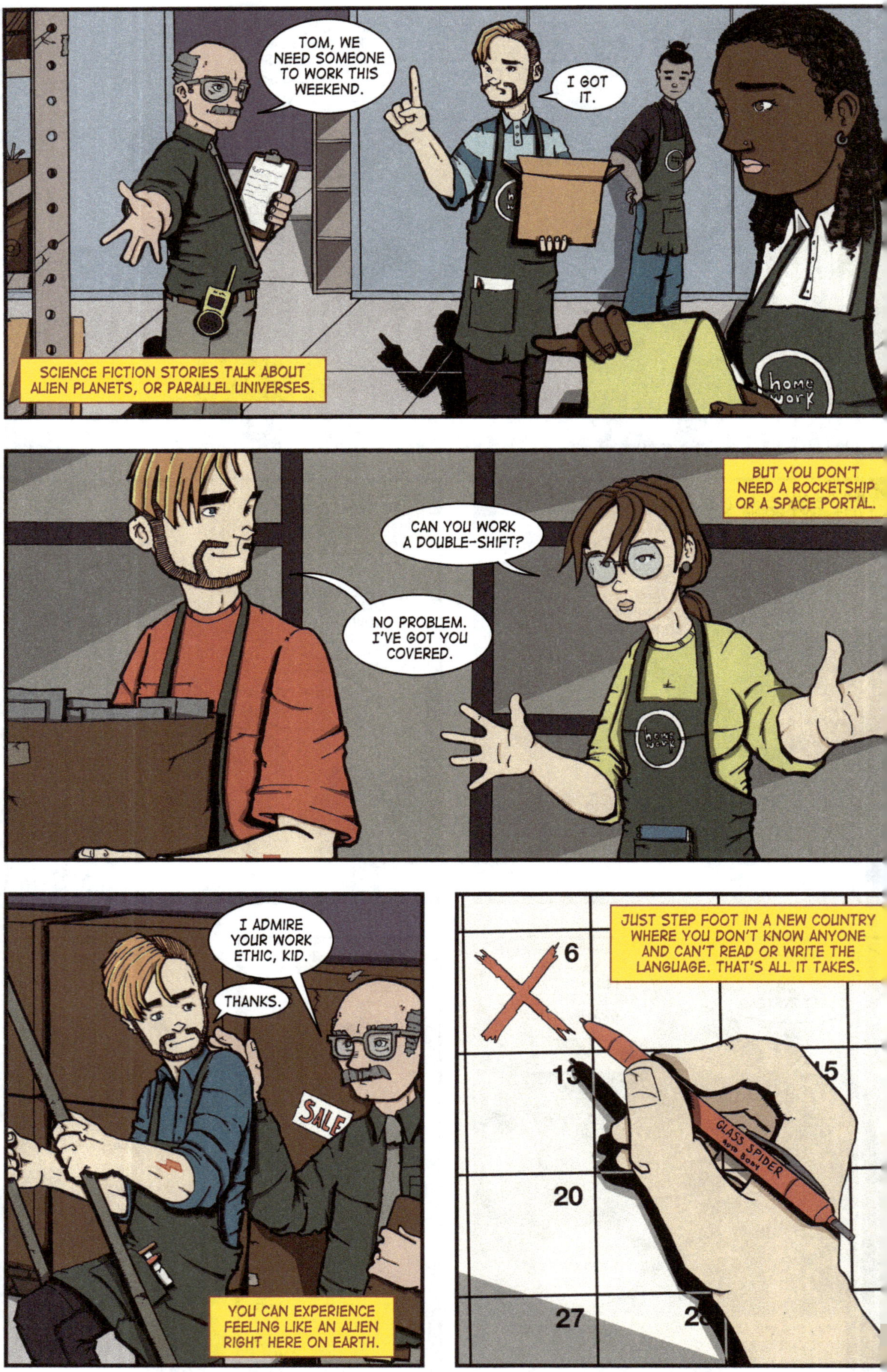
TOM, WE NEED SOMEONE TO WORK THIS WEEKEND.
I GOT IT.
home work
SCIENCE FICTION STORIES TALK ABOUT ALIEN PLANETS, OR PARALLEL UNIVERSES.
BUT YOU DON'T NEED A ROCKETSHIP OR A SPACE PORTAL.
CAN YOU WORK A DOUBLE-SHIFT?
NO PROBLEM. I'VE GOT YOU COVERED.
I ADMIRE YOUR WORK ETHIC, KID.
THANKS.
SALE
YOU CAN EXPERIENCE FEELING LIKE AN ALIEN RIGHT HERE ON EARTH.
JUST STEP FOOT IN A NEW COUNTRY WHERE YOU DON'T KNOW ANYONE AND CAN'T READ OR WRITE THE LANGUAGE. THAT'S ALL IT TAKES.
6
13
20
27
GLASS SPIDER

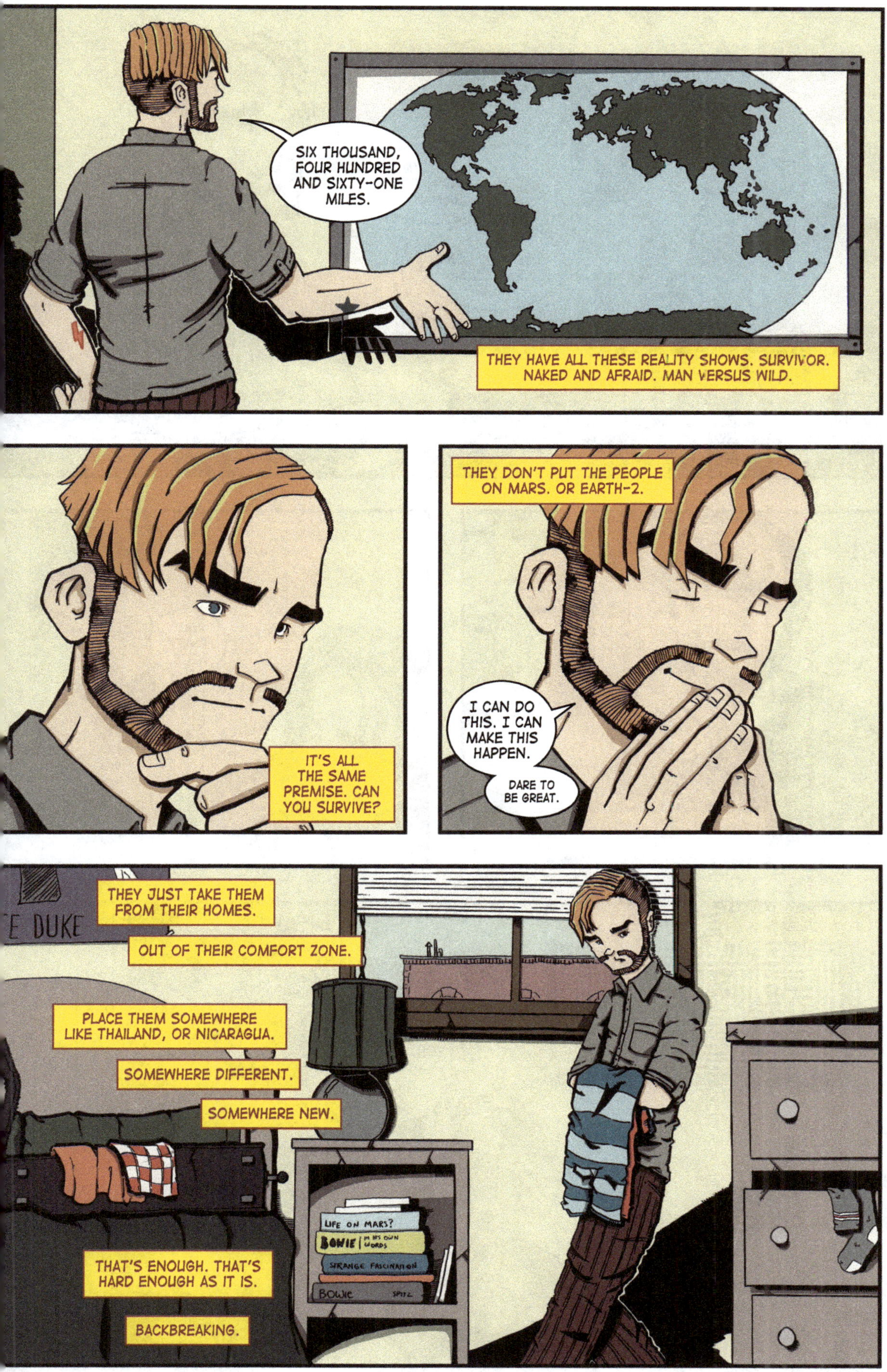
SIX THOUSAND, FOUR HUNDRED AND SIXTY-ONE MILES.
THEY HAVE ALL THESE REALITY SHOWS. SURVIVOR. NAKED AND AFRAID. MAN VERSUS WILD.
IT'S ALL THE SAME PREMISE. CAN YOU SURVIVE?
THEY DON'T PUT THE PEOPLE ON MARS. OR EARTH-2.
I CAN DO THIS. I CAN MAKE THIS HAPPEN.
DARE TO BE GREAT.
E DUKE
THEY JUST TAKE THEM FROM THEIR HOMES.
OUT OF THEIR COMFORT ZONE.
PLACE THEM SOMEWHERE LIKE THAILAND, OR NICARAGUA.
SOMEWHERE DIFFERENT.
SOMEWHERE NEW.
LIFE ON MARS?
BOWIE
STRANGE FASCINATION
BOWIE
THAT'S ENOUGH. THAT'S HARD ENOUGH AS IT IS.
BACKBREAKING.

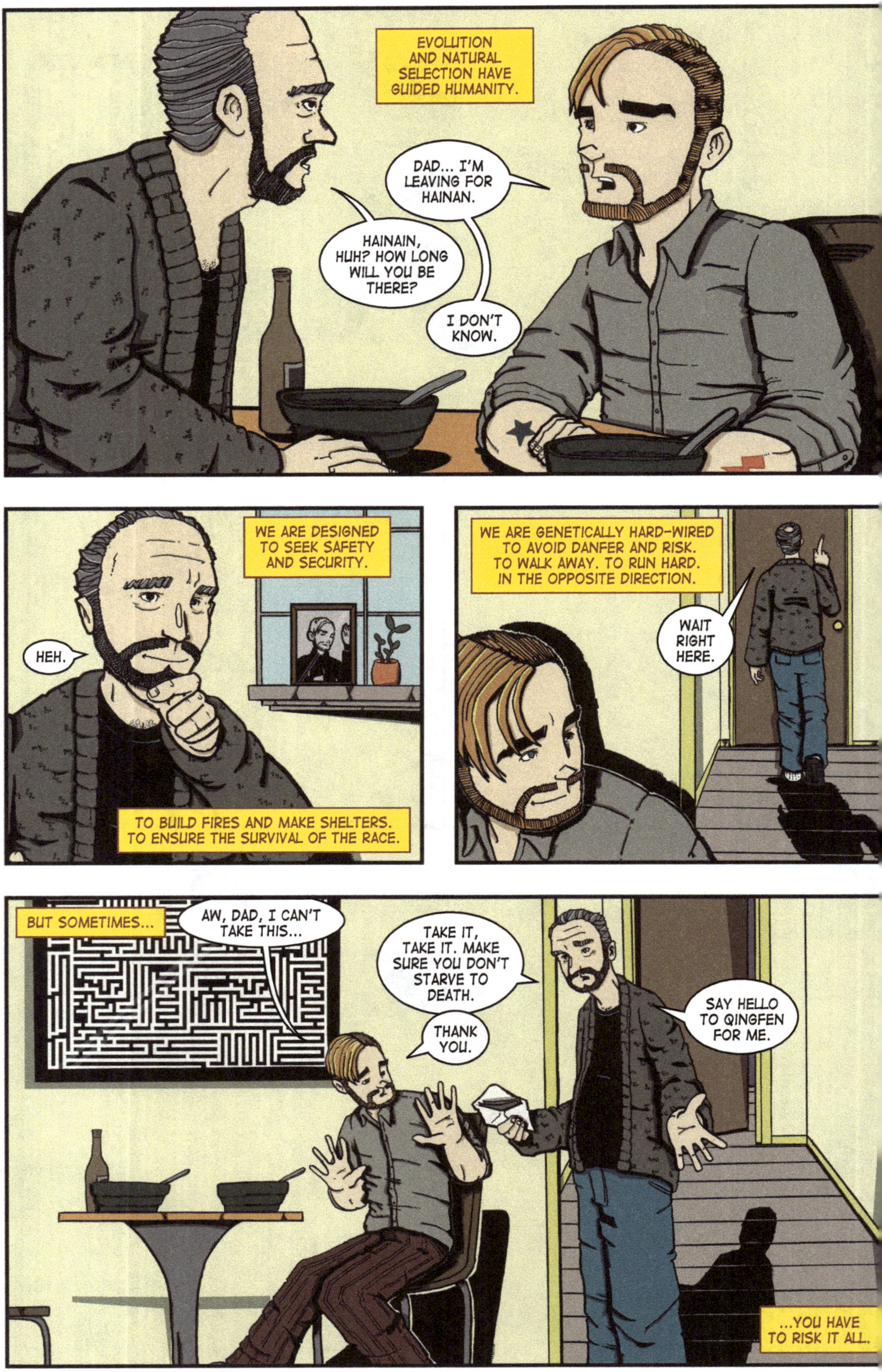
EVOLUTION AND NATURAL SELECTION HAVE GUIDED HUMANITY.
DAD... I'M LEAVING FOR HAINAN.
HAINAIN, HUH? HOW LONG WILL YOU BE THERE?
I DON'T KNOW.
WE ARE DESIGNED TO SEEK SAFETY AND SECURITY.
HEH.
TO BUILD FIRES AND MAKE SHELTERS. TO ENSURE THE SURVIVAL OF THE RACE.
WE ARE GENETICALLY HARD-WIRED TO AVOID DANFER AND RISK. TO WALK AWAY. TO RUN HARD. IN THE OPPOSITE DIRECTION.
WAIT RIGHT HERE.
BUT SOMETIMES...
AW, DAD, I CAN'T TAKE THIS...
TAKE IT, TAKE IT. MAKE SURE YOU DON'T STARVE TO DEATH.
THANK YOU.
SAY HELLO TO QINGFEN FOR ME.
...YOU HAVE TO RISK IT ALL.

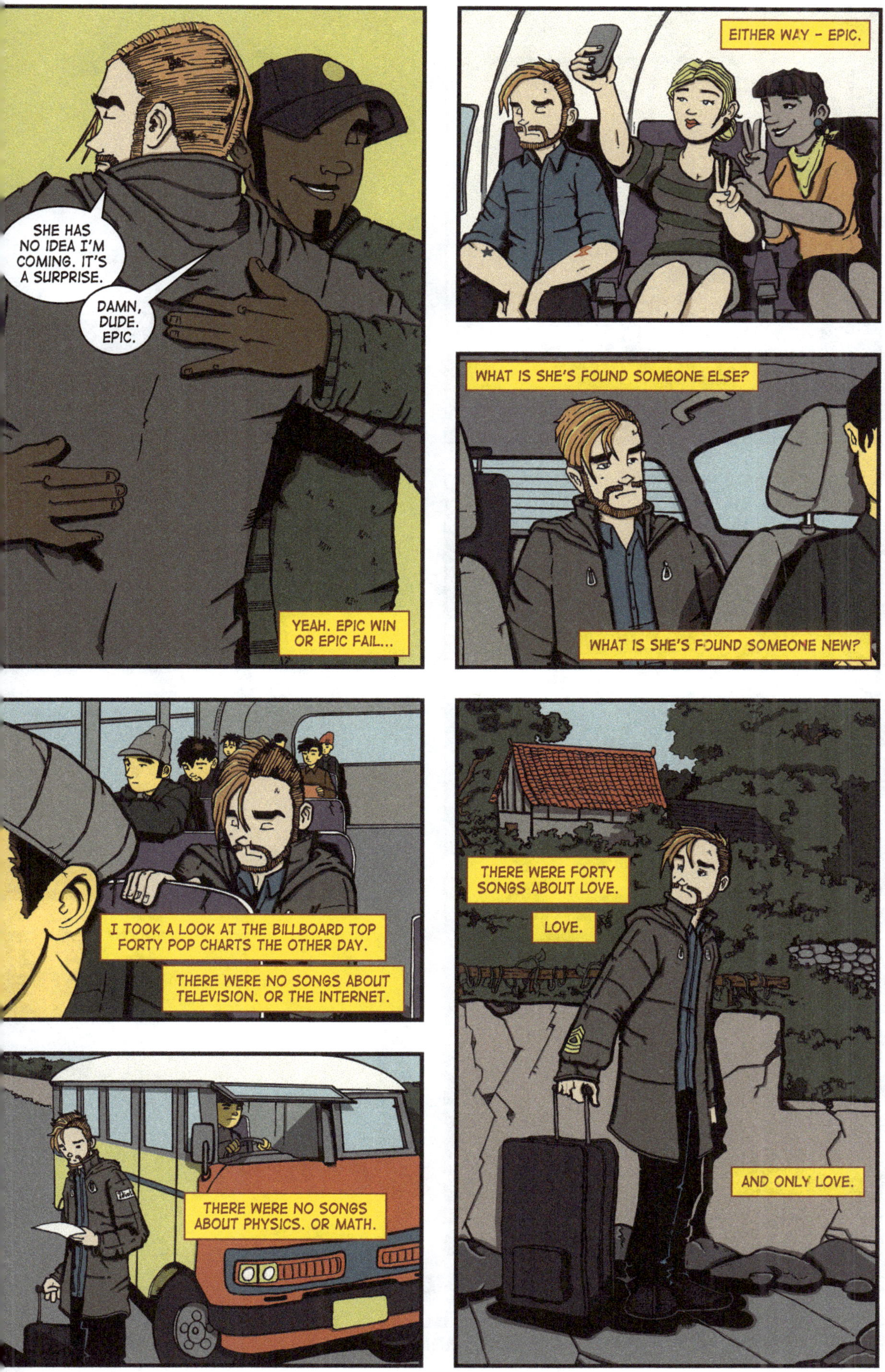
SHE HAS NO IDEA I'M COMING. IT'S A SURPRISE.
DAMN, DUDE. EPIC.
YEAH. EPIC WIN OR EPIC FAIL...
EITHER WAY - EPIC.
WHAT IS SHE'S FOUND SOMEONE ELSE?
WHAT IS SHE'S FOUND SOMEONE NEW?
I TOOK A LOOK AT THE BILLBOARD TOP FORTY POP CHARTS THE OTHER DAY.
THERE WERE NO SONGS ABOUT TELEVISION. OR THE INTERNET.
THERE WERE NO SONGS ABOUT PHYSICS. OR MATH.
THERE WERE FORTY SONGS ABOUT LOVE.
LOVE.
AND ONLY LOVE.

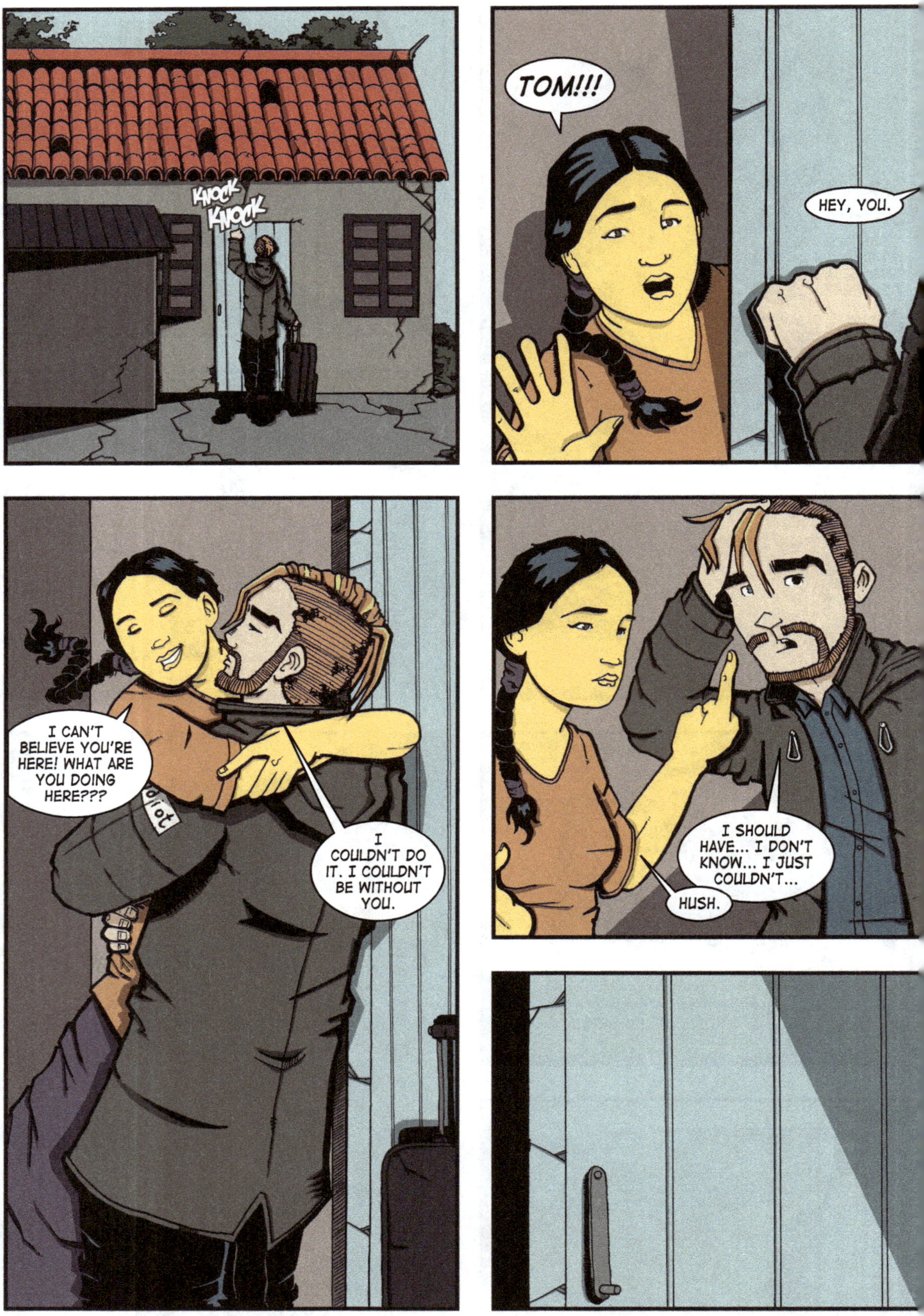

KNOCK
KNOCK
TOM!!!
HEY, YOU.
I CAN'T BELIEVE YOU'RE HERE! WHAT ARE YOU DOING HERE???
I COULDN'T DO IT. I COULDN'T BE WITHOUT YOU.
I SHOULD HAVE... I DON'T KNOW... I JUST COULDN'T...
HUSH.

SIX THOUSAND, FOUR HUNDRED AND SIXTY-ONE MILES

INSPIRED BY DAVID BOWIE'S "CHINA GIRL"

STORY: ROEL TORRES • ART: SCOTT ARNOLD • LETTER ASSIST: MICAH MYERS

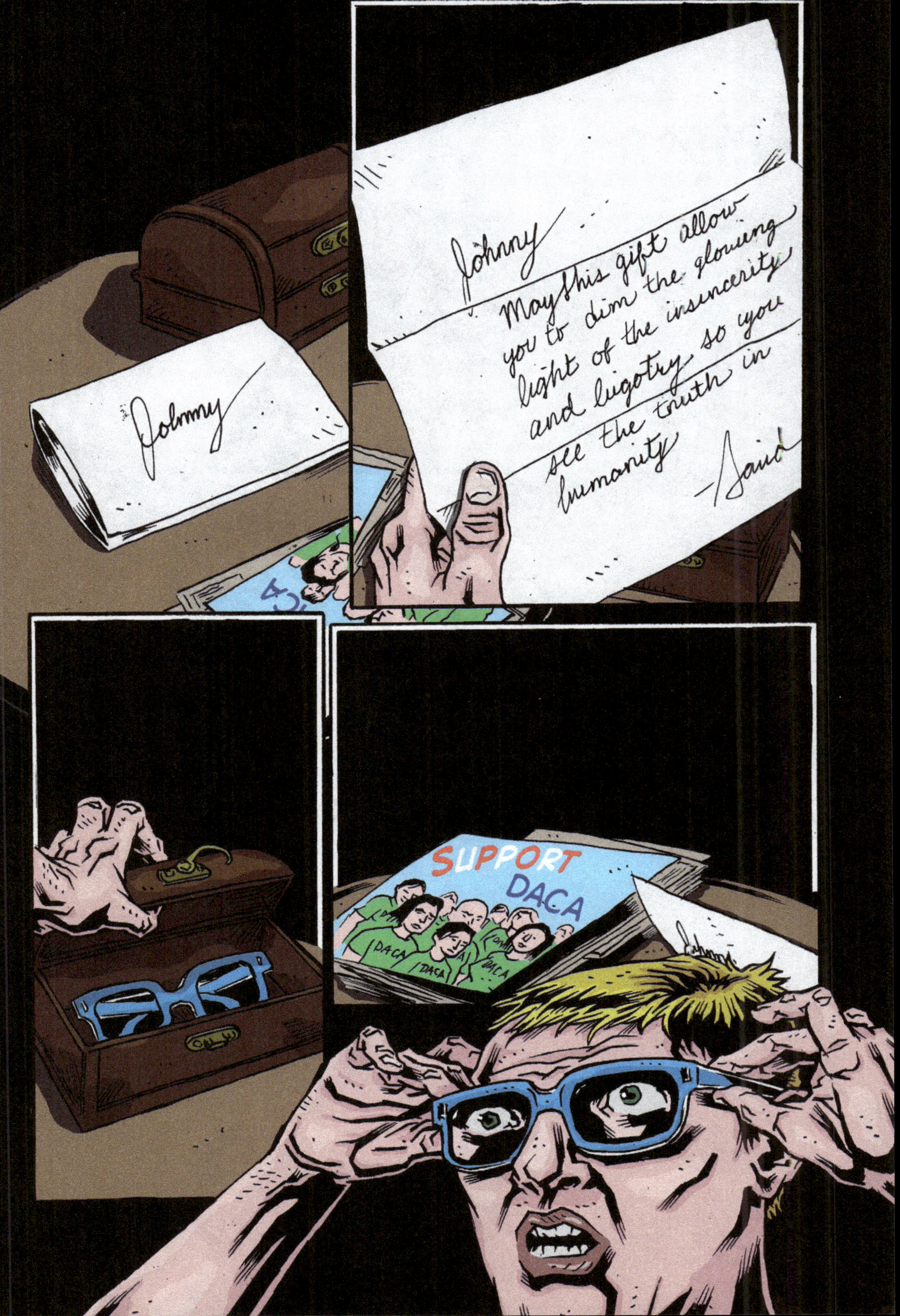
Johnny
Johnny
May this gift allow you to dim the glowing light of the insincerity and bigotry so you see the truth in humanity
-Said
SUPPORT DACA
DACA
DACA
DACA

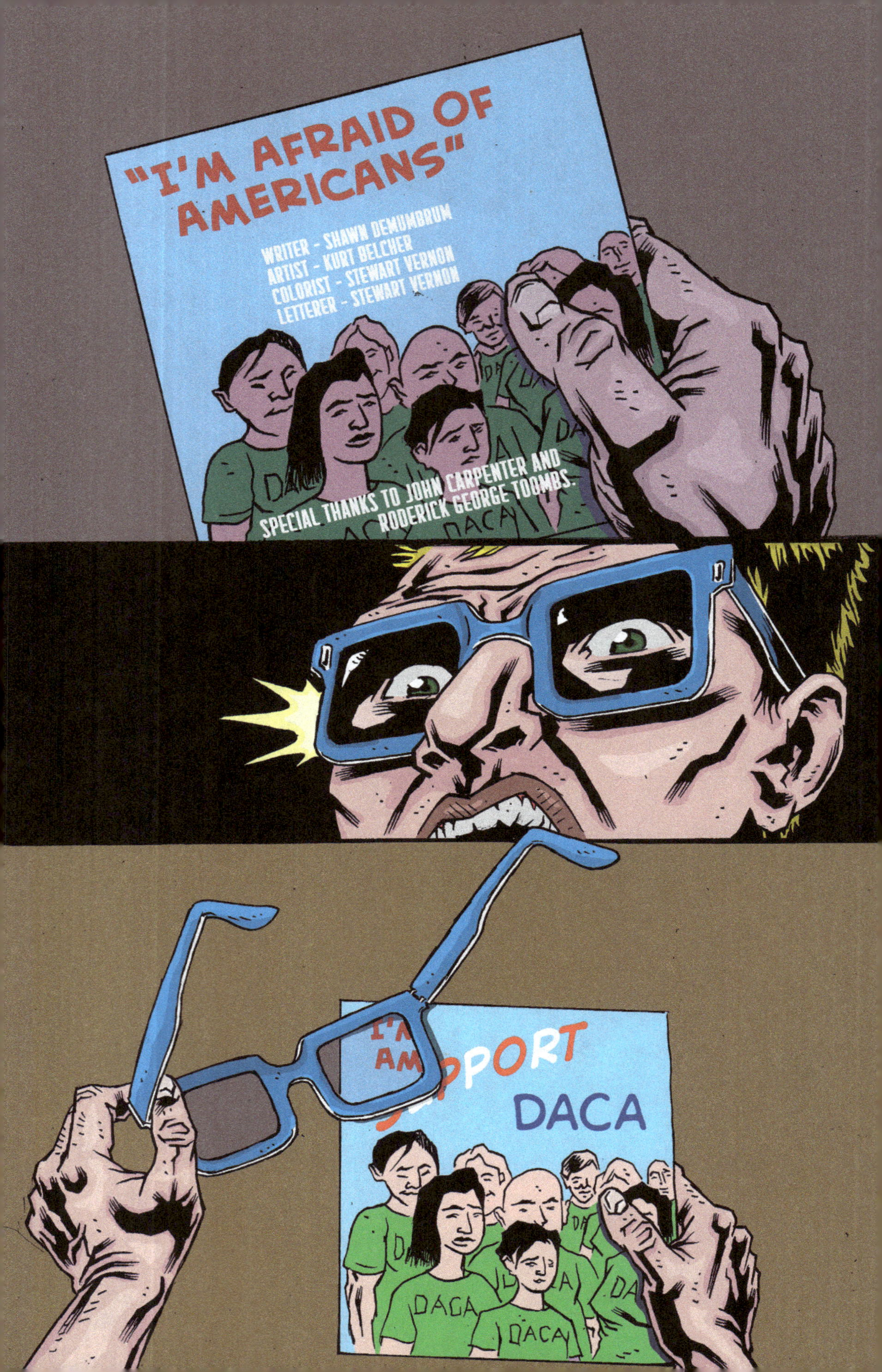
"I'M AFRAID OF AMERICANS"
WRITER - SHAWN DEMUMBRUM
ARTIST - KURT BELCHER
COLORIST - STEWART VERNON
LETTERER - STEWART VERNON
SPECIAL THANKS TO JOHN CARPENTER AND RODERICK GEORGE TOOMBS.
DACA
SUPPORT
DACA
DACA
DACA

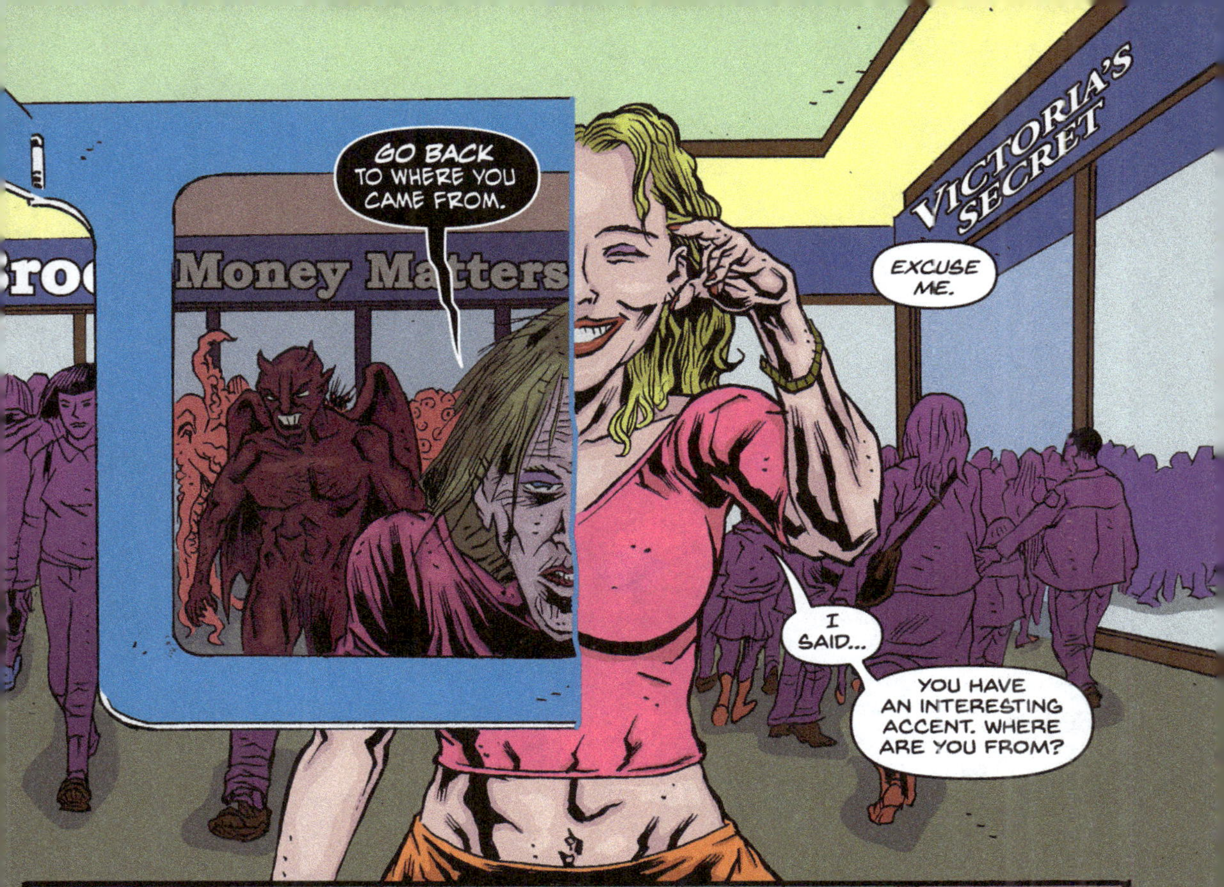
Money Matters
VICTORIA'S SECRET
GO BACK TO WHERE YOU CAME FROM.
EXCUSE ME.
I SAID...
YOU HAVE AN INTERESTING ACCENT. WHERE ARE YOU FROM?

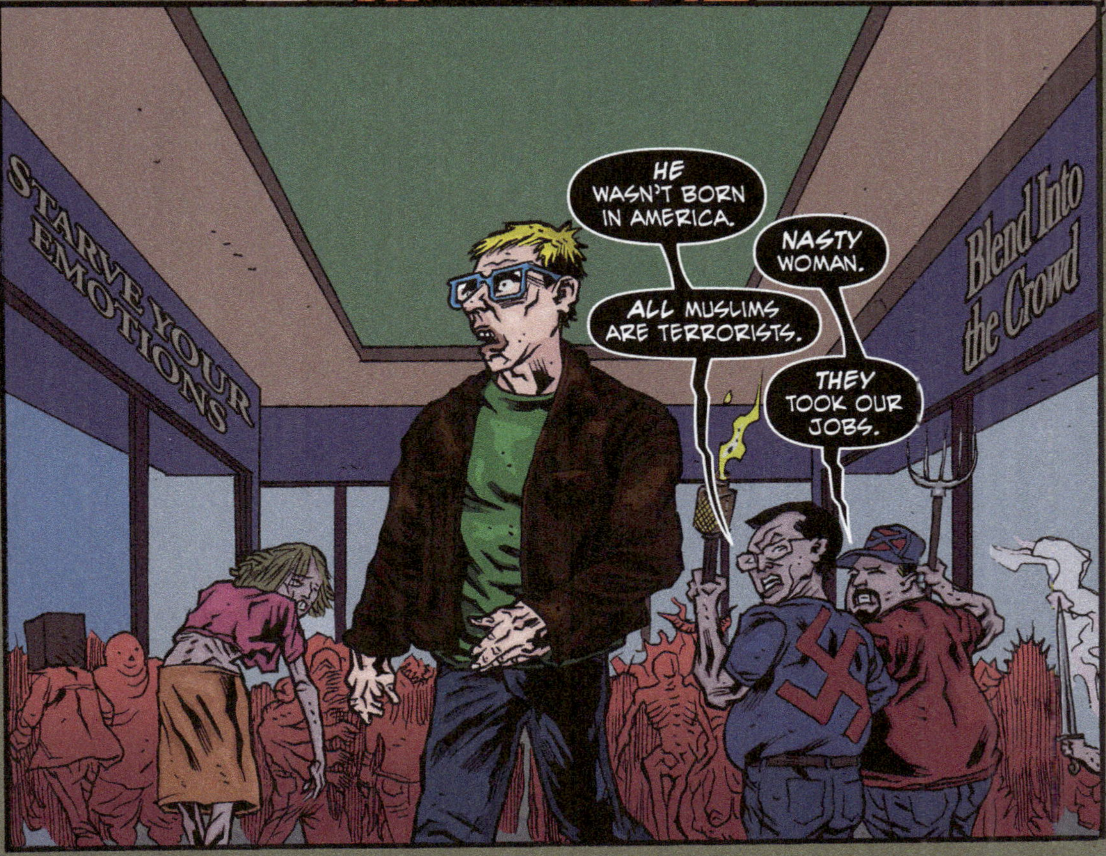
STARVE YOUR EMOTIONS
HE WASN'T BORN IN AMERICA.
NASTY WOMAN.
ALL MUSLIMS ARE TERRORISTS.
THEY TOOK OUR JOBS.
Blend Into the Crowd

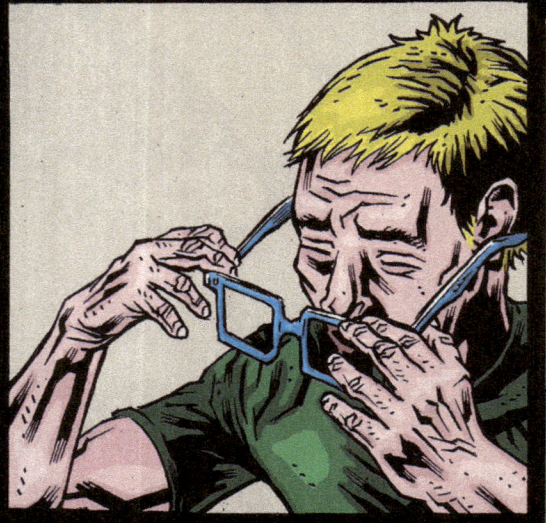

BUT IF I GET ELECTED PRESIDENT I WILL BRING IT BACK BIGGER AND BETTER AND STRONGER THAN EVER BEFORE, AND WE WILL MAKE AMERICA...

HATE AGAIN!

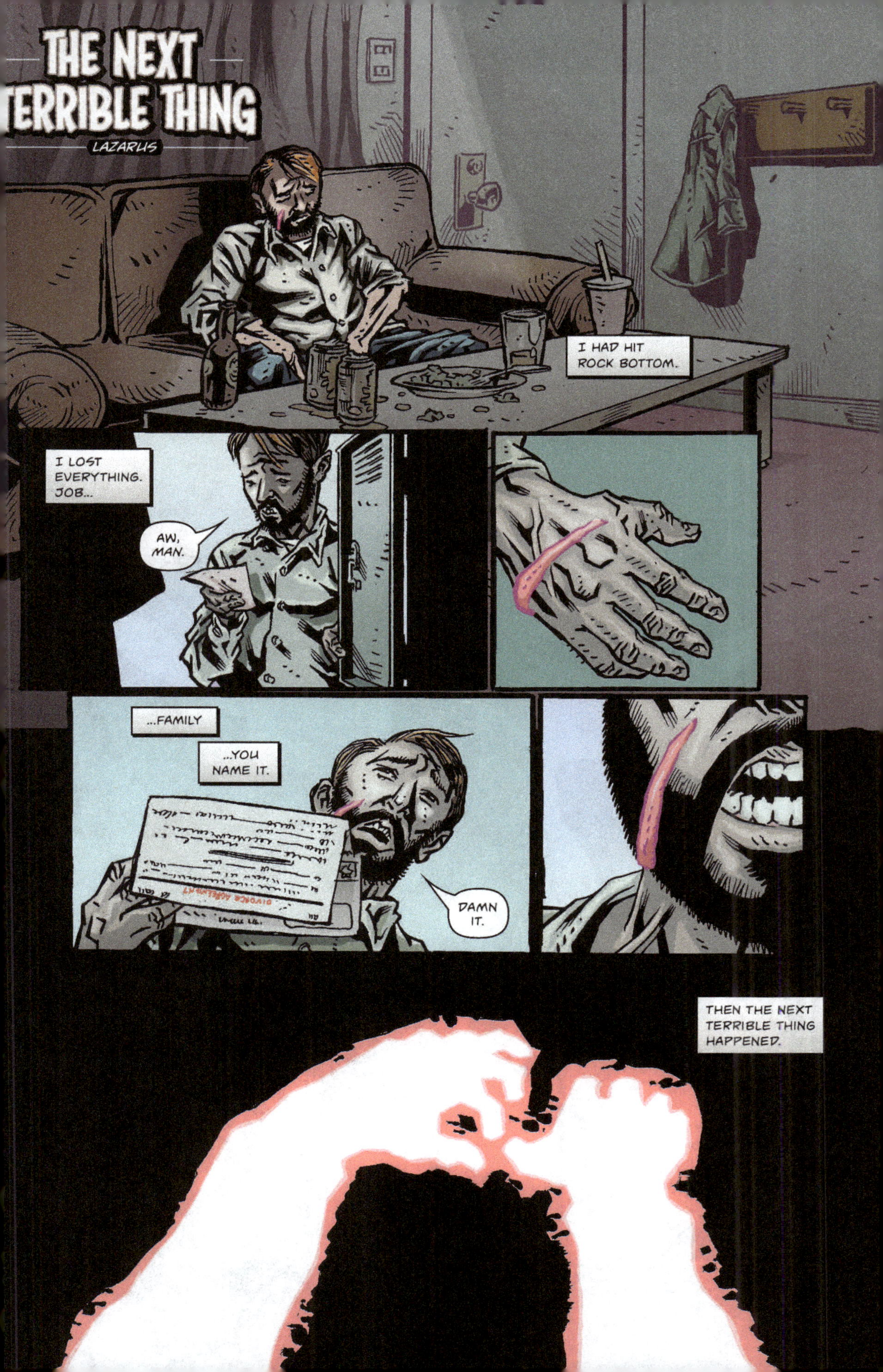
THE NEXT TERRIBLE THING
LAZARUS
I HAD HIT ROCK BOTTOM.
I LOST EVERYTHING. JOB...
AW, MAN.
...FAMILY
...YOU NAME IT.
DAMN IT.
THEN THE NEXT TERRIBLE THING HAPPENED.

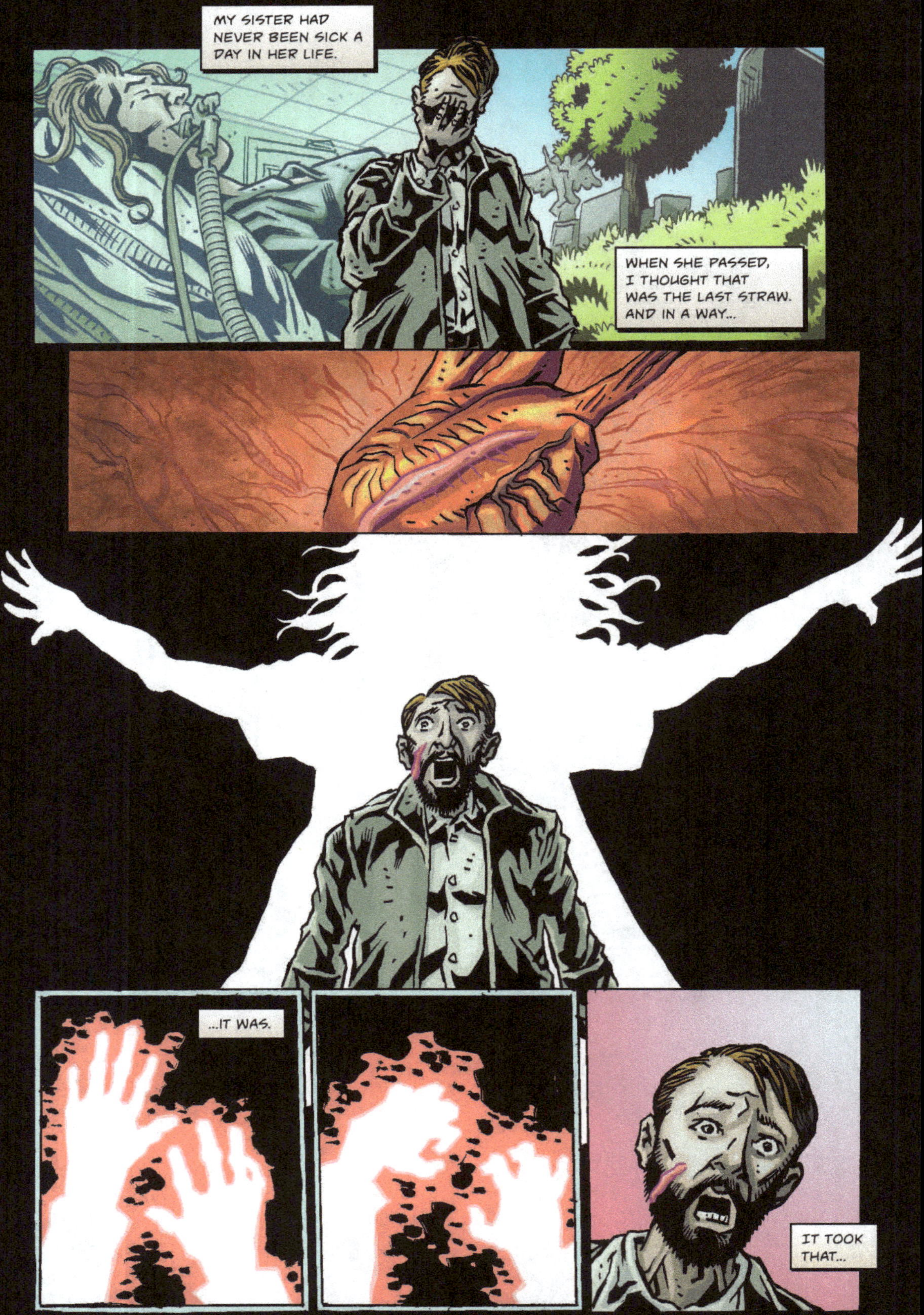
MY SISTER HAD NEVER BEEN SICK A DAY IN HER LIFE.
WHEN SHE PASSED, I THOUGHT THAT WAS THE LAST STRAW. AND IN A WAY...
...IT WAS.
IT TOOK THAT...

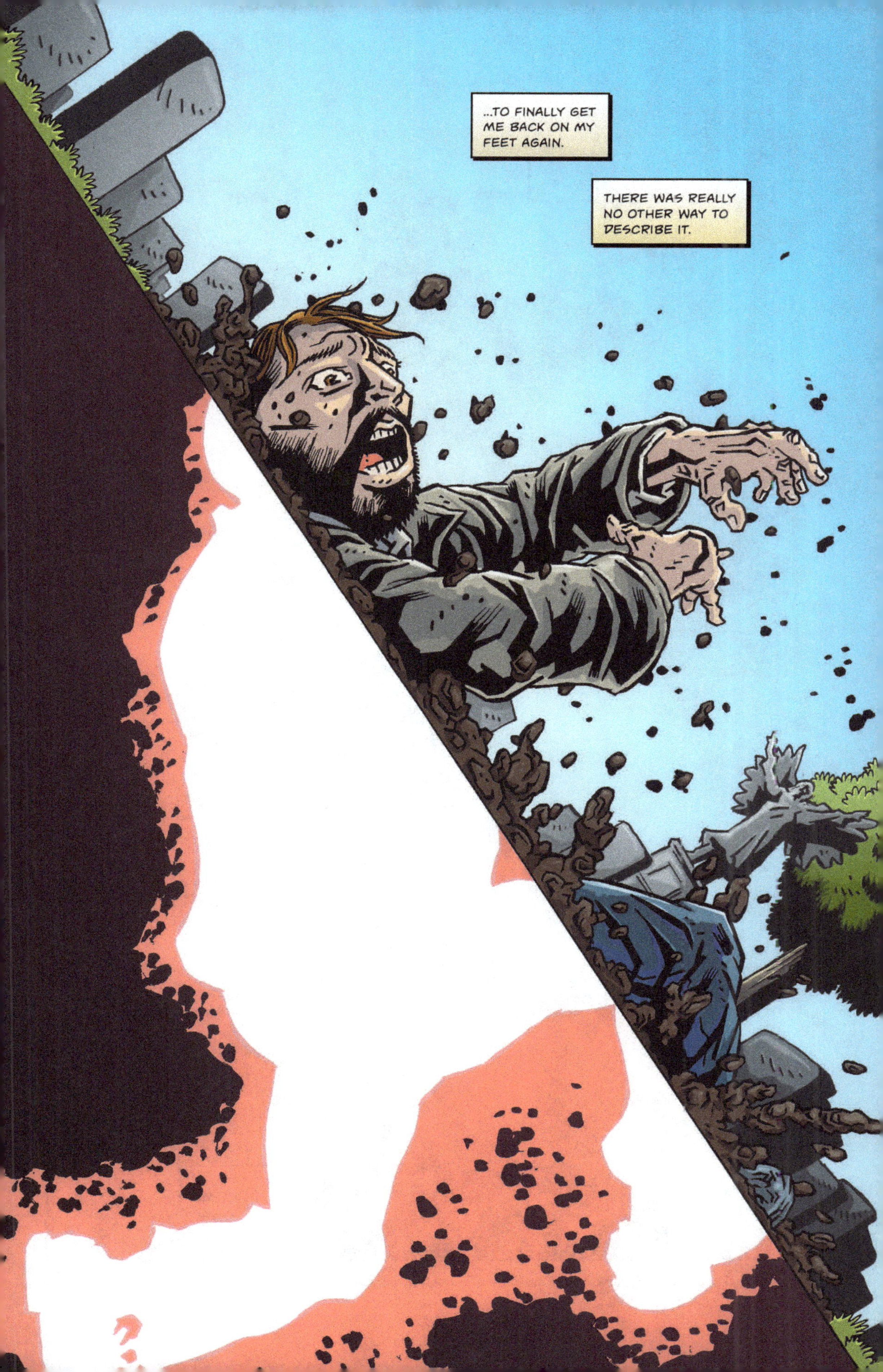
...TO FINALLY GET ME BACK ON MY FEET AGAIN.
THERE WAS REALLY NO OTHER WAY TO DESCRIBE IT.

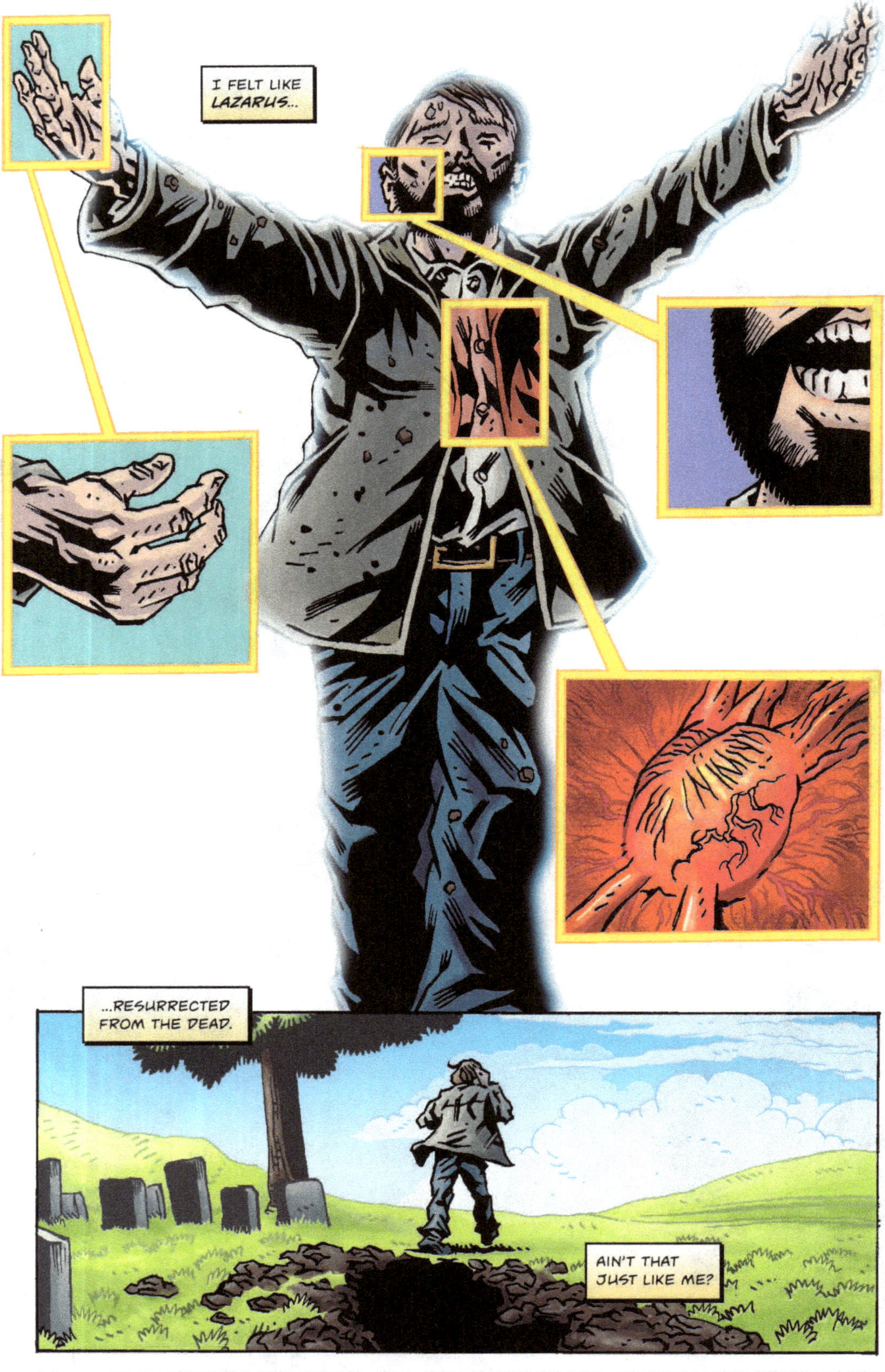
I FELT LIKE LAZARUS...
...RESURRECTED FROM THE DEAD.
AIN'T THAT JUST LIKE ME?

WRITERS: JOHNNY GONZALES & KURT BELCHER - PENCILER/INKER: KURT BELCHER - COLORIST/LETTERER: JEROME GAGNON

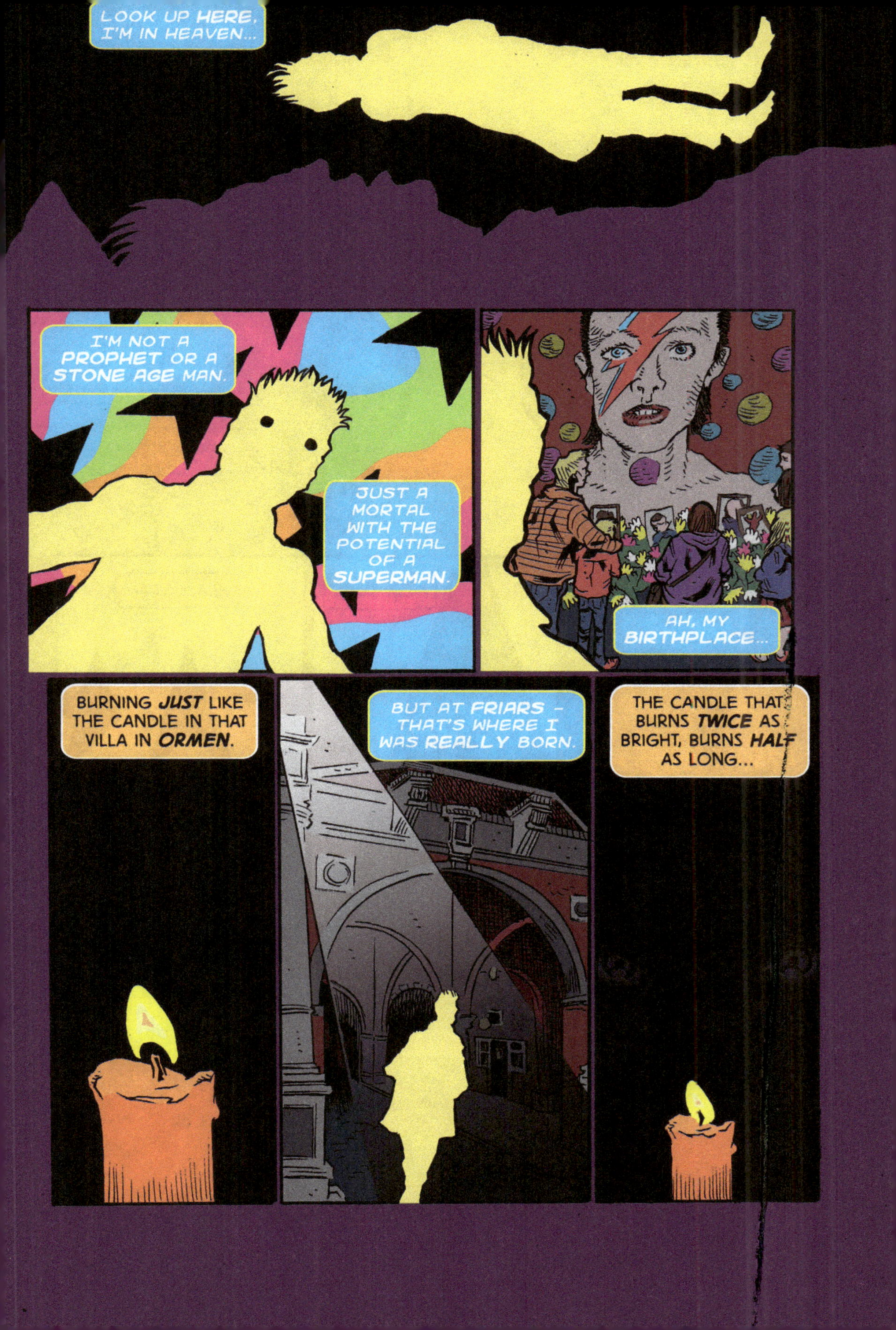
LOOK UP HERE, I'M IN HEAVEN...
I'M NOT A PROPHET OR A STONE AGE MAN.
JUST A MORTAL WITH THE POTENTIAL OF A SUPERMAN.
AH, MY BIRTHPLACE...
BURNING JUST LIKE THE CANDLE IN THAT VILLA IN ORMEN.
BUT AT FRIARS – THAT'S WHERE I WAS REALLY BORN.
THE CANDLE THAT BURNS TWICE AS BRIGHT, BURNS HALF AS LONG...

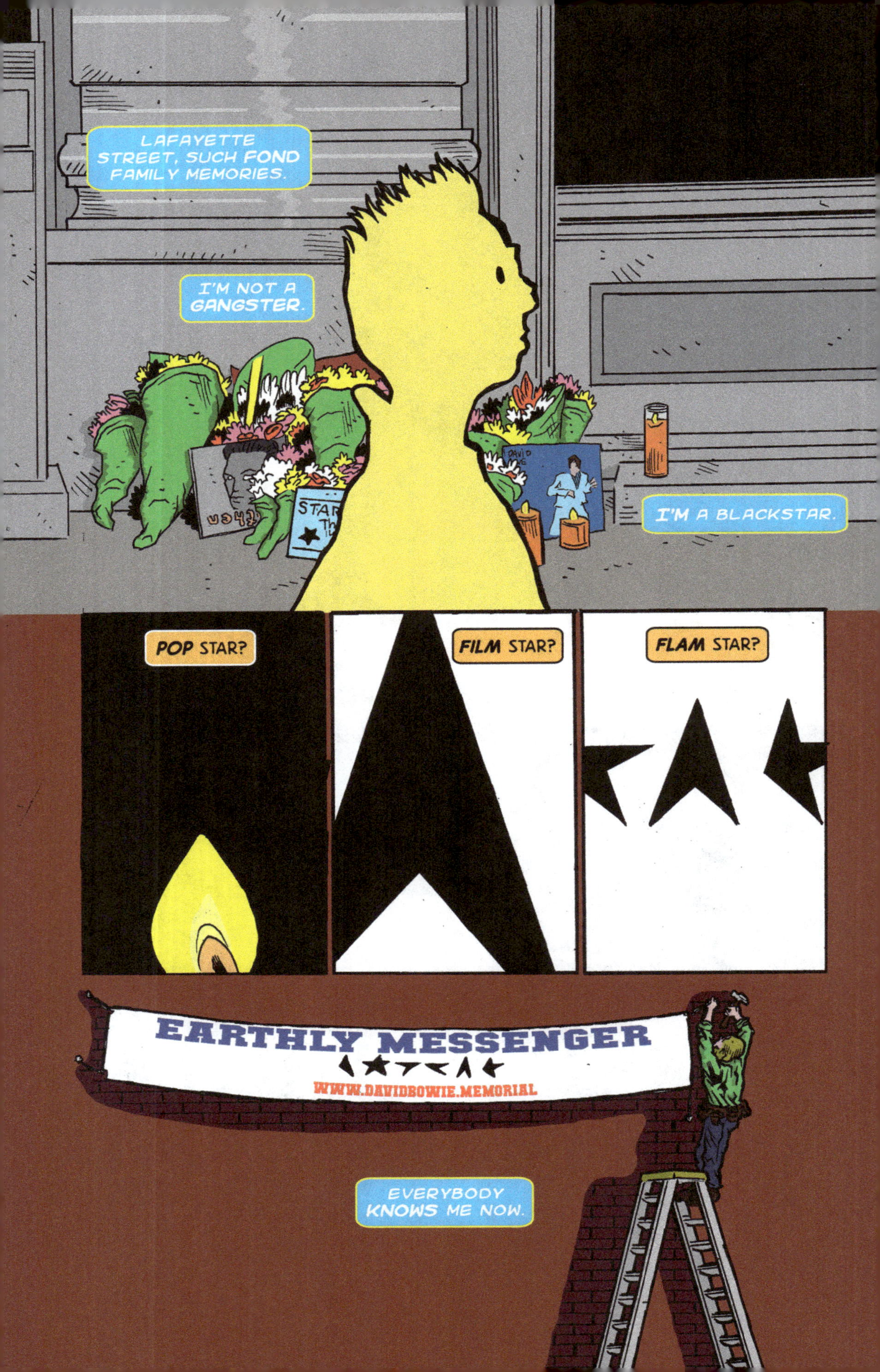

LAFAYETTE STREET, SUCH FOND FAMILY MEMORIES.
I'M NOT A GANGSTER.
I'M A BLACKSTAR.
POP STAR?
FILM STAR?
FLAM STAR?
EARTHLY MESSENGER
WWW.DAVIDBOWIE.MEMORIAL
EVERYBODY KNOWS ME NOW.

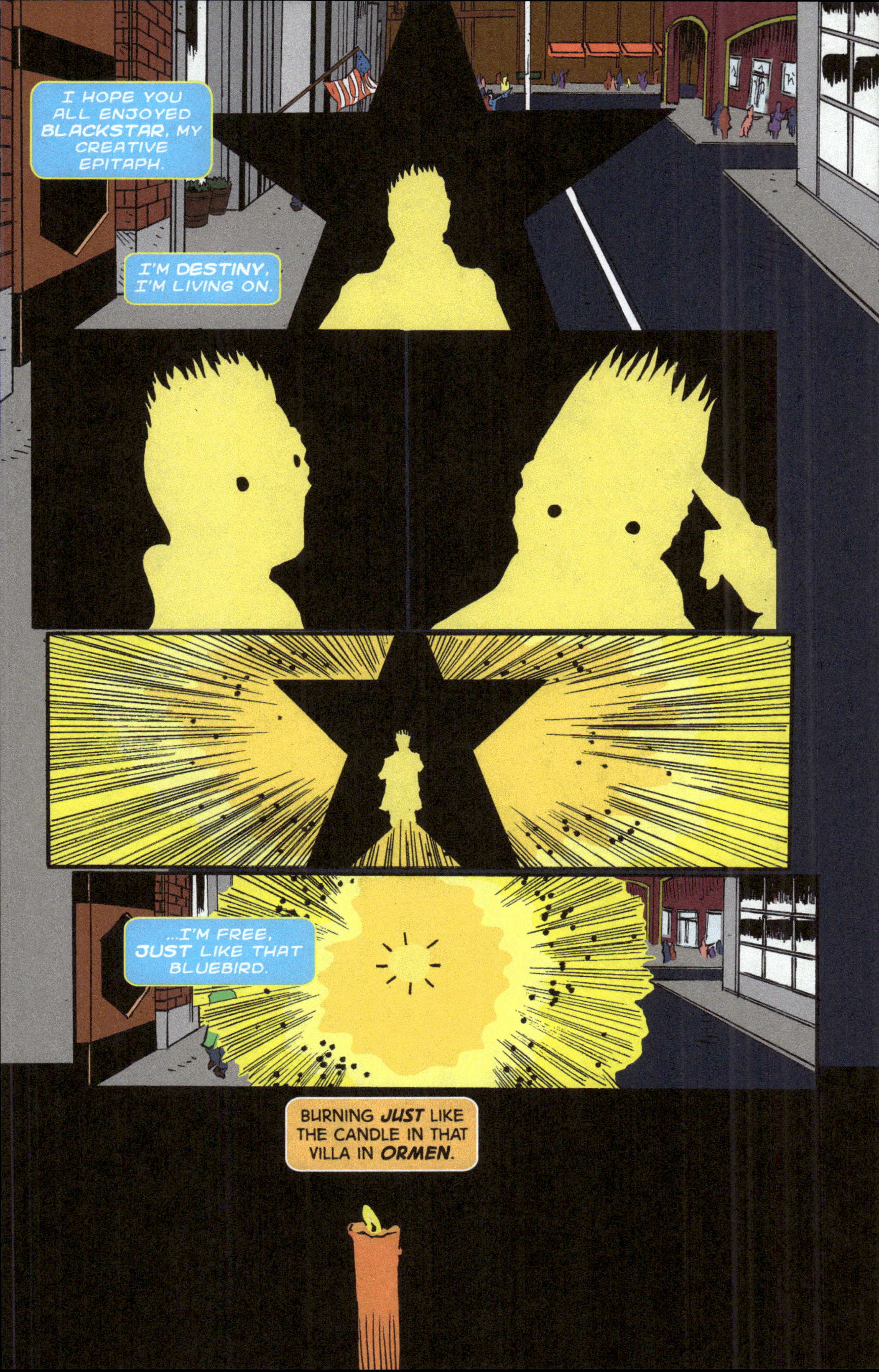
I HOPE YOU ALL ENJOYED BLACKSTAR, MY CREATIVE EPITAPH.
I'M DESTINY, I'M LIVING ON.
...I'M FREE, JUST LIKE THAT BLUEBIRD.
BURNING JUST LIKE THE CANDLE IN THAT VILLA IN ORMEN.

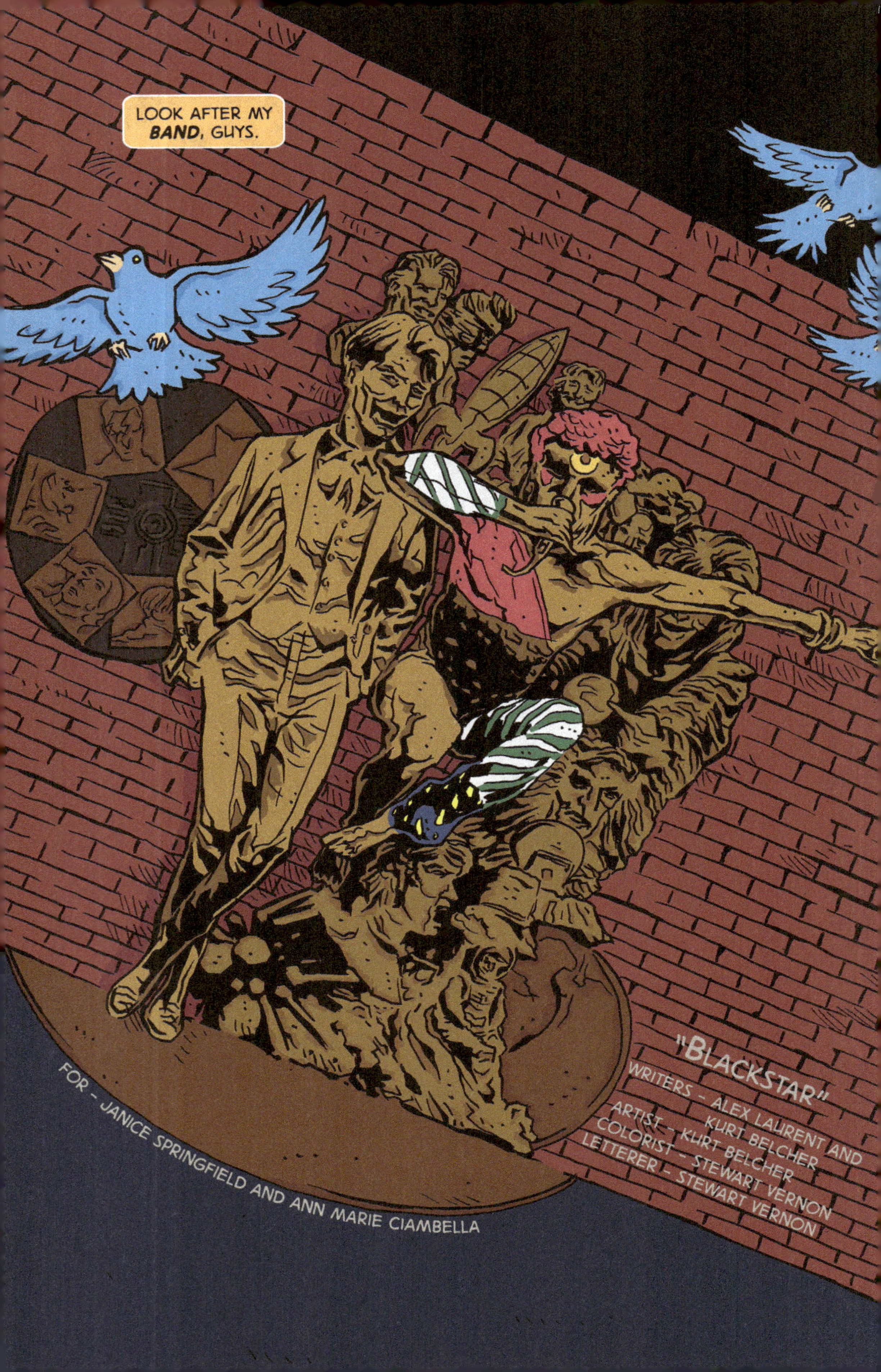

LOOK AFTER MY BAND, GUYS.
"BLACKSTAR"
WRITERS - ALEX LAURENT AND KURT BELCHER
ARTIST - KURT BELCHER
COLORIST - STEWART VERNON
LETTERER - STEWART VERNON
FOR - JANICE SPRINGFIELD AND ANN MARIE CIAMBELLA

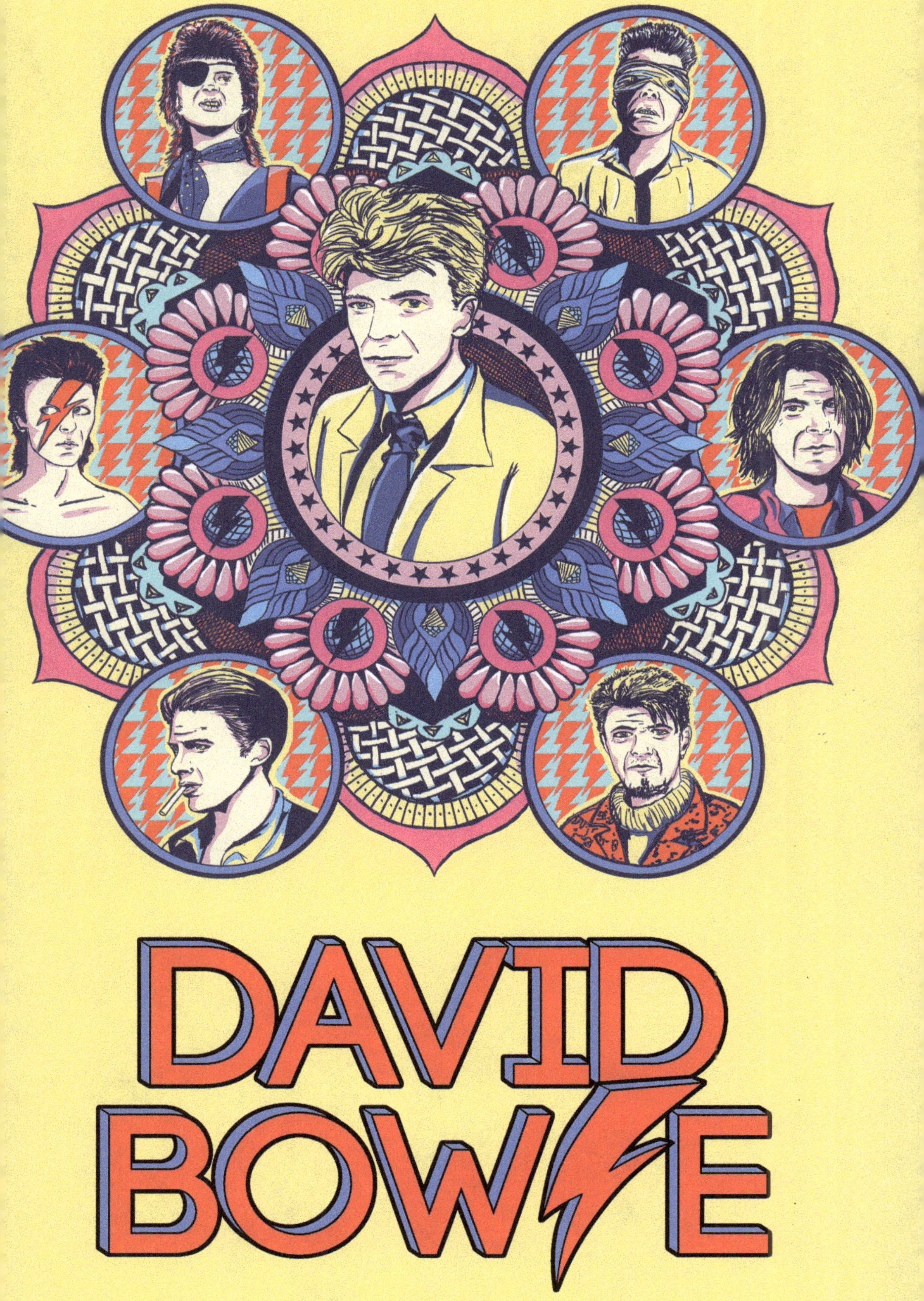

DAVID BOWIE

Spiders & Stardust
a tribute to david bowie

CPSIA information can be obtained
at www.ICGtesting.com
Printed in the USA
BVHW010225090822
644134BV00009B/325